LEADERSHIP AT THE INTERFACE

POLITICS AND PRINCIPLE IN ORGANIZATIONAL LIFE

VERNON STOREY

DETSELIG
ENTERPRISES LTD

Leadership at the Interface:
Politics and Principle in Organizational Life
© 2008 Vernon J. Storey

Library and Archives Canada Cataloguing in Publication

Storey, Vernon J. (Vernon James), 1943-
    Leadership at the interface : politics and principle in organizational life / Vernon J. Storey.

Includes bibliographical references.
ISBN 978-1-55059-348-8

    1. Leadership. 2. Organizational behavior. 3. Leadership--Case studies. I. Title.

HM1261.S76 2008   658.4'092   C2008-900091-9

Detselig Enterprises Ltd.
210, 1220 Kensington Rd NW
Calgary, Alberta
T2N 3P5

DETSELIG
ENTERPRISES LTD

www.temerondetselig.com
temeron@telusplanet.net
Phone: (403) 283-0900
Fax: (403) 283-6947

All rights reserved. No part of this book may be reproduced in any form or by any means without permission in writing from the publisher.

We acknowledge the support of the Government of Canada through the Book Publishing Industry Development Program (BPIDP) for our publishing program.

We also acknowledge the support of the Alberta Foundation for the Arts for our publishing program.

SAN 113-0234
ISBN 978-1-55059-348-8
Cover Design by Alvin Choong

Contents

Foreword 7
The Author 9
Acknowledgments 11
Introduction 13

Part I Understanding the Interface

1 — Fire on the Mountain: 25
The Reality of Politics in Organizational Life

Reality Defined: Micropolitics in Organizational Life 27
First Cousins: Linking Politics and Economics 30
The Reality of Scarce Resources 32
Striking a Particular Harmony 32
No Solitary Effort: The Power of Distributed Leadership 33

2 — Mapping the Ground: 37
Making Sense of Organizational Life

Leaders and Conceptual Frameworks 39
Understanding Micropolitics: A Framework for Action 42
Circumstance as Leadership Opportunity 43
   Urgency and Importance 43
   Leadership Action: Bounded, Considered, Reflective 44
Elements of Micropolitics 45
   Context: External and Internal Environments 46
   Demand: Source and Substance 48
   Interaction: Influencing Patterns and Processes 50
End Results: Outputs and Outcomes 51

3 — Who Leads? Context and Capability 55

Clarifying an Understanding of Leadership 55
Distributed Leadership – More than Delegating 59
Considering Context: A Framework for Study and Practice 62
   Leadership in Governing around Purpose 62

4 Leadership at the Interface

Leadership in Administering toward Goals	64
Leadership in Managing Means	65
Leadership in Delivering Service	65
Understanding Applied	65
The Matter of Competence	66
Completion Competence: Getting the Work Done	67
Contact Competence: Working with Others	68
Conceptual Competence: Seeing the 'Big Picture'	69
Conflict Competence: Understanding the Political Milieu	70
Continuation Competence: Staying the Course	71
Character Competence: Building Trust	72

4 — Purpose in Mind: Power as a Condition of Leadership 77

Addressing the Reality	78
Identifying Power and Influence	80
The Nature of Influence	83
Understanding Interests	83
The Organizational Domain	86
The Personal Domain: High Freedom	88
The Personal Domain: Low Freedom	89
Power and the Moral Character of Leadership	91
The Priority Dilemma	92
The Influence Dilemma	92
The Means Dilemma	93
The Effectiveness Dilemma	93
Organization or Individual? A Perennial Dilemma?	94
The Power of Transparent Leadership	97
Working with the Reality of Power	99

5 — Actors and Agendas: The Human Face of Organizations 103

Understanding Agendas	105
The Public Agenda	105
The Private/Personal Agenda	106
The Hidden/Secret Agenda	107
Origins of Agendas	109
Formal Origins	110
Grounded Origins	110
Unique Origins	111
Working with Interests and Preferences	112
Special Case: Determined Pursuit of a Single Interest	114
A Challenge for Leaders: Whose Interests?	117

6 — Interface Turbulence: Conflict as Leadership Opportunity — 121

    A Perspective on Conflict — 122
    The Possibility of Resolution — 124
    The Place of Difference and Dissent — 125
    Identifying Positions and Interests — 129
    Addressing Conflict: Seeing and Reading — 131

7 — Evidence of Leadership: — 135
Choices, Decisions, and Outcomes

    Decisions Avoided or Delayed and the Search for Consensus — 136
    The Reality of Forced Choice — 138
    Working within Tight Boundaries — 138
    Many Actors and Audiences — 140
    Urgency, Importance, and the Sudden Turn of Events — 141
    A Vision for Action — 143

8 — Vital Engagement: Principled Leadership at the Interface — 145

    The Place of Values — 145
    Grounded Leadership: Foundation for Credibility — 148
    Leadership as Service, Leaders as Servants — 150
    Leadership as Stewardship — 154
    Pressures and the Grounded Leader — 155
    Grounded Leadership as a Guide for Action — 157
    Conclusion — 158

Assertions — 161

PART II LEARNING AT THE INTERFACE

Using Scenarios for Learning — 169

9 — The Demand of Critical Incidents — 171

    Index to the Critical Incidents — 173

10 — Learning through Case Study — 187

    Index to the Case Studies — 189

References — 245

List of figures

Figure 2.1	Using conceptual frameworks	41
Figure 2.2	Micropolitics in organizations: A framework for action	44
Figure 3.1	Contexts for leadership action	63
Figure 4.1	Varieties of power	85
Figure 5.1	A typology of agendas	106
Figure 5.2	Origins of interests, legitimization of agendas	109
Figure 6.1	Steps to group development or dysfunction	127
Figure 8.1	Values and the political process	146

Foreword

This book is itself an act of service: a thoroughly informed and yet thoroughly commonsensical look at the business and the profession of organizational leadership. It is written from the standpoint of the *political*, which the Romans concisely captured in the expression, *Cui bono?* – Who gets what from whom and how?

Vernon Storey provides answers to these questions, but he also gives us a suggestive introduction to a more radical question, Why? Professor Storey is also exceptionally well qualified to discuss the realities of the world of organizational politics as he is intimately familiar with every level of administration in practice and all that that implies.

Whether the reader is well grounded in the realities of administrative action – the stresses and strains, joys and pains – or whether the reader be far removed from those realities by way of theoretical contemplation or academic detachment, there will be profit in the reading. And a profusion of intriguing vignettes and case studies make the reading light and entertaining work.

The book is sophisticating in the original sense of that word: making worldly-wise. Although the book's primary value lies with the novice or aspirant leader who must engage the facts of life at the level of organizational governance or administration, it is of great value for those who have already had their baptism of political fire as well. For both, it provides a vocabulary of political concepts that enhance our understanding of the moral art of organizational leadership.

If one were asked to choose the single central thesis of the book, it could perhaps be captured in one word: thoughtfulness. This reinforces the familiar notion of the *reflective practitioner* by emphasizing the desirability in leadership of thoughtfulness and, even more so, the undesirability of mindlessness. The writer himself is authentically thoughtful and, consequently, authentically conduces thoughtfulness in the reader. Readers who approach this book receptively will be rewarded and encouraged and will extend the scope of their own professional thoughtfulness.

Administration is intrinsically political. Elsewhere I have proposed (asserted?) that "Administration is philosophy-in-action" and that "Power is the first word in the administrative lexicon." Professor Storey is supportive of those contentions. But saying this is also to say that administration is value-laden (one might well say value-saturated) and that politics is the arena in which value conflicts are resolved. So any approach to the study of values and a deeper understanding of them is by no means an impractical exercise but an endeavor earnestly to be desired. Vern Storey clearly traces the line from values to the clash of agendas and the imposition of power in this book and, as such, it can be studied with advantage. Also shown is that value-logic is rarely linear, much less digital. Nietszche's dictum that "There are no facts, only interpretations" is amply brought home even while the case is being made for a foundational stand. To cite another foundational philosopher, Wittgenstein, in one of his typically cryptic utterances: "Philosophy is the disease of which itself must be the cure." We might try substituting any of the words leadership or administration or politics in this quotation and one would then have three further justifications for this author's task, a task that he has efficiently, effectively, and graciously carried to a conclusion in this highly commendable and delightfully illustrated book.

Christopher Hodgkinson
Professor Emeritus, University of Victoria
July, 2007

THE AUTHOR

Vern Storey is a professor of leadership studies within the Department of Educational Psychology and Leadership Studies at the University of Victoria's Faculty of Education. He is well known in the field as a professional whose commitment is to strengthening the practice of leadership in public sector and community service organizations. Vern has many years of experience in education in British Columbia, where he has worked since 1962 as teacher, principal, supervisor, superintendent of schools, and university professor. His research interests include the study of leadership, politics and governance, professional development, rural education, and more recently the history of education. Vern's books include *Learning to Teach* (2003), *The Home* (1998), *Guarding the Trust* (1994), *Building the Parent Partnership* (1988), and *Principals for Tomorrow* (1987). He has been a consultant to a variety of not-for-profit and public service organizations on issues of governance and performance.

The aim of *Leadership at the Interface*, as has been the case for each of Vern's books, is to provide a reference for both students of politics and practicing professionals. His books are designed to be professional development resources for organizational leaders. His education experience, his university work, and his consulting activities come together here to provide a resource for leaders who daily face the reality of all organizations: where there are scarce resources, there will be politics, power, and influence. That reality calls for principled leadership and it demands much from those who answer the call.

Acknowledgements

I am indebted to my colleague Christopher Hodgkinson, Professor Emeritus of the University of Victoria, for his significant contribution to the study of the philosophy of leadership and for the opportunities we have had to consider together the matter of administration, or leadership, as "philosophy-in-action." I have appreciated his clear articulation of the concept of praxis, which he has defined as "ethical action in a political context... behavior informed and guided by purposes, intentions, motives, morals and values as well as the facts or 'science' of the case... conscious, reflective, intentional action."[1] It is praxis, or to borrow a term from business, value-added behavior, that distinguishes the activities of managers of events and circumstances from the actions of leaders of people. This book is about praxis.

This book had its genesis in my book *In the real world* (EduServ, 1997), in which I first grappled with the connection between leadership and politics. I am grateful to EduServ for encouraging me to write that piece and for returning copyright of the manuscript to me when that organization moved out of publishing to concentrate on other core activities of their enterprise. With its parent body the British Columbia School Trustees Association, EduServ for several years played an important leadership role by encouraging the production of professional development materials and activities within the British Columbia education community.

Special thanks are also due to many graduate students, both on and off campus, in courses I have taught on politics in organizations. We have explored together what has become for me, and I hope also for you, an exciting topic. Your perspectives, enthusiasm, and energy, and your toleration and encouraging critique of successive drafts, have made this a rewarding venture.

Vernon J. Storey
Victoria, British Columbia, 2008

---

[1] Christopher Hodgkinson, Education Leadership: The Moral Art (New York: State University of New York Press, 1991), 113.

Introduction

> *In real-world practice, problems do not present themselves to the practitioner as givens. They must be constructed from the materials of problematic situations which are puzzling, troubling, and uncertain. In order to convert a problematic situation to a problem, a practitioner must ... make sense of an uncertain situation that initially makes no sense.*[1]

We often pass over the introduction to a book in order to move quickly into its topical content. In this case, I urge you to read these opening pages carefully – they are an integral part of the text. The aim of this book is to support and strengthen the efforts of leaders in social service organizations – our schools, health care agencies, churches, volunteer or 'third sector' enterprises, and an array of other organizational contexts. Some of you are designated leaders; others are simply recognized and acknowledged for your contributions to the quality of life in your organization. Some are engaged in the formal study of politics in organizations; others will read this book as a professional development resource. All are vitally engaged with communities and are working on their behalf in work that matters much.

Our social worlds are complex, though we do not comprehend every complexity. We acknowledge that leadership is a challenging human enterprise. We understand that in the "21st century, there is a genuine demand for effective leadership,"[2] and sometimes we search uncertainly for leaders to meet that demand. We hear in common conversation that we are facing a leadership crisis, though the evidence to support that notion is usually anecdotal. We demand capable leadership. With that as our preference, the task of nurturing leadership becomes a vital engagement with the complexities and challenges of organizational life. That activity is the focus and commitment of this book.

Leadership is an interface concept inextricably intertwined with the political character of life in organizations. By definition leadership is a political activity. By nature it is also a moral enterprise. Those realities form the ground for *Leadership at the Interface*. The character of leadership stands alongside its political surrounding in a context shaped by forces and influences that daily challenge the values and ethics of its practitioners. Leadership is a powerfully *human* activity. Politics practiced for the common good in our organizations can also be a powerfully *humane* activity.

This introduction includes a short overview of each of the book's chapters. Beyond that it offers a close look at the way this book is constructed: its study and application strands, its use of assertions, and the case studies and critical incidents that are two of its key elements. I encourage you to use this introduction as a key building block in the experience of professional learning and growth that I hope will mark your real-world study of the ideas developed in *Leadership at the Interface*.

This book is for leaders who carry assigned responsibility for guiding the work of organizations and for those who have responded when a leadership need was evident. I have written it for those who recognize that work done by every person carries a leadership component and for those who might consider walking the leadership path. In his argument for a philosophical analysis of leadership, Koestenbaum notes that:

> We live in a common world; we all have needs and hopes, feelings and ideals. We ask, What kind of people does it take to achieve these goals? And, more important, What kind of people does it take to help others achieve them, to create environments and societies – durable ones, sustainable ones – that will facilitate these goals?[3]

Those who offer leadership in our organizations engage directly in pursuing a common mission with their colleagues and with those served by the organization. Their task is often as complex and uncertain as it is crucial. We expect leaders to understand power and conflict. We expect them to possess and to develop further the skills demanded in turbulent human contexts. We ask them to establish and work from a base of authenticity and credibility before an array of watchful audiences. In short, we ask them to be leaders in settings populated in many cases by hesitant partners. Often their work will be scrutinized by skeptical onlookers.

As Christopher Hodgkinson has observed, "The problem is profound.... At stake is the quality of organizational life. We all live in and by organizations, directly as members and indirectly as associates or clientele."[4] Yet accepting the invitation to do the work of leadership often carries with its personal satisfaction the reality of personal cost. It is probably a consequence of that difficulty, and a mark of our times, that some who could meet the challenge are reluctant to lead our organizations. It is also a mark of our times that the question of why we are short of able and willing leaders invites a myriad of possible responses but no clear and enlightening single answer. Perhaps we can aid the effort to identify and develop leadership potential, willingness, and skill by understanding the complexities of the task and the importance of the mission.

With that in mind, I have written this book as a personal learning and professional development tool. It is designed to aid reflective practitioners in their search for knowledge and skill and to support their quests for understanding. Throughout, the focus of the book is on leadership. It is concerned with the interface of leadership and politics in organizations, particularly in the social service and not-for-profit sectors.

The faces of our organizations have changed dramatically in recent years; our recognition of their political character is now well established. There are few exceptions. Layton's comment is even more applicable today than when they were written two decades ago: "Everyone readily concedes that political savvy has become more urgent for [leaders]; indeed, their professional survival is increasingly linked to their degree of political understanding and sophistication."[5] It will be clear throughout *Leadership at the Interface* that its intended readers are reflective practitioners. They are individuals committed to understanding the scene around them as an essential first step toward defining quality leadership action with and for people and their organizations.

The book is developed in two strands: **understanding** and **application**. Part I emphasizes the development and building of understanding. In that strand, my commitment has been to present conceptually strong analysis and synthesis set against a background of defensible theory-like material and assembled into a package that will stimulate reflective thought and offer a building block for professional growth. In that regard, the study component prepares the ground for integration and application – for praxis. The second strand, the application component, focuses on the translation and testing of understanding through the analysis of life-like scenarios, such as case studies and critical incidents.

Part I

Understanding the Interface

The first eight chapters of *Leadership at the Interface* constitute the understanding component. These chapters establish the philosophic knowledge base of the book and situate it within the literature on organizational leadership. Chapter 1 aims to challenge, in fact to debunk, a long-established piece of organizational folk wisdom – that our mission-focused service organizations are above politics. That assertion was described some years ago by Scribner as "the apolitical myth."[6] According to most understandings of the term *politics* as it applies to organizations, that apolitical fallacy is not true now, nor was it ever true. Responsible argument, though, seeks to replace a challenged term or concept with another of greater accuracy, relevance, and utility. *Leadership at the Interface* presents and develops the assumption that three inevitable realities exist where people gather around a common purpose: organization, leadership, and politics. The concern of this book is with the nature and quality of each.

I seek to present in Chapter 1 a clear statement that the reality of organizations as political places is a generality. That pervasive circumstance challenges leaders with a call for skillful action. The value of understanding organizations as political places will become clear as we consider a foundational argument that the skilled practice of leadership can be both principled and supportive of the people who work in and around that organization.

Chapter 1 also presents some basic vocabulary and definitions. Though it is not essential that we all hold precisely the same definition of a term, it is important for our reading of and dialogue about this book that we hold relatively common understandings of vocabulary used to describe topics we are exploring together. Given that there is latitude in the process of defining, I have offered some basic working definitions that reflect an effort to discard less functional meanings and replace them with more helpful ones, at least for the process of working through *Leadership at the Interface*. I have also stated a fundamental value commitment – that leadership capability is distributed among the many rather than the few.

Chapter 2 proposes a conceptual framework for the topical focus of the book. The model I have developed is descriptive and diagnostic rather than prescriptive in nature. Its purpose is to provide a schema for reflective practitioners for understanding the political fact of organizational life. The model can be applied fully or in part to each case study or critical incident in Part II as a lens for viewing the political character of the places in which we work and relate to others.

Chapter 3 situates leadership contextually by addressing the question, "Who leads?" I address that question from a perspective that recognizes and calls for a broad base of involvement in the doing of leadership – the notion that effective leadership is inclusive rather than exclusive. The chapter presents a perspective on dimensions of leadership competence in a way that pluralizes the term and offers the reader a set of markers for practice. Rather than the traditional competence/incompetence dichotomy that often characterizes a unitary concept, I have suggested that for those who would lead there are multiple dimensions of competence: discrete areas of capability that taken together mark the effective practice of leadership.

The content of Chapter 4 is foundational to the overall tone and character of *Leadership at the Interface*. It addresses the idea of purpose-linked power as the application of influence in a context of principled leadership. For many, power remains a major 'nondiscussable,' yet power is both a hallmark and an essential component of leadership. The moral character of leadership is of direct and pervasive importance to the leaders of human, and therefore of political, organizations. Our view of leadership affects our understanding and use of power. We read much and hear often about a perceived crisis of leadership, but we are not short of technical experts; if we find that to be the case, we can train more. We are not short of managers or, fortunately for the schools of management that dot the horizon, those who would become managers. Yet we apply the word *crisis*, which usually suggests danger and urgency, to our organizations in a way that suggests we face a crisis of leadership. Whether or not that is true will be determined by the nature and quality of our leadership practice, by the way we understand and use power. Chapter 4 seeks to develop a clear and substantial understanding of power, focusing on some of its varieties and manifestations and on the principled use of power by leaders.

Chapter 4 completes the foundational component of *Leadership at the Interface*. This chapter offers a perspective on the political character of life in and around our organizations. I have sought to develop a common vocabulary, to provide a conceptual lens through which we can view our work and service lives, and to propose a framework for understanding leadership in those contexts. I have tried to stimulate reflection about practice, to aid the process of praxis. All too often our opportunities to engage in thinking and action of that sort are constrained by complex and turbulent working hours. We face the pressure of matters that, because they must be addressed immediately, are moved to the top of our priority lists even though it is not necessarily our own first choice nor the most important concern. Our challenge is to move beyond simply being aware of that complexity and to develop strategic initiatives that will aid our own professional growth and strengthen the practice of leadership throughout our organizations.

I have noted that human organizations are political organizations in the sense in which this book defines politics. Like all drama, whether real life or staged production, our workplaces include players, roles, plots, and audiences. Chapters 5 through 8 explore specific elements of that life. Chapters 5 and 6 examine the human face of organizations and the interactions that surround our efforts to satisfy interests. We consider the power of agendas and the reality of turbulence surrounding human interaction.

Chapter 5 focuses on the actors who guarantee that politics in organizations will be a reality and that there will always be skirmishing around the allocation of scarce resources. There will be both conflict and collaboration around matters demanding resolution; power and authority will be used and misused as we seek to accomplish our agendas.

Chapter 6 examines the phenomenon of conflict, which has become the focus of much writing, speaking, and training. We know that human skirmishing is inevitable and ever-present. We understand that unresolved conflict around an issue can bring an organization to a virtual standstill. The emphasis in Chapter 6 is on developing a functional understanding of conflict and the skill to identify and characterize it. The focus of the chapter is on diagnosis, sense-making, and the need to understand the nature of conflict in organizations.

The focus shifts in Chapter 7 to leaders themselves and analyzes the dimensions of decision making in complex human settings, the reality of the "no-win" decision, and the urgency and importance of understanding the consequences and implications of our decisions, because we know that they will affect the working lives of others. I consider decision making and action to form an unbroken unit. By definition, decision includes action. At its heart, leadership is about change in organizations and in people as we gather to achieve purpose. Regardless of the processes used to reach decision points, leaders and leadership are charged both with the task of deciding and with the responsibility for action. Chapter 7 addresses that reality with the intent of strengthening leaders' capacities to understand and to act.

Chapter 8 examines the moral character of leadership. We consider the idea of leadership as service and the more profound notion of leaders as servants. Each of those concepts rests on the assumption that leadership in organizations involves stewardship – caring for the assets and interests of others. If that is the case, our search will be for grounded leaders whose actions rest on a foundation of values and commitments that enable transparent, principled leadership.

Throughout the book I present several **assertions** – forthright 'as if true' statements intended to provoke readers to thought and discussion. These assertions have two purposes. First, they are intended to provoke agreement, disagreement, and further questions and ideas from readers.

Their second purpose is to reframe some ideas developed in the text in order to stimulate reflection, study, and debate about those ideas. In some instances, the assertions have been written in light-hearted language (perhaps another way to make a point and to increase the likelihood that the idea will be remembered). These statements provide discussion points throughout the book, capturing the essence of some but not all of the ideas presented. It may be useful, if your perspective on an assertion differs, to write a counter-assertion to a statement I have presented in the book or to add assertions that crystallize your own ideas. For ease of reference, I have listed all of the assertions again at the end of Part I following Chapter 8.

PART II

LEARNING AT THE INTERFACE

The second component of *Leadership at the Interface* presents a set of opportunities to practice applying, albeit in simulated form, the concepts gained through reading the book. The emphasis shifts to the development of skilled practice and reflection on that practice. Here the process of using knowledge as a bridge to understanding is extended through discussion and reflection using real-world vignettes. This active professional learning component includes two types of narrative, **critical incidents** and **case studies**. I describe these components at the beginning of Part II.

The critical incidents in Chapter 9 are small vignettes applicable at various points throughout the text. Each is based on a single, seemingly discrete event or decision, and each involves very few characters – usually no more than one or two. The case studies in Chapter 10 are more obviously complex. They often involve several characters, greater complexity, and some passage of time. The cases invite detailed study and the creation of various 'what if?' scenarios. In both the critical incidents and the case studies my intent has been to provide opportunities for you to reflect, analyze, synthesize, and apply the content of this book.

How might you use *Leadership at the Interface*? Your work with the text may be solely your individual learning project. On the other hand, this material might become the focus of a group's collaborative professional development effort and process. If a particular purpose for writing this book stands out, it is to encourage groups of professionals to gather around a common task and learning agenda, aided by a core of content that all identify as relevant. *Leadership at the Interface* also provides opportunity for a blended approach; your own individual and private study should be supplemented and enriched through interaction with your colleagues. In some instances, the critical incidents and case studies in Part II will lend themselves also to the 'realities' created through role play and simulation. Whatever the application, the book can provide the framework for an important professional development activity and a significant element of your professional learning portfolio.

I have not referenced the case studies and critical incidents to particular portions of the book. Individual readers and study group facilitators will often find that a vignette has more than one point of applicability. Some themes, such as the notion of power, may appear in several cases. The stories themselves are practice-based and experience-referenced; they are not accounts of actual people or circumstances.

Quite deliberately, and after seeking advice from colleagues, I have chosen not to provide study and discussion questions to accompany the critical incidents and case studies. I recognize that we are accustomed often to addressing someone else's questions when we engage in analysis, and there is a place for that strategy. However, it can also limit some otherwise creative and divergent thought and subsequent dialogue. The risk inherent in predesigned questions is that they may narrow rather than broaden the scope of our thought and discussion. The bridge built by a writer's questions may be a perfectly good bridge. On the other hand, it may cross at the wrong point or act more as a dam than a bridge. Often there is more to be gained from the richness of experience-rooted dialogue and debate than from question-and-answer exercises.

As one study aid, the conceptual framework presented in Chapter 2 can provide a useful means of analysis and problem diagnosis. You and your colleagues may wish to apply the model to specific scenarios and workplace regularities. The process of reflective thinking might suggest generally applicable questions for those who prefer that mode. With any of the critical incidents or case studies the following questions might be posed. What is really going on here? What does it mean? What action is possible and appropriate? How does this scenario relate to the context in which it is being discussed or to some other point in the book? Beyond that, particular and specific questions will interest individual readers, especially when a colleague group is available to offer insights and discuss possibilities.

Whether your study of this book is an individual pursuit, a group project, or a combination of the two, it can be strengthened by the use of a personal learning journal. Such a journal might include your own notes to add value to your reading and to your analysis of the case studies and critical incidents. Where group study is involved, your journal will be enriched by the notes you develop after reflecting on the deeper dialogue that often arises from bringing to the debate a variety of perspectives, experiences, and understandings.

Leadership is not a solitary quest. It is a personal venture carried out in collaboration with colleagues and associates who themselves practice leadership. Almost always leadership will be strengthened and fully realized as a joint pursuit. My purpose in writing this book has been to offer a contribution to our effort to ensure that the leadership practiced in and around our organizations will be guided by sound, reflective thinking buttressed by the active support and participation of colleagues who understand both the scene and the pressures. My hope is that *Leadership at the Interface* will be experienced by leaders at the interface of organizational task and organizational politics as a useful tool, that the process of studying it will be a rewarding venture.

END NOTES

[1] Donald Schon, *The Reflective Practitioner* (New York, NY: Basic Books, 1993), 40.

[2] Peter Northouse, *Leadership: Theory and Practice*, 2nd ed.(San Francisco, Jossey-Bass, 2001), xiv.

[3] Peter Koestenbaum, *Leadership: The Inner Side of Greatness; A Philosophy for Leaders* (San Francisco, Jossey-Bass, 2002), xiii.

[4] Christopher Hodgkinson, *Administrative Philosophy: Values and Motivations in Administrative Life* (Tarrytown, NY, Elsevier Science, 1996), 84.

[5] Donald Layton & Jay Scribner, *Teaching Educational Politics and Policy* (Tempe, AZ, University Council for Educational Administration, 1989), 25.

[6] Ibid., 33.

PART I

UNDERSTANDING THE INTERFACE

Chapter 1 — Fire on the Mountain: The Reality of Politics in Organizational Life

It started with lightning. Early on August 16th, 2003, a bolt ignited in Okanagan Mountain Provincial Park, south of Kelowna [British Columbia, Canada]. As the fire spread, it became a rank six firestorm, the highest possible level. In just four days, the fire had destroyed the park, jumped a 50 metre-wide fireguard and was approaching Kelowna. Nearly 30 000 Kelowna residents were eventually evacuated. In one night alone, 223 houses were lost. . . . the most destructive wildfire in B.C.'s recent history. Can we salvage anything from such destruction? [1]

It is difficult, some would say meaningless, to compare the destructive power of a major rural-urban interface fire to the realities of daily life in an organization. Yet the idea of interface, that place where independent systems and environments meet, communicate, and act on each other, applies also to our experience in workplace and community.[2] Social systems exist alongside each other; they interact and often they collide.

Sometimes activity at the interface is destructive; sometimes it strengthens people and their organizations. Always it involves the human dimensions of those organizations; cooperation and collaboration as well as competition and conflict are realities that mark our life in community. Always it involves economics and politics – the reality of locating and allocating scarce human and material resources. Always life in our organizations involves leadership – the movement of people around purpose. This book focuses on leadership at the critical interface of politics, principle, and organizational life.

Organizations are political systems. We accomplish our collective goals through organizations, that is, the structured social entities in which we gather to accomplish purpose. Dahl and Stinebrickner, speaking primarily of large-scale politics, have argued that

> whether a person likes it or not, virtually no one is beyond the reach of politics.... Politics is an unavoidable fact of human existence. Everyone is involved in some fashion at some time in politics, and politics has consequences in everyone's life. We cannot really escape politics – though we may try to ignore it.[3]

The same applies to our organizations, although we often profess to find both the idea and the activity of politics distasteful. We have argued historically, perhaps less vigorously in recent days than before, that our schools, churches, and community-based social service organizations are, or at least they should be, beyond and somehow above politics. The very notion of politics somehow carries a Machiavellian flavor, a taste that does not blend easily with the idea of working ethically toward the greater social good.

Perhaps some of our discomfort has originated with the term *politics* itself. The politics we usually have in mind seem somehow unpleasant and undeserving of involvement by principled leaders. After all, our concern is with organizational mission and purpose and with the interests of those on whose behalf we work. Surely such a compelling focus leaves no room for activities that carry images of intrigue, skirmishing, manipulation, and power. Yet we know that though we sometimes reject these concepts and prefer not to acknowledge them as characteristic of our work, they really do exist and they demand our attention. We understand that the strategies and processes which sometimes threaten our best efforts are real. We realize that defeat and disappointment, when they come – and they *will* come – sometimes are indicators of our own need for greater knowledge, understanding, and skill.

We realize also that when we reach agreement, when we have made decisions, and when we succeed, usually it comes about through something other than the brightest person having found the one best way. In short, we realize that our organizations are political places populated by people with interests and shaped by the character of their interactions. That observation carries clear implications for leaders – both those who lead today and those who will lead tomorrow – in terms of our expectations for their knowledge, skill, and understanding. It calls for a philosophic and an ethical base for the practice of leadership in these complex human settings. Our 'inside' stories of impressive success and catastrophic failure make it clear that "anyone aspiring to lead...must acquire some considerable political sophistication."[4] That process of knowledge acquisition and skill development must begin with a search for clarity and precision in our understanding of the phenomenon we call politics, at least insofar as the term applies to the social service and not-for-profit organizations in which we work

Success in our work is multifaceted and often difficult to calculate. The obstacles are sometimes formidable; they are not often of our own making. It is vital that we understand the scene around us, that we develop considerable facility not only in sense-making but also in decision making. Accomplishing that demands we grasp essential terms and concepts for thinking about, discussing, and applying principles of political systems and activity.

Much of the material helpful in the early stages of this quest comes from writers whose primary frame of reference is politics in its traditional and most common conception. Those writers are concerned with the governing of states and countries and issues related to connections between these entities and other bodies. Many of the principles discussed by such writers as Crick[5] and Dahl and Stinebrickner[6] in regard to the dynamics of national and international relations bear a clear and direct relationship to the patterns of interaction that we see in the organizations with which we are familiar. In each case the actors are people and their agendas are human agendas.

REALITY DEFINED: MICROPOLITICS IN ORGANIZATIONAL LIFE

The phenomenon of politics emerges in settings where people gather to accomplish *purpose*, a term that implies commonality when discussing organizational life. Ensuring shared understanding of, common commitment to, and joint action around a purpose is a fundamental leadership challenge.

A more straightforward task is to define the term *politics* as we will use it in this book. In this discussion, I will define **politics** with four criteria in mind: the definition will be clear, it will be useful to readers, it will enable discussion based on common understanding, and it will be supported by current thinking. Beyond that my intent is to assist readers to develop a working vocabulary of politics.

Assuming that two or more people are involved in an activity and that their intent is to accomplish a common purpose, we can identify three related social phenomena: leadership, organization, and politics. Each has a particular focus. The concern of leadership is the movement of people toward purpose; the concern of organization is the structural context for that movement; the concern of politics is the human interaction involved in these processes. When we consider political activity in organizational settings, we move to a more bounded set of activities often described as **micropolitics**, which is defined by Blase as follows:

> Micropolitics refers to the use of formal and informal power by individuals and groups to achieve their goals in organizations. In large part, political actions result from perceived differences between individuals and groups, coupled with the motivation to use power to influence and/or protect. Although such actions are consciously motivated, any action, consciously or unconsciously motivated, may have political 'significance' in a given situation. Both cooperative and conflictive actions and processes are part of the realm of micropolitics. However, macro- and micropolitical factors frequently interact.[7]

Pirie has described micropolitics as the "process of examining the resistance of interest groups," noting that

> this approach does not sit easily with those who prefer policies to be ethically straightforward, and who think the proper activity should be to convince others of what is right, and then do it. Theirs is a completely honorable and defensible position. The micropolitical approach strives to accommodate entrenched interests, and to craft policies which will be popular as well as right. It is more complex, but it can produce impressive results.[8]

The possibility of action by two or more people around a common purpose is a fundamental and essential precondition for leadership. Typically, that action will be carried out through some system of organization, by some means of assembling the participants. In that circumstance, values, interests, preferences, and agendas will mark the context for leadership. It is a micropolitical context commonly marked by scarce resources and by the human dynamic of power surrounding resource allocation: cooperation, collaboration, competition, and conflict. I propose a principled approach to the study and practice of micropolitics by organizational leaders, an approach that seeks both to acknowledge existing reality and to suggest that we will be defined or confined by that reality only as we accept it as tolerable or inevitable.

In this book, I define politics in organizations, or *micropolitics*, as (a) activity surrounding demand for support of values and interests and (b) authoritative response to demand. While that definition does not capture the richness and worth of politics in its broadest sense, it does provide a basis for study and the elements of a framework for analysis and understanding. Throughout this discussion I will use the term *politics*. Whether I refer specifically to the process of civil government rather than to an organization will be made clear by the context.

Authoritative response will not necessarily end demand. That reality complicates the political process and invites leadership. Finite resources, the need to share those resources, and the recognition and conciliation of special interests that is always part of activity in organizations, make decisions necessary. Regardless of the process used to reach decisions, ensuring that they *are* made is a leadership task. The process, unless it is entirely arbitrary and owned by a sole and unchallenged decision maker, is a political process. Its locus is within a political system, defined by Dahl and Stinebrickner as "a collection of elements that interact with one another and that individually and collectively exercise influence over the individuals and collectivities that make up the elements or parts of the system."[9] Our organizations are political systems and leadership activity occurs at the interface of organization and environment.

We sometimes prefer not to discuss politics in organizations, feeling somehow that it is outside the parameters of humane and ethical leadership. After all, politics implies manipulation and control. Yet if politics is a reality, and if it is a feature of human behavior in an organization established to accomplish a stated purpose, the issue is one not just of control but of control properly exercised; not just of influence but of appropriate influence. It is a matter not just of power but of legitimate power; not just of formal authority but of ascribed authority. Politics is an element, a component, and an integral part of leadership. Skilled political analysis and ethical political behavior are essential for effective leadership.

Assertion 1.1: Leadership and politics are inextricably bound, and that is reasonable.

Assertion 1.2: Politically skilled, humane leadership is not an oxymoron.

Politics is a part of life in and round our organizations. But when accurately understood and effectively practiced, politics is a positive component of leadership. If insightfully handled and rightly experienced, politics can enrich life in organizations. Crick has described it as "the positive experience of diversity."[10]

Assertion 1.3: The fact of scarce resources is an ever-present organizational reality. Wisdom in searching out reasonable ways of sharing resources is a leadership imperative. Effectiveness in implementing resource allocation decisions is a political skill.

We can assume that there will be many interests and that frequently those interests will compete and collide. In short, politics sounds as though it could be a messy business, if not a downright dirty game, and it can. Whether or not that is the case will be determined by those who play the game, by the rules they make and follow, and by the extent to which all players have opportunity to succeed.

I have sketched some broad outlines of the concept of micropolitics in organizations as a way to begin thinking about the idea. I have suggested that politics is a leadership activity both foundationally important and morally rooted. It is also closely related to another area of human endeavor and organizational reality – economics.

FIRST COUSINS: LINKING POLITICS AND ECONOMICS

The first relevant stop on the road toward enriching our thought about organizational politics – even before we listen to what others have said on the subject – is almost certainly economic theory or economic analysis. If nothing else, it is important that we agree on some working terminology. While it may be difficult to disentangle economics from politics, Dahl and Stinebrickner's explanation of the difference is important to our discussion:

> Economic analysis is primarily concerned with scarce resources and with the production and distribution of goods and services ... political analysis focuses on the exercise of influence and on patterns in the exercise of influence. Activities of human beings or groups of human beings can simultaneously have political and economic aspects.[11]

When we focus on scarce resources or just on resources generally in connection with the idea of distribution, the intimate connection between economics and politics becomes clear. As Bernard Crick has observed, "A political doctrine I take to be simply a coherently related set of proposals for the conciliation of actual social demands in relation to a scarcity of resources."[12] The idea of scarce resources is central whether we are discussing economics or politics. The process of making economic decisions in a democracy adds a further guarantee that politics will be an integral part of the process.

Assertion 1.4: Economic theory and political theory are working partners in the leadership enterprise, whether or not our leadership actions are overtly financial in character.

At least three ideas inform our understanding of the link between economic theory and politics in organizations: **resources, scarcity**, and **distribution** or **allocation**. For each of these ideas, standard definitions provide a useful starting point. In the case of **resources**, the idea of 'a supply that can be drawn on' is particularly helpful, precisely because it begs the question, "A supply of what?" In answering that question we can include any or all of monetary, material, and human resources. Further, we can broaden our conception of each term to ensure its relevance. Human resources, for example, can include numbers of staff and volunteers, their scheduling or, said differently, their time as a resource, and also their assignments. Perhaps the most helpful answer to the question above is to identify resources as "Whatever is needed to accomplish purpose."

The idea of **scarcity** is central to our understanding of politics as a human activity. We use the term in connection with resources. It indicates that in almost all cases the supply, however we have defined it, is finite and limited – there are boundaries. For leaders, an immediate illustration of this idea is the departmental or organizational budget. We often see available resources as too few to meet the array of demands, usually defined as needs. Frequently, we have little or no control over that reality. The matter is complicated by the fact that ideas of what is adequate and sufficient will vary considerably from person to person. When we link ideas of resource supply and human interest with demand and introduce the dynamic of human behavior, we cross the bridge to politics.

The third idea, expressed either as to **distribute** or to **allocate**, means to give shares of or to deal out. The term implies that there are multiple potential recipients for each of an organization's finite resources. Those resources, whether money, time, expertise, or staff, must be shared. To this point, and until we introduce the intricacies and dynamics of human activity, the idea of distributing scarce resources might seem a purely rational exercise, rooted in one's particular conception of economics and able to be systematically and clearly described, explained, and implemented. Quickly though, we discover it is not that straightforward. Interests are revealed, competition begins, strategies are employed, and often there are winners and losers.

THE REALITY OF SCARCE RESOURCES

When we consider, plan, and carry out the distribution of scarce resources, the application of economic theory becomes the practice of political activity. Immediately two additional variables are introduced: **interests** and **competition**. We will explore these dimensions throughout the book, particularly through the critical incidents and case studies in Part II. For the moment two observations by Hodgkinson will provide a useful introduction. He points out the reality that "each institutional subsystem has its own built-in intrinsic value problem, namely, competition for scarce institutional resources which have alternative uses and claimants."[13] The value-rich question is "How, to whom, and according to what guidelines will the resources be distributed?" The question could be made simpler still: "Who gets what, and how do we decide?" The milieu in which answers to that question are formulated and the nature of the answers will define the political complexity of the organization.

As Hodgkinson notes, it is reasonable to suggest that as a general principle of human activity in organizations, "each level and group will militate for maximum rather than optimum allocation of resources for its own interest."[14] We use the terms **stakeholder** to acknowledge the legitimacy of individual or group interests, and **vested interest** to suggest a degree of caution, cynicism, or mistrust of those stakeholders. In either case we accept the reality that participants have interests. We hope to learn what those interests are and we often direct efforts to that end.

We understand that our work is bounded by the critical matter of resource scarcity. It is also marked by the challenge of ensuring that decisions for which we are responsible are fair and equitable in both substance and process. We expect to decide by whatever means and processes suit the circumstances whether, how, and to what extent various interests will be satisfied. In the terms we are using in this book, we understand that we will engage in political activity. Further, we expect to engage in principled political action.

STRIKING A PARTICULAR HARMONY

Crick has defined politics simply as "the activity by which differing interests ... are conciliated by giving them a share in power in proportion to their importance to the welfare and the survival of the whole community."[15] He was writing of politics at the national and international levels but the principle applies equally to the work of organizational leaders in micropolitical contexts. Crick recognized also the unique nature of political activity, even – or perhaps especially – when it is well grounded and when its necessary pragmatism has a strong moral base:

> A political doctrine is thus just an attempt to strike a particular harmony in an actual political situation, one harmony out of many possible different (temporary) resolutions of the basic problem of unity and diversity in a society with complex and entrenched rival social interests.[16]

Crick's conception of politics recognizes the temporary nature of the resolutions we craft as we seek to negotiate the common good in intense and complex human settings. His choice of the term *resolution* rather than *solution* conveys the idea of progressing from dissonance to consonance, of dealing successfully with a matter. In the reality of daily life, that progress will often be an ongoing process. For leaders in organizations, the paradoxical challenge is to stand firmly on a temporary footing, understanding that life at the interface involves processes that by definition are fluid. The political process is characteristic, not episodic; interests will always differ and resources will almost always be scarce.

We often use phrases such as *pure politics* or *political decision* in connection with the policy decisions of government or other authorities. Our associated feelings and connotations are often negative (unless the decision happens to suit our interests). Clear definition of terms and concepts is essential for those who must engage in the art of politics in its close association with leadership. In fact, if the ideas presented in this book are plausible and acceptable, it is reasonable to ask the question, "Which of our decisions are not political?" If we answer "None, or very few" that does not suggest we lack principle or offer flawed leadership.

NO SOLITARY EFFORT:
THE POWER OF DISTRIBUTED LEADERSHIP

Chapter 3 addresses an important question regarding the losuc of leadership – who will lead, when, and how? It is important to grasp from the start an important theme and value commitment of this book – the assumption and belief that each of us carries leadership capacity. Each can contribute to accomplishing an agreed upon purpose, whether the task at hand is to extinguish a fire on a mountain or to deal with the daily complexities of life in an organization.

We demand of our designated leaders that they have a clear, 'big picture' vision of our organization's future. We expect to play a part in shaping, clarifying, and accomplishing that mission. For some, though, the dream has died or, perhaps, has never been considered. In regard to organizational leadership, we must reject two positions as ethically unacceptable. First, we must challenge a designated leader's assertion that "I cannot lead." That assertion often comes with a careful delineation of barriers and obstacles standing in the way or with a list of factors that limit the speaker's leadership effectiveness. Second, an individual organization member's assertion "I am not responsible to lead" and his or her disavowal of the right or responsibility to lead is equally unacceptable. I suggest that in the profoundly moral enterprise of working in concert with others to achieve social goals, we will stand on firmer ground when we ask and seek to answer the better question: "How will I lead?" or "What will mark my leadership contribution?"

This chapter began with an analogy of politics as forest fire. Yet throughout *Leadership at the Interface*, our focus will be not on the fire but on the interface, on those critical points of intersection that demand our intervention and participation. Throughout this book, the focus is on leaders who are prepared to be *first responders*, leaders who seek always to understand interface complexities. The goal of *Leadership at the Interface* is to aid that effort. Chapter 2 focuses on an early leadership task – making sense of our organizational context and identifying its complexities and characteristics.

END NOTES

1. Natural Resources Canada, "The State of Canada's Forests 2003-04," *Natural Resources Canada*, http://www.nrcan.rncan.gc.ca/cfs_scf/national/what-quoi/sof/sof04/views01_e.html.
2. *Mirriam-Webster Online,* http://www.merriam-webster.com/dictionary/interface.
3. Robert Dahl & Bruce Steinbrickner, *Modern Political Analysis*, 6th ed. (Englewood Cliffs, NJ: Prentice-Hall, 2003), 3.
4. Christopher Hodgkinson, *Educational Leadership: The Moral Art* (New York: State University of New York Press, 1991), 34.
5. Bernard Crick, *In Defence of Politics*, 5th ed. (London: Continuum, 2005).
6. Dahl & Stinebrickner, *Modern Political Analysis*.
7. Joseph Blase, *The Politics of Life in Schools* (Thousand Oaks, CA: Corwin, 1991), 11.
8. Madsen Pirie, "Adam Smith Institute and Micropolitics," *Adam Smith Institute*, http://www.adamsmith.org/blog-archive/000902.php.
9. Dahl & Stinebrickner, *Modern Political Analysis*, 28.
10. Crick, *In Defence of Politics*, 153.
11. Dahl & Stinebrickner, *Modern Political Analysis*, 33.
12. Crick, *In Defence of Politics*, 16.
13. Hodgkinson, *Educational Leadership*, 35.
14. Ibid., 37.
15. Crick, *In Defence of Politics*, 7.
16. Ibid., 17.

CHAPTER 2 — MAPPING THE GROUND:
MAKING SENSE OF ORGANIZATIONAL LIFE

Framing: a quality of communication that causes others to accept one meaning over another. . . . people become leaders through the ability to manage meaning. Indeed, all truly great leaders have mastered the skill of framing.[1]

A conference speaker opened by asking a group of senior organizational leaders, "Show of hands, please – how many of you want more pain on the job?" The audience response was predictable – no one raised a hand. Yet all understood the significance of the question, and probably each knew the reality of work-related angst. For some the difficulty of making sense of one's surroundings in turbulent times, in what Vaill has described as "permanent white water," may have been near the top of the list.[2] For others, the sustained pressure of multiple, often conflicting demands was a critical element. For leaders in complex surroundings, intensity is a fact of life. Still, "despite the stress they are under, they are all being urged to innovate, to look for ways to improve the operation of the system, to upgrade their own skills, and to work more effectively with each other."[3]

Leaders face challenges and uncertainties similar in nature and intensity to those realized by that conference group. For some, virtually all of their primary and traditional reference groups – their communities of interest – have changed profoundly in recent years. Those changes have been reflected in similar shifts throughout society. Staff groups typically are organized; many groups have broadened their missions to embrace a much broader social mandate than simply bargaining for salaries and benefits. In the third sector, members and supporters assert their right to have a voice and a place in organizational affairs beyond volunteering their assistance. Many groups are highly aware of and skilled at exercising their own strategic roles on the platform of organizational micropolitics. They are faced by those anxious to give them space at center stage and by others who would prefer to restrict the entry and participation of those they term 'outsiders.'

The realities of organizational life – ever-present uncertainty and its related tensions and challenges – nurture the challenge facing leaders. Those are commonalities, not circumstances limited to particular settings. In fact, the experience of leaders is more likely to be shared than unique. Wherever we work, if we are engaged in human enterprises, we face a world unimagined by our earlier colleagues. Our quest, like that of our predecessors, is to make sense of the sometimes puzzling circumstances that surround life on the shifting sands of our organizations. As we search specifically and personally, it is vital that we maintain a dialogue with others who face similar challenges. Understanding what the leadership craft demands of its practitioners will help us to understand the demands of our particular context.

It is common to read in leadership literature about the importance of vision and the need for leaders to possess it. Often, though, the underpinnings of that sort of direction-focused thinking are undefined. We attach a variety of meanings to the term, some of them less than useful. Perhaps we expect that by definition leaders are visionaries – that line of thinking will usually send us back to search for a less challenging definition. If we try to live up to the illusion we hope that our disguises will not fall away and allow others to discover that we are less able than we should be to discern the future and chart the course.

Because we cannot know the future with certainty, we rely on our capacity to make and help others make the best and most plausible approximations, to make reasonable sense of our surroundings. We frame our ideas as concepts we can plausibly present to others. Hodgkinson has captured both the importance and the possibility of this dimension of future-focused leadership in his assertion that "the leader can and must try to sense the spirit of the times and the direction of trends, and fulfill a duty to match the organizational culture with the larger culture that surrounds and sustains it."[4] Hodgkinson presents a leadership task that does not begin with immediate circumstances or the urgent pressures of the moment. It is rooted instead in a disciplined effort to gain a much broader grasp of circumstance, setting, and context.

Most of us accept that we may not be unusually intuitive either at trying to crystal-ball-gaze into the organization's future or at seeking to shape the future we envision for our organization. With that realization in mind, we might focus more usefully on the idea of sense-making, of searching for conceptual clarity regarding the circumstances in which we are immersed and in which we must survive. In this way, we are able to help ourselves and our organizations to grow.

We might think of experimentation and the development of theory as a sequenced effort to observe circumstances, explain data, predict future occurrences, and control events. Yet we have learned that the scientific process, especially as it relates to people in organizations, is not as neat, ordered, or reliable as we would prefer. In fact, the action-outcome connection may not only be tenuous but also unpredictable and surprising. In his classic work, Galbraith suggests that logic and data will not always lead to outcomes that we have anticipated or planned:

> The connection between any particular action and its result is uncertain at best and quite frequently unknown... Power... regularly passes to those who are able to assert the unknown with the greatest conviction. Power accrues not to the individual who knows; it goes to the one who... believes that [she or he] knows and can persuade others to that belief.[5]

We are pointed toward an ethical question and a potential dilemma for the individual who is called upon to lead: "What will form the basis of my call to others who might follow or join with me in the leadership initiative?" I assume that our answers will be rooted in good data, sound judgment, and a standard of behavior that reflects a concern for the welfare of others. Our sense-making must be soundly rooted in a moral base that will usually ensure legitimate outcomes. I assume also that leadership demands a better-than-average ability to make sense of things and to convey that sense meaningfully to others engaged in the enterprise at hand.

LEADERS AND CONCEPTUAL FRAMEWORKS

The authenticity of a leader will be established in part on the basis of the ability she or he has to analyze and assess surroundings and circumstances. We are used to hearing (often in university courses) about **conceptual frameworks**. Sometimes we walk away from those conversations with a less-than-satisfying realization of what the term means despite a sense that understanding it may be important to our leadership effectiveness. Simply put, a conceptual framework is a mental picture of the circumstance we are considering.

The analogy of a pair of glasses through which we can view events and circumstances has been used, but it can be a flawed analogy. It suggests that if we are not wearing a particular set of conceptual glasses, we will not have a conceptual framework. The reality is that in regard to any phenomenon to which we can relate with some degree of understanding (i.e. a chair) the human mind *will* have a picture of that concept or set of concepts – we will have a conceptual framework. Asked to sketch our conception of a chair, we will draw different pictures from those of others because we diverge in our experience, our preferences, our values, our biases and, perhaps, even in our ability to see with the particular conceptual glasses we are wearing. If we are unable to see at all, we will rely on our other senses to create a conceptual framework. Our conceptual frameworks may be useful, or flawed and unhelpful, but they will not be absent. If we can apprehend some meaning for the term or concept we are exploring, we will view it through a metaphorical lens. We can never think without using a conceptual framework.

We rely on conceptual frameworks to make even limited sense of our worlds. Our sketches of a chair will differ in appearance and usefulness, but in the end, after bringing to bear our experience and perhaps testing the chair for strength and reliability, we will choose it as a place to sit. Believing in the validity of our understanding, we choose to risk. If someone else also sits because of our suggestion, perhaps even that may provide a crude and primitive validation of our leadership capability! On the other hand, if the chair collapses when we sit on it, we will need to address another set of issues and perhaps rethink our conceptual framework.

We might agree on the ubiquity of conceptual frameworks, but that says little about the utility of any given view. Our understanding of an event, a circumstance, or a pattern may be full and complete. On the other hand, it may be incomplete or flawed. We may have a conceptual framework that is useful or one that is not. Almost certainly it will differ from another person's perspective; that is part of the richness of creative human thought. The leadership imperative is to demonstrate that on balance our conceptual frameworks, our understandings, and our interpretations can provide a useful foundation for our leadership decisions and actions.

To this point, we have defined conceptual frameworks in descriptive terms using vocabulary that would permit a photograph to be classed as a conceptual framework. Life in organizations demands more than that – it expects that we will analyze, interpret, and value. Usually our conceptual frameworks are more public than private because that is how we communicate in order to share our understanding and influence the course of events. This is particularly the case when the task is one of leadership and especially so when the context is political. In order to to lead we must first be able to *read*, that is, to read what is around us in the way of events, circumstances, and behaviors. Fairhurst and Sarr assert that "leadership is about taking the risk of managing meaning. We assume a leadership role, indeed we become leaders, through our ability to decipher and to communicate meaning out of complex and confusing situations."[6]

This book focuses on the reality of micropolitics in organizations and on the implications of that reality for leaders and leadership. I have noted that we vary in our understanding of situations. Our conceptual frameworks will often differ from those of our colleagues. The leadership imperative in this regard is that we strive for useful analyses of circumstances so that our conceptual frameworks – our ways of thinking about things – will be useful both to ourselves and to others. This is especially the case in the organizational context, where it is essential that leaders be able to manage meaning, to see, to make sense of circumstances, and to act.

If we are to lead capably, the initial leadership challenge is

To know what we
SEE
when we
See
What we
see.

The further challenge is both

To choose and to know what we
DO
when we
Do
what we
do.

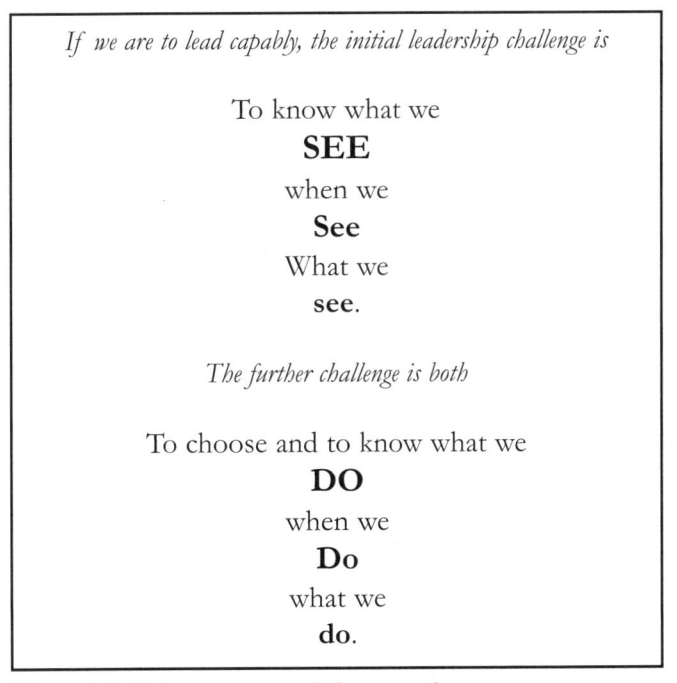

Figure 2.1 Using conceptual frameworks.

The leadership challenge is to develop skill in understanding what we often term the 'big picture', to understand what we **SEE** when we **See** what we **see** (Figure 2.1). Insight and understanding permit us to **SEE** the big picture, the broad patterns and regularities. We **See** emerging regularities and tentative shapes in the single events that we **see**. The hard work of analysis takes place around our efforts to **SEE**. Beyond that though, leaders face a moral challenge – to know and to choose what they **DO** when they **Do** what they **do**. The hard work of addressing dilemmas takes place around the business of choosing. Few would argue against either Machiavelli's ability to see or his clarity about what could be done to deal with what he saw. Yet we are not anxious to be identified as *Machiavellian*.

We understand that both in specific circumstances and over time, the nature of our leadership practice will be examined for the degree to which it reflects our ability to see and to help others see. It will also be assessed for the quality of what we do and avoid doing and what we influence others to do or not do. We understand that there are times, perhaps more often than not, when we are compelled to **do** before we are able to **see** clearly. We do not always have adequate opportunity to survey our options for action and choose the most credible and defensible alternative. In those instances we must rely on the strength of a vital third dimension of leadership understanding – knowing what we **VALUE** when we **Value** what we **value**.

Understanding Micropolitics:
A Framework for Action

When we work in complex circumstances, we inevitably experience some puzzlement and lack of comprehension as we seek to make sense of what we see. We will not always know immediately how to interpret a situation, how to usefully describe it, how it fits with our value framework, or precisely what to do about it. My primary purpose in this chapter is to offer a way of thinking about political complexity, a framework for understanding and acting on what faces us. You will be able to practice your understanding through the critical incidents and case studies that appear in Chapters 9 and 10.

The nature of systems theory and of micropolitics requires us to engage in the hard task of understanding the complexities and intricacies of organizational life because, finally, we must *act*. We can assume variability and unpredictability to be the norm in many of the circumstances we face. We cannot assume that the actors and audiences we identify as the only people involved in events leading toward a particular decision are in fact the total group of stakeholders. Similarly, we cannot be guaranteed that those constituencies will remain static throughout the life of a situation. With those caveats in mind though, we can use the model depicted in Figure 2.2 as a basis for thoughtful action in a broad range of situations and circumstances.

CIRCUMSTANCE AS LEADERSHIP OPPORTUNITY

Not much about politics in organizations is neutral, but the word **circumstance** comes close. It is defined in the Oxford dictionary as time, place, manner, cause, location or surroundings of an act or event; external conditions affecting or that might affect action. That definition prevents us from choosing inaction as a leadership alternative. Being paralyzed by circumstance simply is not an option. That said, circumstance is the context and crucible for leadership choice and action. Leaders must assess, weigh, and consider. They must be alert to options and to the implications of their options in a broad array of circumstances (Figure 2.2, center circle).

Urgency and Importance

Not all circumstances carry equal weight. Some circumstances can be ignored or postponed, and occasionally that is our reasonable choice. Some, however, demand our attention; they simply cannot be overlooked, even for a time. It is helpful to classify circumstances for purposes of planning and decision making; we might identify them as either **urgent** or **important**. What we consider **urgent** cannot wait. We cannot afford to delay our response, or there will be consequences. There are risks both ways, and that is captured in the evaluating. To decide that a circumstance is not urgent often carries immediate and sometimes painful consequences if we have misjudged or if others do not agree with our judgment. Sometimes the consequences are minor and ignoring them seems worth the risk. In other instances our response must be immediate; the greater good demands that we act.

Other circumstances, while they are not urgent, clearly are **important**. We may delay the start of our action, and its pace and direction may vary. Some circumstances can be addressed in a short time, while others will take on the character of a project or a program. Delayed action may be necessary, and it may be appropriate in some situations. However, if we decide that an action is important it must remain on the list for action. The consequences of inaction may not be immediate or acutely painful, but they can be broad and far reaching.

Yet these two types of circumstances can overlap; they are not mutually exclusive. A situation or problem may be both **urgent** and **important**. In fact, that is frequently the case in organizational life. We rely on our experience, we consult with colleagues, and we engage in professional development programs and activities. We watch, we listen, we read, and we assess. At our best, we consider sense-making a pursuit, a lifelong learning opportunity carried out in the micropolitical context of leadership action. The nature of our circumstances will affect the nature of that leadership action.

Leadership Action: Bounded, Considered, Reflective

Sometimes there are few alternatives. Smoke in the hallway demands that we call the fire department and clear the building. Legislation, policies, and salary agreements will structure aspects of our daily life in organizations, sometimes decreeing how we must act in particular circumstances. In many cases, these structures are deliberately designed to limit our options. We understand that reality, usually we accept it, and sometimes we welcome it. In those circumstances, our initiatives and responses are constrained; our leadership alternatives are **bounded** (Figure 2.2). If however we intend our leadership practice to be thorough

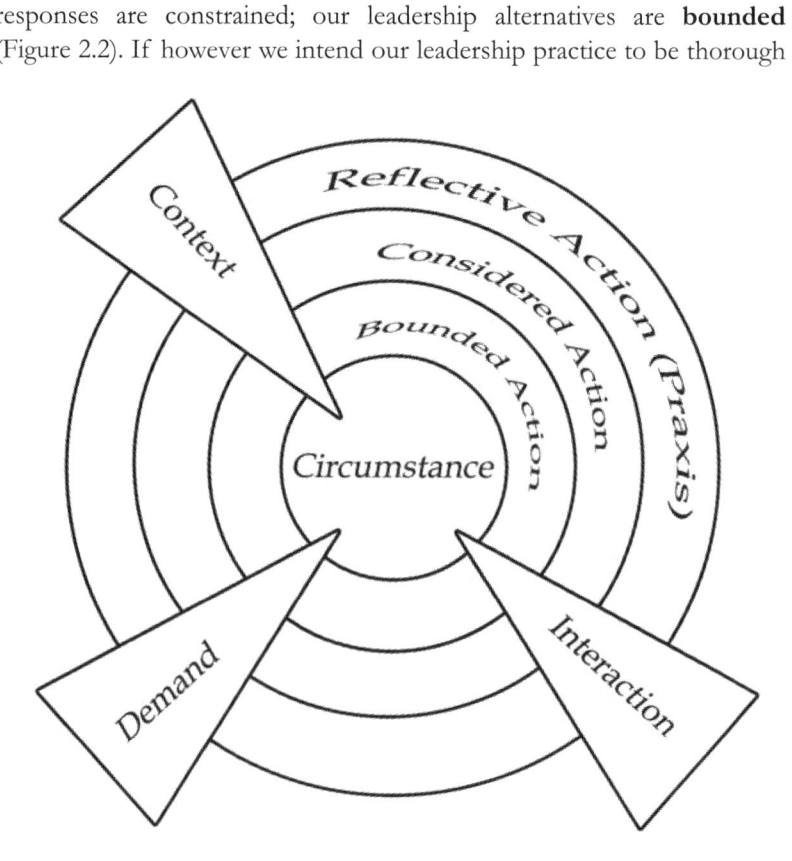

Figure 2.2 Politics in organizations: A framework for action

and defensible on behalf of our organization and its people, we may not immediately accept boundaries as real or necessary. At times we may test and challenge boundaries on behalf of those we serve. Our testing and checking is in itself leadership activity. Eventually we must act, even when the possibilities are bounded.

Leaders are always pressed by circumstances. Fortunately that pressure rises and falls; we have opportunities to exercise judgment and create opportunities. Those around us expect that we will be thoughtful and will engage in legitimate decision making processes. They expect opportunities to be engaged with us in those processes, some more than others. Whatever characterizes the decision process, they eventually expect that the resulting actions will be **considered**, that they will be characterized by thoughtfulness and by legitimate processes.

When we are involved in **reflective** action, and sometimes those opportunities seem less frequent than we would prefer, we are engaged in **praxis**. To be true to the term, we might think of praxis as a seamless, indivisible process of practice and reflection on that practice, always with growth and development in mind, always engaged in the search for possibilities. Praxis is truly a lifelong state of being and becoming, a hallmark of leadership that really does make a difference in the lives of those it touches. Praxis is not detached, it is attuned and attentive. We are familiar with the term *reflective practitioner*. Lightly, we might coin the term *praxitioner* to capture the essence of reflective action.

I have depicted these action alternatives in Figure 2.2 as a set of three concentric circles surrounding the circumstance. The smallest circle, representing **bounded action**, lies closest to the immediacy of the circumstance, offering fewer degrees of freedom for leadership response. The second circle broadens the range of possibilities, allowing opportunity thoughtfulness and **considered action**. Finally, the outer circle suggests 'big picture' opportunities for **reflective action**, that is, for **praxis**.

Whatever the nature of our leadership action – bounded, considered, or reflective – we carry it out in settings marked by complexity. In short, to function effectively in the human context of our organizations we must understand and engage with the **micropolitical** nature of our setting.

ELEMENTS OF MICROPOLITICS

The key process elements of micropolitics (Figure 2.2) fall into three categories: **context** (the external and internal environments), **demand** (both source and substance), and **interaction** (influencing patterns and processes). We will examine each of these categories, leaving unanswered for the moment the question of **outcomes**, which will be discussed at the chapter's end.

Context: External and Internal Environments

In systems terms we identify an organization's context as its environments, both internal and external. Almost always environments are complex and consist of multiple, often overlapping components. To be as aware as possible of the parameters or boundary conditions of those environments and their accompanying circumstances is a leadership imperative. At an entry level, regardless of the degree of skill we have developed in understanding and working through the challenges of politics in organizations, we understand that **constraints** and **pressures** are endemic. If we accept the notion that resources are finite, we will also understand that limiting factors will affect and in some cases even determine our actions. Actual constraints and pressures will vary; they may change without apparent intervention or warning during the life of the matter at hand. Wirt and Kirst, in a reference to schools and school systems that can easily be applied elsewhere, have identified "three broad stimuli" that affect organizations:[7]

> The *state of the economy* greatly influences the amount of resources available and their allocation.... *the power of new concepts*, particularly those centered on social change.... [and] *crystallizing* events that capture core constituencies and dramatically generate new demands.[8]

The meaning of the first phrase is self-evident – a glance at television news tells us that the financial scene facing both our industrial and our social plans is a major determiner of our courses of action. We are barraged with reports of events we did not contemplate as possibilities. New concepts can have either a focusing or a distracting effect on the business of organizational work. Crystallizing events will sometimes change our plans, our decisions, even our way of life. We are faced daily with an array of new ideas and possibilities. Often those are accompanied by pressures on leaders to respond.

Each of these stimuli carries great potential to create constraints and pressures. Viewed from a political perspective, the circumstances to which they relate will usually have strong human connections also. Whether or not there is sufficient money to fund a government or a service organization initiative provides a case in point. Often the answer is "No," but almost always that answer is greeted with a full range of responses regarding the asserted merits of a particular request and the perceived veracity of the individual or body denying it. We may be presented also with an array of alternatives and modified possibilities for action that may be regarded as acceptable compromises. The leadership imperative is to arrive at a reasonable understanding of circumstances most likely to affect the decision making process, the final outcome, or both, and to act on our understanding.

> **Assertion 2.1: Understanding of constraints facing the parties remains incomplete unless those parties hold a common data base. Even then, holding common data does not necessarily ensure common interpretation and understanding, let alone agreement.**
>
> **Assertion 2.2: Analysis of a constraint will remain incomplete until we have gained some understanding of why it is seen as a limiting factor.**

By definition politics involves human participation. Even the majority of influences that originate in the surrounding environment are people-mediated. Each differs from others in its relevance to the decision at hand. Life in organizations is lived by **actors and audiences** – participants, stakeholders, and onlookers. I include onlookers since both in the theater and in the real world of daily life in an organization interested onlookers can play a significant role in both process and final outcome. Beyond that the lines will often blur, both on the stage and on the street.

Active resistance to remaining simply an onlooker is characteristic of our society, especially when we have a vested interest in a process and its outcomes. Lack of awareness of that fact, or determining that some onlookers should simply remain spectators, is a key part of some of our current conflicts – witness the struggles we have seen between a city council and neighborhood residents over matters of parking and paving.

In many organizational contexts, the initial listing of parties is straightforward: governors or trustees, administrators, members, staff, clients, donors, to name some of those most directly interested in the organization's activities. The full list of potential parties may be longer and membership may vary among circumstances. Not all are or will become active, but all have attachments of interest and preference. From time to time, depending on the issue, parties may change their affiliations. We will discuss actors and audiences further in Chapter 5.

Every organization is located in a context of **resource availability**. We typically think of resources as a key constraint; I have identified them as a unique and powerful contextual element. To this point, resources are to some extent an abstraction: the amount we have becomes relevant only when we juxtapose it against what we assert is our need for a resource.

In most cases we set boundaries around resources by identifying a **policy context** – an array of decisions we have made to guide resource allocation decisions. In an earlier time, those decisions would often have settled the matter. We understand now that our policies are living statements that not only offer a basis for action but can also be revisited and modified, even discarded and replaced.

Each of these realities shapes and influences the policy context of our organizations. Even before we contemplate new initiatives or decide whether and how to respond, our present context itself becomes a variable. A food bank must change its strategies when a major employer ceases doing business. Schools in an area will be affected by declining enrolment or a growing number of families in crisis. While the term *first responder* may not apply in these circumstances, those who lead our organizations face another imperative – a critical need to be informed early and in relevant depth about looming and urgent developments likely to affect those organizations.

Constraints and pressures, actors and audiences, resource availability, and the policy context: these are just four examples of elements of an organization's internal and external environments. The leadership challenge is to understand these and other complexities that surround and make up the contexts within which leaders work. Making sense of and engaging in dialogue about these environments challenges leaders to add richness to the process of developing and growing both our organizations and the people within them.

Demand: Source and Substance

The constraints and pressures that surround and mark our organizations – in other words, the larger social and economic patterns that affect their operation and the lives of their inhabitants – commonly translate into **demand**. In terms of resources, we identify our wants and perceived needs as the first step in articulating our demands for a share of what is available.

We present our demands, even when they are shaped as mild requests, to communicate what we hope to secure. Often we are less overt about the origins of those demands, sometimes because we desire to keep that quiet or because we are not at all clear about their source. However, our demands fundamentally originate in the **values** we hold. Hodgkinson has described values as "concepts of the desirable with motivating force."[9]

Our values might also be considered the fundamental 'because' that drives our actions.

Assertion 2.3: Values are most likely to be revealed by evidential indicators, not by being announced or claimed.

Our values will shape our **interests**. In terms of the concepts we have explored, it is useful to think of our values as providing a foundation for our interests and preferences. Given the immensity of the task of discerning values, identifying interests and preferences will usually present a more manageable challenge. At minimum, our conversations about interests and preferences may contain more *discussables* than *nondiscussables*; this openness may be less likely when we probe a person's values. We might infer that a particular value is held by an actor or an audience. Interests and preferences are more likely to be made explicit.

Assertion 2.4: We can spot preferences, and we can often elicit interests, but values are a more complex and elusive target.

Assertion 2.5: Uncovering interests is important to understanding preferences, but the process may be difficult and our conclusions sometimes uncertain.

When multiple ways to achieve our interests exist, we will sort them according to our preferences. By definition, the terms **interests and preferences** exclude the possibility of a neutral or disinterested observer. In fact, we could restate the terms as "interests, *therefore* preferences" to underline the fact that parties who prefer a particular outcome are more likely to sit at a table labeled 'I care' than at one marked 'I don't care.'

Assertion 2.6: Preferences are more likely to be flexible and open to alternative possibilities than are interests.

Having clarified our preferences, we can begin to solidify our demands by clarifying our **commitments** to selected possibilities. We would rather choose one path than another and we will often search for allies that will share our leanings. Our commitments move us to a final course of action as we translate values into measurable outcomes. This in turn develops our **agendas**, which will shape our efforts.

Whatever the value basis, whatever the source of our demands, those demands will be displayed as **substance** and captured as a **decision focus**. In most cases the end point of our deliberations will be to allocate value, often described as distributing scarce resources, but at this point we are some distance from that outcome. Identifying a decision focus is in itself a political task, for we will often have an interest not only in the outcome of the decision but also in the processes leading to that outcome.

If our interest is in gaining an additional staff position in our department, for example, we will view enhanced staffing levels as the focus of the decision. We would rather not see the debate focus on equipment acquisition, especially if it is unlikely that there will be enough money for everything.

> **Assertion 2.7: Knowing what is to be decided is prerequisite to further action.**
>
> **Assertion 2.8: Even to agree about what must be decided is likely sometimes to be difficult.**
>
> **Assertion 2.9: When we believe that agreement exists, it is probably worthwhile to check carefully that our perception is shared.**
>
> **Assertion 2.10: The decision reached may address the initial decision statement, or it may not – circumstances and preferences change.**

Interaction: Influencing Patterns and Processes

Activity at the interface, which we might call **interaction**, forms the life and turmoil of the micropolitical scene in organizations. That scene is characterized by an array of **influencing patterns and processes**, including **cooperation, conflict, collaboration,** and **compromise**.

The politically astute leader will be skilled at *identifying* patterns and processes of interaction and influence. She or he will be competent in *working* in the influencing arena and will stand on an ethical base that makes sense of the *identifying* and guides the *working*.

Politics exists in organizations that are in motion – places of deciding and choosing, accepting and rejecting, valuing and prioritizing. Each of these activities is human at the core. Organizations do not decide; people decide. Organizations are simply conduits for conveying and representing the actions of people, even though we often designate those actions accurately and reasonably as the organization's position or policy. Where actions are directed at organizational goals or at an acceptable blend of organizational and personal goals, we recognize them as legitimate indicators of interests and preferences and as evidence of power and influence. The leadership challenge is to ensure that we safeguard the use of power and influence in ways and toward ends that are positive and constructive.

Assertion 2.11: Organizational decisions provide some indication of values, but the moral heart of leadership is most clearly visible in the influencing patterns and processes that lead to those decisions being implemented.

END RESULTS: OUTPUTS AND OUTCOMES

Our circumstances exist in social contexts, the environments within and around our organizations. Those contexts are marked by demand and we address demand through interaction. We seek to influence output and outcome through process. The model presented in Figure 2.2 is a process model. Rather than including end results as a component of the model, I suggest that its leadership-focused goal is to change a circumstance, to create a new reality and a new circumstance.

The creation of new realities and new circumstances, because it is a political process, will ensure a continuing need for skilled, morally competent, political leadership. Conflicts once thought resolved may resurface in a new circumstance as conflicts that now need to be *re*-solved. The achievement of end results cannot necessarily be considered as the final outcome of a linear process. We may achieve certainty, but we might also discover it to be a temporary certainty or even a new uncertainty. What seems initially to be a final outcome may turn out to be the beginning of a new process. That is the reality of leadership in the micropolitical context.

When we achieve a result, though it may be incremental and temporary, we have allocated value. Usually, we will also have allocated resources. Even so, it is important to remember that while the terms *value* and *resource* are connected, they are not synonymous. Resource allocation decisions are perhaps better described as evidence that value has been assigned or that the effort to resolve a matter in one's interest has been won or lost. The term **value allocation** describes the results, or the outcomes, of values-based decision making. Perhaps extra funding is awarded for a special initiative or a request for more staff is granted. The initial value criterion is not that resources have been allocated but that an identifiable decision to do so has been made. Obviously the value action is not complete until decisions have been implemented. Moreover, though it may be tempting to believe that a particular value action signifies the end of the matter, that will not always be the case. It could in fact be argued that will seldom be the case. Some of the reasons for this will become clear as we examine the other elements of the model.

Reaching a shared understanding of what is to be decided is an essential early task. Establishing this commonality is an important part of our ongoing effort to address the conflict that inevitably will arise when value-rich decisions are made. Clarifying the decision focus gives parties with differing interests two opportunities: first, to ensure that they are clear about the actual substance of the decision(s) being considered; and second, to seek in the early stages to influence the nature of decisions. That dynamic precedes and also may affect the chances that 'right' decisions will be made.

> Assertion 2.12: In most resource allocation decisions, chances are good that someone will perceive inequity.
>
> Assertion 2.13: To avoid viewing shaping and decisions as wins and losses is a perpetual leadership challenge.
>
> Assertion 2.14: The values revealed by a decision will be perceived differently. There may be as many views on what the decision *means* as there are people offering comment.

A closed view of decision making in a micropolitical context might suggest that understanding will be attained once a matter has been concluded. Unfortunately for many former incumbents of office, that is not the case, leaving the former holder of an office or position with a classic and unanswered conceptual question, "Why didn't I see that?" Awareness in advance of the range of possible outcomes, and a productive canvassing of the possibilities, demand a thoroughgoing competence. That competence is built through knowledge of the task at hand and of the organizational and political context of decision making. Despite possessing that knowledge and the competence of preparation and experience, our familiarity with organizational life suggests that we will not always be able to predict all of the actual outcomes of decisions.

> Assertion 2.15: Time pressures and the tyranny of the urgent can threaten one's ability to see outcome implications.
>
> Assertion 2.16: A selective tendency of decision makers to ignore outcome implications, even obvious ones, is to be expected as a possibility, perhaps even a frequent occurrence.
>
> Assertion 2.17: There is not necessarily any correspondence between the perceived importance of a realized implication and its actual effects.

We will not always understand clearly the circumstances that characterize our working lives. We have a leadership obligation nonetheless to seek that understanding. We can be aided in the venture by our colleagues; by structuring opportunities to build our knowledge, understanding, and skill; and by personal commitment to do the hard work involved. Each of those strategies however has an enemy. First, we often disclose less rather than more to our colleagues, because we see an element of strength in our professional privacy and because we know that they are busy too. The loss comes when we fail to seek out colleagues with whom we can build trusting and mutually supportive working relationships. Second, we are often less than satisfied with our professional development experiences, sometimes because quality is lacking or because we have not matched our needs and interests with appropriate experiences. Sometimes the opportunities we desire simply are not available. We may feel the loss in our gradually decreasing capability to cope with rapidly increasing complexity and challenge. Finally, we often acknowledge, most often privately and internally, that we do not always work hard on our own professional growth. The loss in this case lies in our own view of ourselves as leaders. That is both a personal and a moral loss.

This book is about understanding the realities of leadership in contexts that are profoundly political, particularly in this chapter. We have identified a framework that might aid our effort to understand these terms, a way of looking at politics in our organizations. We have focused on identifying elements of a model that we can apply in a variety of situations as an aid to analyzing, deciding, and acting. Armed with this understanding, we will be better equipped to design and to deliver to ourselves our own competence-building plan of professional growth and development. When we do that we develop a deeper understanding of politics in our organizations and equip ourselves and others to lead more effectively.

End Notes

1. Gail Fairhurst & Robert Sarr, *The Art of Framing: Managing the Language of Leadership* (San Francisco: Jossey-Bass, 1996), xi, xiv.
2. Peter Vaill, *Learning as a Way of Being: Strategies for Survival in a World of Permanent White Water* (San Francisco: Jossey-Bass, 1996), 4.
3. Ibid., 7.
4. Hodgkinson, *Educational Leadership*, 83.
5. John Galbraith, *The Anatomy of Power* (Boston: Houghton Mifflin, 1983), 41.
6. Fairhurst & Sarr, *The Art of Framing*, 2.
7. Frederick Wirt and Michael Kirst, *Schools in Conflict* (Berkeley: McCutchan, 1992), 20.
8. Ibid., 20-21.
9. Hodgkinson, *Administrative Philosophy*, 110.

Chapter 3 — Who Leads?
Context and Capability

> *Infusing purpose, harnessing human energy, and orchestrating the many tasks and groups involved in guiding the affairs of... [an] organization are challenging endeavors. They require a diverse set of talents, a great deal of patience, an exceptional amount of strength and stamina, a deep sense of caring, a sensitivity to the diverse needs and concerns of a wide variety of stakeholders, and many other skills and competencies. [Leaders] live in a world of demands and public expectations, a world that sometimes seems irrational, always presents competing pressures, is occasionally more exciting than the occupations wish, and is constantly changing.*[1]

Where we gather around purpose and goals, we seek to accomplish both through leadership. Leadership and politics are inextricably intertwined throughout that endeavor. I suggest that our politics can be anchored in a solid moral base of thoughtful, reflective leadership practiced in ways that that will better the human condition. Leadership, I propose, is a broadly based human activity open to the many rather than restricted to a few. The nature and effectiveness of our leadership practice will be tightly linked to the character of our political wisdom and skill.

Clarifying an Understanding of Leadership

The notion of leadership is at once alluring, elusive, and frustrating. We have studied much, written much, and asserted much. We believe we recognize leadership when we experience it, yet we do not always agree on what we have seen or what the term means. We understand intuitively, or at least we believe, that there are capable leaders among us. We may count ourselves among them. We are deeply concerned when there appears to be a lack of leadership in places that are important to us, yet we are sometimes reluctant to grant others the opportunity to lead. Our reluctance may be rooted to some degree in ego. Equally, it may reflect our discomfort with the fact that we lack a clear, precise, widely accepted understanding of leadership, a phenomenon complicated by its symbiotic relationship with politics.

Issues surrounding the definition, study, and practice of leadership are widely recognized and have been long standing. Fullan has pointed out that leadership has been the focus of "countless articles over the past decade," an observation that might suggest we have access to a growing body of systematic and reliable knowledge.[2] He acknowledges our progress on some fronts, noting that we "have mapped out much of the territory, including broadening the concept of leadership."[3] Yet in regard to the present state of affairs, Fullan asserts there is "a shortage of qualified leaders at all levels in the educational system."[4] One might reasonably infer that his statement applies also to other fields of endeavor. Common conversation suggests that this situation has not improved substantially in recent years and that it is replicated across many organizational settings. It is not uncommon to hear reference to a presumed 'crisis of leadership' in our schools, hospitals, churches, or government. Maxcy's assertions, which may relate to that reality, arguably remain current:

> It is clear that there has been no long-standing consensus as to what the leadership concept means.... We have seen that talk of leadership is conceptually flabby and under-developed. The term 'leadership' is used in so many and varied ways that rigor is seriously restricted.... Despite the huge literature, no clear-cut generalizations regarding leadership seem to hold.... The lack of proper theoretical grounding of the leadership concept has had the result of allowing muddled and contradictory research on leadership to become the norm rather than the exception.[5]

If our primary task is to practice leadership in our work and social settings, we owe it both to ourselves and to those touched by our actions to give a scrupulous effort to practice leadership that is both expert and humane. The journey demands that we develop a clear notion of who we will identify as a *leader* and in what contexts we might observe leadership. Yet our search will always be made more complex by the ever-present reality of politics.

Typically, we have narrowed our conceptions of the locus and nature of leadership. In terms of locus, we have often restricted our consideration to those individuals we formally designate as leaders, usually those who occupy senior positions in our organizations. In terms of its nature, we have often restricted our designation of leadership to matters of governance and policy. Hodgkinson, for example, has argued that the "term is commonly associated with administration. Sometimes it is identified with it.... administration is leadership and leadership is administration."[6] More recently, Fullan has asserted that "we are forcefully reminded that the notion of leadership must not be confined to those holding formal leadership positions. All leadership, if it is effective, must have a strong component of *sharedness*.[7]

We struggle with the vocabulary of leadership. Sometimes meanings vary between North American, European, and other settings, which may be simply a matter of linguistic convention. Often however, the root of the difficulty is more than a matter of usage. Sometimes we are bound by notions of role that stand in the way of a robust understanding of the term itself. As an example, Northouse has struggled to clarify the concept:

> Leadership is a process that is similar to management in many ways. Leadership involves influence, as does management. Leadership requires working with people, which management requires as well. Leadership is concerned with effective goal accomplishment and so is management.... But leadership is also different from management.... Management is about seeking order and stability; leadership is about seeking adaptive and constructive change.[8]

Perhaps we must separate the notion of what leadership *is* – its definition – from ideas about where we might locate or situate leadership. We need to be clear about what constitutes the work of leadership. Hodgkinson has stated clearly and helpfully that leadership is "the moving of people towards goals through a system of organization."[9] However, even that seemingly simple definition of leadership suggests a range of complexities surrounding the act. Therein lies the opportunity to direct our efforts at preparing and strengthening leaders in regard to those complexities, recognizing that leadership has a fundamental reason for being – the achievement of purpose through people.

Hodgkinson has contributed significantly to the field by clarifying for those involved in the study and practice of leadership that there are fundamental differences in the work to be done within organizations. In a manner particularly helpful to practitioners, he has distinguished clearly between two primary functions, asserting that

> an important conceptual difference exists between the terms administration and management.... by administration we mean those aspects dealing with the more value-laden issues and the human components of organizational life and by management we mean those aspects that are more routine, material, programmatic, and amenable to quantitative methods.[10]

Hodgkinson has acknowledged the persistence of the definitional problem, noting that "the mix of administration-management...will naturally vary, in complex and sometimes imponderable ways."[11] He is clear as to the distinction:

> Generally then administration is the broad art of determining organizational goals and motivating towards them while management is the ancillary, auxiliary, and subordinate science of specifying and implementing means toward the achievement of the same goals. Administration is ends-oriented, management means-oriented.[12]

That clearly articulated separation of function lends itself to further analysis and explication. However, Hodgkinson also asserted the synonymous character of two other concepts, implicitly raising the troublesome question of who may lead:

> Administration *is* leadership. Leadership *is* administration.... In short, good leadership entails good administration and bad administration entails bad leadership and leadership is what administration does, either successfully or otherwise. It follows that the philosophy of administration is also and always the philosophy of leadership.... To put it differently, both leadership and administration are the moving of people towards goals through a system of organization. This can be done well, or done badly, or done indifferently, but it cannot not be done at all.... But for our more technical purposes the terms "administration" and "leadership" merge and become synonymous.[13]

I propose a broader, more inclusive conception of leadership "for our more technical purposes" that I believe is supportable alongside Hodgkinson's text. I differ not at all with his depiction of the practice of administration as constituting leadership, as philosophy-in-action. He has asserted convincingly that "leadership pervades organizations and is intrinsic to their structure"[14] and that within organizations "no one can escape leadership acts and responsibilities."[15] Listing a variety of occupations within an organization, Hodgkinson has observed that "all may have to make exquisitely difficult value judgments, and all will be making crucial organizational decision, leadership acts."[16]

The capacity for leadership exists throughout our organizations but it must also be developed and encouraged within our organizations. Fullan observes that "adaptive solutions must be generated and carried out by scores of committed participants.... The scientific study of leadership has never been greater, nor has the recognition that broad-based leadership is the only way forward."[17] Wheatley also supports the idea of a broad, well-populated context for leadership:

> If we are to develop organizations of greater and enduring capacity, we have to turn to the people of our organization. We have to learn how to encourage the creativity and commitment that they wanted to express when they first joined the organization.... figure out how to reengage people in the important work of organizing.[18]

In a manner consistent with trends elsewhere in the emerging literature, Wheatley suggests a more widely accessible basis for leadership activity, noting that "organization occurs from the inside out, as people see what needs to happen, apply their experience and perceptions to the issue, and use their own creativity to invent solutions."[19] Throughout the literature, leadership is characterized as activity, as a *doing*. Hodgkinson describes leadership as "an event, not an attribute of personality. It is a description given to a dynamic complex of action.... Leadership is the conjunction of technical competence and moral complexity."[20]

> **Assertion 3.1: Organizations require leadership to accomplish purpose. Considering how to ensure that outcome creates a context for creating structures and appointing personnel.**

DISTRIBUTING LEADERSHIP – MORE THAN DELEGATING

If we agree that leadership is a vital activity and that its specific character involves the moving of people toward goals through a system of organization, then we open the door to productive discussion around the *doing* of leadership. Who will engage in the practice of leadership in our social services organizations – our schools and school systems, not-for-profit organizations, churches, societies, and others throughout the third sector? How will we utilize our knowledge to enhance the practice of leadership? If leadership is broadly based, are there opportunities for useful intra- and inter-organizational study? How will we assess the quality of leadership? Our questions demand answers, responses based on a solid conception of leadership that will be relevant to the organizational life we encounter daily. As a foundation for those answers, we might consider a model that assumes a broad base for leadership, a nonexclusive model that acknowledges the presence, relevance, and value of leadership situated at many points within the full range of organizational activity. The model draws in part from the emerging literature on **distributed leadership**.

The idea of distributing leadership within an organization is enticing. It also is frequently misconstrued. The well-intentioned implementation efforts of organizational leaders can easily become little more than a patriarchal assignment of duties to those for whose work the leader is responsible. However, if we adopt a sharply focused definition of leadership as the movement of people around purpose we can expand our understanding of the possibilities of distributed leadership. Bushe has asserted that

> a person provides leadership when they do something that helps a group or organization achieve its goals or increase its effectiveness. Anytime anyone helps a group of people increase their clarity or come to an agreement, they are providing leadership. You can provide leadership whatever your position in an organization.[21]

We use an array of what we might call 'D words' to describe our efforts to develop a stance on and a style of leadership. We delegate, we devolve, we decentralize, and we democratize. In the process though, we can easily forget that what we call delegation may be seen by others as simply handing off work without reward. Until we nurture the actual practice of leadership as purpose-focused change encouraged and enabled throughout our organization, we are simply rearranging.

In their survey of the literature, Bennett, Wise, Woods, and Harvey have developed a conception of distributed leadership that differentiates it from other characterizations.[22] Their conception may not appeal to all, perhaps because it challenges some deeply held values and beliefs. Our normative conceptions of leadership served us well for a time, but present social and organizational realities demand that we re-examine and challenge existing practice and 'find a better way.' Bennett and his colleagues draw on the work of Gronn and others to offer a three-element leadership perspective that may help in that search.[23] Three questions arising from their work inform our quest; those questions relate to **origins**, **boundaries**, and **capacity**.

In terms of **origins**, we can ask "Where have we found leadership for our organization?" Typically, we have focused our search on likely individuals – we need a company president, we have a vacancy for a school superintendent, or our advocacy organization lacks an executive director. If our search is effective, we can often see positive results in a short period. Our challenge beyond that is to nurture leadership that can be sustained over the long haul. For that to develop, we need organizations broadly committed to the sort of change that ensures our shared purpose will be accomplished. We need value-added leadership that is the multiplied product of organization-wide effort; leadership that reflects the contributions of the many rather than the few. Gronn refers to this as concertive action, or "the demonstrated or presumed structuring influence attributable to organization members acting in concert."[24] This demands we value the efforts of the many in building the leadership capacity of our organization.

In terms of **boundaries**, we might ask "Who might engage in leading our organization?" Organization members, particularly executives, will sometimes refer to *the leadership*. Sometimes those outside the inner circle will refer in similarly depersonalized terms to *the administration*. Both terms suggest that leadership is a function of the few. Distributed leadership, on the other hand, "is predisposed to widen the conventional net of leaders, thus in turn raising the question of which individuals and groups are to be brought into leadership or seen as contributors to it."[25]

How far will we go to build leadership capacity in our organization and within its members and clients? Speaking of schools, for example, Bennett and his peers ask, "In particular, what is the role of the parent or student body in relation to distributed leadership?"[26] In churches and voluntary organizations we might ask that question regarding those often referred to in similarly nonleadership terms as *the membership*. In both cases, the question can be answered by determining who should have a role in ensuring that our common organizational purpose will be accomplished.

In terms of **capacity**, the question arises "How broad is the potential leadership base for our organization?" Because our inclination is usually to look at those who have demonstrated leadership capacity, we can easily overlook "the idea that numerous, distinct, germane perspectives and capabilities can be found in individuals spread through the group or organization."[27]

The idea of distributed leadership can challenge our values and beliefs. In subtle ways we can both endorse and distort its practice. Fundamentally, distributed leadership is about simultaneous commitments to the organization's purposes and to its people. We can clarify those commitments by examining the contexts in which we can search out and seek to develop leadership capacity in our organizations.

Considering Context: A Framework for Study and Practice

In our social service organizations (and plausibly, in our business enterprises), we can identify four major activity sets that require the presence and practice of leadership: governance, administration, management, and service delivery. We might describe these as the organizational contexts for leadership. In a manner dependent on the nature of an individual's work, leadership in each of those settings will be characterized by different patterns of activity and by different knowledge and skill set requirements. Regardless of the specific nature of one's activity, the practice of leadership will be concerned with attaining organizational purpose. The practice of distributed leadership will also be concerned with engaging others in that venture.

The tasks of analysis, learning, and practice outlined in the following model proceed on the basis of several assumptions. The first is that we will endorse the notion of leadership as a shared enterprise in which many can and will engage. That conception is displayed in the format and content of Figure 3.1. The second assumption is that it will be useful to differentiate among some important contexts for leadership in organizations. Figure 3.1 identifies four such contexts. The third assumption is that systematic learning is both a key element of leadership activity and one that pervades and surrounds all four contexts. In some instances, context-relevant learning will bring us together for initiatives of common interest. On other occasions, our learning about practice will be specific to the nature of our work in governance, administration, management, or service delivery; we will group ourselves accordingly. The assumptions I have identified highlight the importance of working from a base of strong understanding regarding each of these four leadership contexts. They hint at three important questions: Who can lead? Who may lead? and Who will lead?

Leadership in Governing around Purpose

Organizations exist where people are gathered around a common purpose. Broadly speaking, our social service organizations exist for the purpose of bettering the human condition. Each has a societal focus; each addresses purposes related to human need and benefit. Our schools and school systems, for example, focus on the educational growth of children, and we expect them to fulfill that mandate.

```
         GOVERNING            DELIVERING
        around purpose          services

              ┌─────────────────┐
              │   CONTEXTS FOR  │
              │   LEADERSHIP    │
              │     ACTION      │
              └─────────────────┘

         ADMINISTERING          MANAGING
         toward goals            means
```

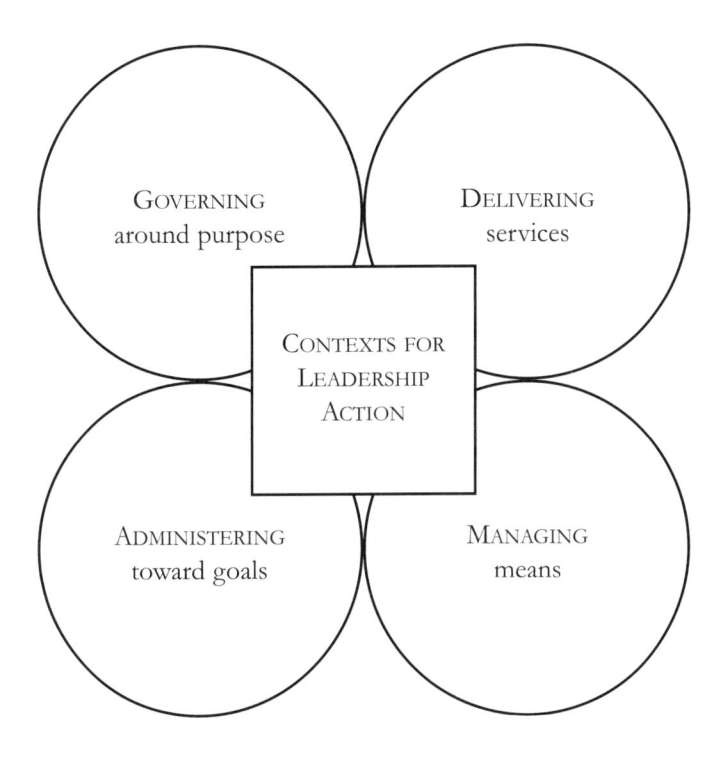

Figure 3.1 Contexts for leadership action

In many cases we have selected representatives to act on behalf of those whose interests are to be served. We entrust that work to individuals who will act together in the pursuit of common purpose. Typically, we have entrusted the work of schools in our local communities to those whose titles reflect the character of their task, trustees. We may call them by another name, perhaps directors, but we assemble them as corporate boards to work on behalf of education. We offer them little by way of preparation and we ask them to carry out their work under our close scrutiny. We rely on them to have a broader vision of the task at hand and to ensure that our schools fulfill the charge we have given. Fundamentally, we ask our boards to govern on behalf of those they serve; their work is to accomplish the organization's purpose.

What then of leadership in governance? The work is unique because of its character – governance occurs in a group setting. Our knowledge of leadership suggests that it will be strengthened as we broaden the base of involvement; governance demands that broadening and usually mandates its specific nature.

The uniqueness of governing leadership lies in its focus on basic purpose and direction – the long view, the 'big picture'. We expect our school boards to point schools toward what is at the horizon and beyond, to set the course for public education. John Selden, seventeenth-century British jurist, understood that the task of trustees was to seize the rudder, to determine direction. In an often-quoted excerpt from his memoirs, Selden observed that "they that govern most make the least noise. You see, when they row in a barge . . . he that governs sits quietly at the stern, and scarce is seen to stir" (1689/1885).[28] In regard to boards, the challenge is often to insist that they *will* govern despite pressure from those who would have them administer, manage, or deliver a service. The risk and sometimes the reality is that they will engage in one or more of those activities, each of which is properly assigned to others.

Leadership in Administering toward Goals

In the lexicon of leadership-related terms, *administration* and *management* are often contextualized and redefined, sometimes without adequate clarification, to the point that it can be difficult ensure common understanding. I identify the fundamental concern of administration as being about goals or ends. The primary focus of management, then, is on the means to achieve those ends.

Leadership as administration is closely associated with leadership as governance. Its essential task is to be clear about the organization's fundamental purposes and about the boundaries of executive action toward ensuring their realization. Beyond that, the administrator is concerned with communicating and accomplishing purpose. She or he is charged with engaging others across the organization in understanding, interpreting, and accomplishing the organization's intents. The administrator serves the vital linking function of ensuring voices for those affected by the identification and selection of purpose – voices of suggestion, of critique, of support, and of change.

The risk for the administrator is that she or he may invade governance or meddle in management or service delivery. In some cases, the nature of organizational reality is such that either of these errors may become attractive, perhaps almost compelling. Therein lies the risk. The challenge for the administrator is to maintain a broad view of how to accomplish the stated purpose, to focus on work around the organization's reason for being, and to refuse the distraction of shifting his or her main focus to work intended primarily for others.

Leadership in Managing Means

Frequently management is described as carrying out the executive function, hence the common reply, "I'll have to refer that to management." We often identify management, or managers, as carrying overall responsibility for the behavior of the organization, and we may have difficulty altering that popular conception. For purposes of this chapter, though, that characterization is less than useful. In the terms I have used in this discussion, the executive function is properly the primary role of those whose task is to administer. The core function of management is to ensure the means, to provide the tools, and to enable activity toward the stated purpose. Those who govern will determine the destination; those who administer will identify targets and strategies for reaching those targets, and those who manage will ensure that accomplishment is enabled and supported. As such, the work of managing involves leading.

Leadership in Delivering Service

At all times leadership is about purpose. Differentiation is possible because we have different roles to fulfill, but those efforts are always directed at achieving an organization's purpose. In some important ways, those who deliver service offer us a primary measure of whether organizational purpose is being achieved. In many cases, they are the most public presenters of the organization, seen by many as primary indicators of the extent to which the organization is fulfilling its mandate. Because of their proximity to those being served and their specialized preparation, they are frequently trusted as the sources of expertise and information.

In the school, the child's teacher is usually a parent's most important primary point of reference. We measure our organizations by the manner in which they deliver on their promises, and we look for tangible indicators that the work is being accomplished. Our organizations, especially when they are large, are often remote and impersonal; the service provider offers a human voice that in many cases offers us the evidence we expect.

UNDERSTANDING APPLIED

There are few 'pure' models in human endeavor. Even our best frameworks are only approximations intended to facilitate our thinking and discussion. Not every activity of a person designated as administrator will be administrative in character; not every action will be explicitly and singularly goal directed. In fact, nested within each quadrant of Figure 3.1

we might imagine a mini-version of the full model. That characterization frees us to assert a broad conception of the leadership function. The emphasis is one not of singularity and rigidity in a context of exclusiveness, but of emphasis and balance as we identify and embrace a more inclusive understanding of leadership.

Who can lead? If that is the question, and if accomplishing purpose through people is the intent, I suggest in concert with Hodgkinson that the answer is "Any of us." The operative and, perhaps, more relevant question is "In what contexts will leadership occur?" Our answers can encourage us to be increasingly clear about our roles, how we will fulfill them, and how we will engage in improving our practice. Our answers can lead us to reflect on our practice, to learn about leadership.

We have committed much time and effort in the study of leadership to defining roles and boundaries. Perhaps our work could also emphasize breaking barriers. I offer for consideration the conception advanced in this chapter, that leadership is broadly based and legitimately accessible to each of us in the work we do in pursuit of organizational purpose. With that in mind, there is reason to shape the character of our activities in ways that will invite others to engage with us in the study of leadership.

THE MATTER OF COMPETENCE

We understand that intelligence is a complex concept, one that cannot be reduced to a simple two-digit (or preferably a three-digit!) number on an IQ scale. Humorous stories abound of individuals who are brilliant and gifted in one area of human endeavor and challenged in another. While we may or may not consider ourselves among the most brilliant and gifted, we recognize that our intelligences vary widely. Together, we participate in weaving the diverse tapestries that form our organizations and our society.

The differences that we have come to expect among the varieties of intelligence may be found also in regard to **competence**, a word for which we usually hold a narrow understanding. Even in the narrow sense, we understand that the question, "Is he or she competent?" carries a different answer when we are hiring pilots than when we are searching for a physiotherapist. We also know that the physiotherapist who is not also a pilot is likely to be more adept at manipulating a muscle than at handling a rudder. Unfortunately, we may continue to limit our understanding of the term by focusing solely on technical skills. This is not sufficient for leadership. In many cases, it is not sufficient even for what we might call job performance. In the same sense that humans are complex, their endeavors also are complex. The intelligence that we use for those endeavors is multiple rather than single, and holding to a narrow understanding of what we mean by competence is less of an option today than it was yesterday. That is particularly the case when our focus is on leadership.

We know that leadership capability can not be measured solely in terms of the leader's technical grasp of the business of the organization, yet we have difficulty even agreeing on a definition of leadership That may preclude for now the possibility of arriving at a universal measure of leadership competence. Both definition and measurement are ongoing tasks; both will be aided by the dialogue and debate that characterize our search for clarity. The concluding section of this chapter will focus on six plausible dimensions of leadership competence: **completion, contact, conceptual, conflict, continuation,** and **character.** That is a partial list; its purpose is to stimulate personal reflection and dialogue among colleagues through consideration of what leadership might mean in practice.

Completion Competence: Getting the Work Done

Completion is the interpretation of competence that traditionally we have come to understand as its defining function: the standard, narrow, unitary notion of competence. Completion competence is the ability to get the job done to the standard expected, within the time allocated, with the resources available, and by using acceptable means. We can reasonably assume that most leaders are competent on the completion dimension; they have had to establish that as a basic career criterion. Yet even the struggle to remain technically competent is continuous – things change. Leaders in many of our organizations accept that the standards of competence and expectations held for them in their workplaces regarding acceptable levels of performance are rising steadily. We glean from others; we read, we engage in dialogue with colleagues; and we establish both formal and informal learning and feedback networks to help us keep our currency. We seek to remain competent in our ability to complete the work.

Where our choice is either to take charge of today's reality and tomorrow's change or to be defeated by it, we expect that completion competency – the ability to get the job done – will be a collective norm. We expect that all in the organization will be able to meet the requirements of their work. In a changing environment this will demand that completion competence allow for the reality that there will be turbulence, upheaval, and the unexpected. None of these factors will be recognized as sufficient reason for not getting the job done. At least, the expectation that there will be continuous growth and improvement in completion competence is more likely than before to be the normative expectation.

We expect leaders to initiate, to *seize the day*. This ability will extend beyond simply having a baseline repertoire of knowledge and skills. It will involve choices, many of them perplexing and difficult. It will demand the ability to work not only with routines but also with opportunities and surprises. Many of these circumstances will be undefined until the intervention of leadership with the ability to describe the reality and point to a path. Improving our workplaces is about addressing it all, making changes in tiny, incremental ways that over time and with the support of others will change the nature of the enterprise. To accomplish this, we will need leaders who can complete the task, leaders who know their field, leaders who we judge as competent to lead the way. Beyond leaders with the requisite package of knowledge and skills we will need those with heart, with a commitment to ensure that the job gets done in the service of both organization and individual.

Contact Competence: Working with Others

In a rather limited definitional way, we can think of contact competence as a 'human relations' approach to working with others or, with somewhat more currency, a 'human resources' approach. Today and tomorrow, though, leadership will demand a broader understanding, one that encompasses a commitment to listen and hear, to serve the interests of those whose voices we have heard. It will create working communities based on that commitment, and it will build responsive organizations that will "guard the trust on behalf of those they are commissioned to serve."[29]

Contact competence speaks of collaborating in the pursuit of our goals in order that each person will be strengthened and equipped to accomplish them. It will be useful periodically to assess our contact competence: Are we listening? Are we hearing? For whom, internally and externally are we a listening and a hearing audience? More importantly, contact competence suggests we have moved well beyond what we have always called *good relationships*. We have developed a view of the others in our organization as members of a team, a family of professionals and support staff engaged together in an enterprise that is beyond the capability of any of us alone.

Conceptual Competence: Seeing the 'Big Picture'

When speaking about conceptual competence we often use descriptors to clarify a term for which we hold at best an imprecise understanding. We speak of the ability to 'see the big picture', the capacity to understand the broader context of activities we plan and choices and decisions we make. In the complex world of today's organizations, there are few easy answers, few simple line drawings. Earlier in this book, I described conceptual strength, applied in the context of organizational and therefore political life, as the ability to know what you *SEE* when you *See* what you *see*. If we add to that the dynamic of living leadership practice, we might also speak of the ability to know what you *DO* when you *Do* what you *do*. In that sense, whether we work inductively or deductively, our goal is to understand and to act, which means to *see* and to *do*. In our dialogue with others in the political context, it is also essential to know what you *HEAR* when you *Hear* what you *hear*. Leadership demands that we understand what we encounter, not only in individual instances, but also as patterns. Beyond that, we must be able to give shape to the whole of the phenomenon we are considering and to integrate the dimensions and components of the realities that are part of our lives in organizations.

Metaphors of leadership are analogous to pairs of glasses – what we see is determined by the viewing lens. In some cases we see a right that is clearly different from the wrong. Sometimes there will be a valid that differs from the invalid. More often, though, our metaphors are simply the tools of our work, each useful in its particular application, each an aid to accomplishing the task rather than simply an end in itself.

When we talk about our work, and especially as we search for answers to the challenges that arise daily, our usual first recourse is to those who work in organizations similar to our own. Each of us has a network of colleagues who form our first line of external support. Beyond that, when we begin to reflect – to conceptualize and analyze – we will benefit from at least three kinds of cross-communication and conversation. First, we need those who work in different settings and can describe their reality in terms that help us to understand our own. Second, we need those who think differently than we think and whose perspectives we will respect. Third, we need colleagues who can challenge our motives and strategies and from whom we will accept those challenges.

First, our efforts to gain a broader and clearer understanding of the organizational, political, and social contexts within which we work will be aided by our contact with colleagues in diverse settings. At the closest proximity, that might take the form of consultation with our colleagues in parallel positions and with their counterparts from other jurisdictions. At another level, our conversations will be with leaders from other kinds of organizations with which our own have much in common – health administrators, leaders of not-for-profit organizations, and business leaders – as we seek both parallels and variant patterns against which to test our ideas.

Second, we will benefit from dialogue with others who see the world differently than we see it. The concrete-sequentialist needs the stimulus and challenge of the divergent thinker who offers another view, another way to plan the work and work the plan. Whatever our profession, we must guard against the ever-present risk of *group think*, against prevailing patterns of thinking that will nudge us toward homogeneity rather than toward uniqueness and originality, toward selecting the comfortable 'what works' over plausible yet untried alternatives that 'just might work.'

Third, we will need colleagues of the soul-mate variety; friends who will stimulate us to think about the way we do our work from the perspectives of motive, value, and ethic. Those are rare associations. They take work and time to build. To our dismay, we have found that cultivating and developing these relationships often takes second place to the tyranny of the urgent. Many leaders' working lives explode the myth that greater seniority brings with it greater freedom and autonomy, and we need alongside us those who have earned the right to challenge our plans, our decisions, and the way we work with others. We need those to whom we will listen for support and guidance, and those to whom we will respond with a depth of honesty that speaks well for the quality of our leadership.

Conflict Competence: Understanding the Political Milieu

The dimension of conflict competence relates most directly to the content of this book. Some might have used the word *combat* to title this section, and that would not be entirely inappropriate. When we speak of politics in organizations, we can on the one hand describe it neatly as the process of allocating scarce resources and, on the other hand, we might paint a clearer picture if we reflect the negotiation, skirmishing, and intervention, and the conflict, compromise, and use of power and influence that surround our efforts to allocate value when not everything can be valued equally and some things will not be valued at all. In fact, we might affirm with Bennet and his collaborator's that

> at its lowest level, organizational life is a sort of daily combat. Even here, however, the deadliest weapons in the administrative armory are philosophical: the skills of logical

and critical analysis, conceptual synthesis, value analysis and commitment, the power of expression in language and communication, rhetoric and, most fundamentally, the depth of understanding of human nature.[30]

There is little doubt that the notion that an organization can be *above politics* was coined either for a forgotten, perhaps mythical organizational of yesteryear or by someone who simply was unable to read the surrounding terrain. As distasteful as military metaphors may be, our organizations *are* battlegrounds for competing interests, each determined to win the day. Without broadly based competence in the areas we are discussing in this chapter, leaders will lack the skill and credibility to work successfully within their organizations in turbulent times.

We live in a world that is undergoing profound transformation on many fronts. We face new and unfamiliar events and patterns that are all too real sometimes. One of our new realities is a significant shift in the way we think about the allocation of public resources, whether they are secured from government or from donors. We have relied on economic theory for models that will guide us in thinking about the allocation of those resources, but we will need to understand political theory and develop the political skills of leadership to influence their actual distribution. We may have a theoretical base or a model to suggest how we might allocate the value implicit in our distribution of scarce resources, but we will succeed only to the extent that we understand and can manage the processes of power and influence.

Continuation Competence: Staying the Course

A thoroughgoing competence based on the capabilities described here will show itself in a continuing commitment to the welfare and development of those engaged in ensuring quality performance in our organizations: a commitment to the achievement of mission. As part of that effort, leaders will continue the work until it is done or until we have given all we can. We understand also, though, that continuation is not always in one's own control. Some leaders have known when it is time to move elsewhere and pursue different goals. In the political maelstrom of organizational life today, leaders sometimes have left before they have chosen to go. In other settings, commitment often makes itself known by the leader's willingness to stay for the betterment of the organization because much of the mission remains to be accomplished.

This is not an argument for long service as the primary measure of competence of commitment. It is rather an argument for leaders to make the decision to stay or to leave on the basis of commitment to basic purposes they have helped to shape and goals for which they have worked to win acceptance. Commitment is currently a popular word, continuation less so. Both words often hold relatively little power alongside ambition and opportunity. The argument is not that we should choose always to continue, but that when we decide whether to continue or to move on, we will consider the qualitative dimensions of purpose and service alongside the quantitative dimensions of advancement and status, and that we will attach weight to both. Organizations have forgotten in some cases the benefits of a continued service that grows in depth and strength over time.

The best of our organizations are engaged in a quest, in a pursuit that identifies their reasons for being and guides their efforts. Each is on a journey with much distance to go before arriving at the destination. For leaders, the journey is seen as an ongoing saga. They are committed to continuing in the pursuit of a mission they understand because they have created and legitimized it together. They are determined to do their work with quality, not simply to look better than another organization but to ensure that their own today and tomorrow will be better than their yesterday.

In some respects, sustained commitment and healthy continuation represent the other side of opportunism. For leaders, there is always a quest and there is always a journey. There are always reflective opportunities that will allow us to examine again the organization, its mission and its circumstances. We can assess the quality of our leadership by asking the difficult question: "Am I in the best place and in the best role, doing the best that can be done with and for this organization, its programs, and its people?"

Character Competence: Building Trust

We can reach only a modest level of agreement about what constitutes character. It is that somewhat undefined quality we expect in the leaders we will trust most to walk with us where we know we must go and to help us build the path. Our definitions will vary but we need little more than an opportunity and an invitation to identify those who in our view best represent character. Similarly, negative examples are easy to find. Although we might achieve greater clarity and precision by exploring the territory within our own organization to determine how its leaders are supported, we can usually find a measure of agreement around some of the words we use to describe character: consistency, trust, dependability, and honesty. Those are the characteristics and behaviors that inspire us when they are present and perplex us when they are absent. In short, we ask for leaders with whom we will be prepared to undertake the journey.

END NOTES

1. John Mauriel, *Strategic Leadership for Schools* (San Francisco: Jossey-Bass, 1989), 314.
2. Michael Fullan, "Introduction," in *The Jossey-Bass Reader on Educational Leadership* (San Francisco: Jossey-Bass, 2000), xix.
3. Ibid.
4. Ibid.
5. Spencer Maxcy, *Educational Leadership: A Critical Pragmatic Perspective* (Toronto: Ontario Institute for Studies in Education, 1991), 48-50.
6. Hodgkinson, *Administrative Philosophy*, 30.
7. Fullan, "Introduction," xx.
8. Peter Northouse, *Leadership: Theory and Practice*, 8-9.
9. Hodgkinson, *Administrative Philosophy*, 78-79.
10. Ibid., 27.
11. Ibid., 30.
12. Ibid., 28.
13. Ibid., 78-79.
14. Ibid., 30.
15. Ibid., 78.
16. Ibid., 79.
17. Fullan, "Introduction," xx.
18. Margaret Wheatley, "Good-bye, Command and Control," in *The Jossey-Bass Reader on Educational Leadership* (San Francisco: Jossey-Bass, 2000), 345.
19. Ibid., 341.
20. Hodgkinson, *Administrative Philosophy*, 85.
21. Gervase Bushe, *Clear Leadership* (Mountain View, CA, Davies-Black, 2001), 11.
22. Nigel Bennett, Christine Wise, Philip Woods, & Janet A. Harvey, "Distributed Leadership," *National College for School Leadership*, http://www.ncsl.org.uk/media/3C4/A2/distributed-leadership-literature-review.pdf.
23. Peter Gronn, "Distributed leadership," in *Second International Handbook of Educational Leadership and Administration*, eds. Kenneth Leithwood and others (Dordrecht: Kluwer, 2002), 28.
24. Ibid., 28.
25. Bennett and others, "Distributed leadership," 7.

26 Ibid.

27 Ibid.

28 John Selden, "Table talk," in *Memoirs of John Selden*, ed. G. Johnson (n.p., 1835).

29 Vernon Storey, *Guarding the Trust* (Vancouver, BC: EduServ, 1994), 6.

30 Hodgkinson, *Educational Leadership*, 112.

CHAPTER 4 — PURPOSE IN MIND: POWER AS A CONDITION OF LEADERSHIP

> *A reference to power is rarely neutral; there are few words that produce such admiring or, in the frequent case, indignant response.... Yet power, per se, is not a proper subject for indignation. The exercise of power, the submission of some to the will of others, is inevitable in modern society; nothing whatever is accomplished without it. It is a subject to be approached with a skeptical mind, but not with one that has a fixation of evil. Power can be socially malign; it is also socially essential. Judgment thereon must be rendered, but no general judgment applying to all power can possibly serve.*[1]

Many discussions of leadership focus at least in part on the matter of power. That is a difficult reality for some of us. Our discussions about politics acknowledge the inevitable reality of power and we have strong feelings about its use and legitimacy. Leadership, politics, and power are inextricably linked, although perhaps *interwoven* is a more appropriate word than *linked*. The relationship is not a simple serial connection of separate and distinct items and events. Hodgkinson has observed that "for the administrator, the executive, the leader, there is an added charge and a greater responsibility because all organizations and all politics involve the exercise of power over others."[2]

Where people gather around common purpose, there will be leadership. Where there is leadership, there is power. Where there is power, it will be demonstrated as influence mediated through political processes. In other words, the existence of purpose ensures the presence of politics and power. Consideration of the idea that politics pervades life in organizations must be qualified in a single instance only – where rule is absolute, and that is virtually the nonexistent case, we will not find politics. In those instances of tyranny and oligarchy, no effort is required to negotiate the satisfaction of interests in response to demand, because "the method of rule... is to clobber, coerce, or overawe."[3] Yet in any work or social setting we experience it is reasonable to say that where we find people organized around purpose, we will find leadership. Where we find leadership, we find power. And where we find power evidenced as influence, we find politics. Crick has described "the political method of rule [as] to listen to... other groups so as to conciliate them as far as possible, and to give them a legal position, a sense of security, some clear and reasonably safe means of articulation, by which... groups can and will speak freely."[4] This is the context in which this discussion of power is framed.

Addressing the Reality

When power is the focus of discussion, we often observe a quiet retreat from candor and disclosure. Generally speaking, we are inclined to take the negative view of power. We tend often to attribute power-holding more to others than to ourselves. That may change if the need to achieve our purposes sends us on a quest for someone with sufficient power, albeit perhaps of dubious origin, to accomplish the task. Individuals try in some cases to avoid the overt display of power, acknowledging that "much exercise of power depends on a social conditioning that seeks to conceal it."[5] It is reasonable to assert that leaders and leadership have much to gain from holding a thoroughly competent understanding of power and from developing a healthy perspective on its use and practice. Similarly, there is much to lose from flawed understanding, from holding unhealthy perspectives, or from less-than-capable practice. At the most basic level of understanding, we might describe power as resulting in behavioral change through **influence**. I will use the term *influence* to describe both the application and the evidence of power.

> **Assertion 4.1: A leader without power has no influence.**
> **To deny having power is to misrepresent leadership.**
>
> **Assertion 4.2: A leader without influence has no power.**
> **To avoid influencing is to decline leadership.**

I noted earlier that for many people power and politics are important nondiscussable topics. Perhaps in part this is because they are often cast in negative terms. Yet most acknowledge that among people in groups, not much beyond self-motivated individual effort (and that should not automatically be denigrated or discounted) can be accomplished without the use of power.

My concern in this book is with leadership, politics, power and influence in the organizational domain. My primary emphasis is on the roots, then the origins, and the character of what we do. It is on strengthening our understanding rather than on developing the trappings and tactics of politics and power for their own sake. I do not propose or even list specific strategies and tactics for dealing with what we might call the 'dark side' of power and politics. That will be addressed by readers individually and in groups through the critical incidents and case studies in Part II and in the discussion and debate around those scenarios. For organizational leaders, beyond the need to recognize what lies near us and what surrounds us as the context of our work, the issue is why and how we seek to influence others. We are called to the ethical use of power.

Perhaps our difficulties arise in part from the pariah-like character we have attached to common notions of power. Like the word **manipulation**, power is semantically a neutral term. In the case of both power and manipulation, though, issues arise in the application. For the leader an understanding of these issues and the variables surrounding them is essential. Once we understand the nature of power we can turn our thinking more usefully to considering its quality and character rather than focusing simply on its presence or its relative absence. Power lies close to the heart of both leadership and politics.

Organizational leadership is about the attainment of organizational ends. We understand, or at least we usually say we believe, that in the legitimate pursuit of those ends people are both primary and essential. People are identifiable as ends in themselves, not solely as the means of organizational goal attainment. We know that in today's organization, success is dependent on the skill and support of all those involved, not on solo performances by single actors. Yet even today's term *human resources* impersonalizes that characterization. We speak of 'the human factor' as an 'element' to be considered. While those terms are descriptive and somewhat useful they can also contribute to our recent and culturally produced tendency to technologize and depersonalize our vocabulary. In the process, we risk losing our grasp of the richness and complexity of human interaction in organizations and failing to develop understanding that will strengthen our ability to work with those involved.

I presented in Chapter 1 a preliminary perspective on politics as a basis for a closer look at the term and the concept of power. To understand leadership fully requires that the leader understand politics in organizations as a reality. To practice leadership effectively demands that our leaders be politically skilled. Our challenge is first to be clear on the concept of politics in organizations and then to understand its relationship to the concepts of power and influence.

As we continue our search for clarity and understanding, it is important to be specific and consistent in the words we use, at least for this particular commitment of our time to reading and study. Throughout this book, I have refered to the politics *in* organizations rather than *the* politics *of* organizations. The latter suggests that there are different varieties or brands of politics, one of which might be a particular politics related to formal organizations. My treatment of politics in this book proposes an important and relevant distinction. My point is simple: politics is a fundamental dimension of human behavior, not an aspect of organization. At its core, the idea of politics as others have defined it and as I will describe it here is characterized by some fundamental concepts. In that sense, it does not matter whether we are describing politics as displayed in the decision making processes of government (although we are likely in the usual case to see that as a distinct and separate phenomenon) or the political realities faced by the chair of a community board or the minister of a church. It will be useful in both cases to establish a definition of politics as we are discussing it here – politics in the context of organizational life.

For the purpose of developing a useful definition, let us step back momentarily from the idea of distribution of scarce resources to consider a more fundamental understanding. The call for a share of scarce resources arises in many cases from the values and interests of an individual or a group. For example, a group of parents who believe that learning a second language is an essential experience for their children will bring that value to the table as a request or a demand. It may be a value held for its own sake; the parents believe that it will be beneficial for their children to understand more than one language. Beyond that, they might consider second language capability as acceptable evidence that the larger value of general cultural enrichment is being recognized. Perhaps they will express it as 'a well-rounded education'. They might also believe that second language capability will enhance their children's career possibilities. That is the demand side of the equation.

IDENTIFYING POWER AND INFLUENCE

Earlier I asserted that politics and leadership are inextricably linked. It is almost self-evident, and certainly it is also clear in the definitions offered by other writers, that both leadership and politics are tied to the idea of power. We describe elected political parties as being in power; we assess heads of state as powerful people; we watch premiers and governors shifting the balance of power by changing the composition of their cabinets. That idea is no less true in our social service organizations – we accomplish ends through the use of power. It is true also that ends are often accomplished through the misuse of power. If we are to be clear, though, we will need first to distinguish between two words that very often are used synonymously – **power** and **influence**.

This task is not as straightforward as it might seem. Dahl and Stinebrickner comment that "unfortunately, in neither ordinary language nor political analysis is there agreement on the definition and usage of what might be called 'influence terms'."[6] They note that

> political scientists use a variety of words that they frequently do not define; when they do define their terms, the definitions frequently do not agree. One writer's influence is another's power, and it is difficult to pin down precisely what we mean.[7]

Scruton suggests that influence is "one of the basic concepts of political science but, like many such concepts, extremely difficult to define."[8] The leadership challenge is to ensure that the meanings we attach to the terms we use are clear and relevant.

We routinely measure power as capacity, or as potential. A vehicle motor might be rated at 250 horsepower. A household electrical circuit might be described as carrying 220 volts. In these and other cases, we have developed precise indicators of meaning, often in terms of assessed potential. We know, or at least we can find out, what we may be able to accomplish in a particular situation with a 250 horsepower motor or a 220 volt circuit. Even though we may not be students of mechanics or electricity, we will choose not to stand in front of a moving car. We will not touch a bare wire, particularly with wet hands. However, we are glad to have a car to drive, and our computers demand a source of electrical power. We note the actions of organizations and their leaders and we understand that in various ways they have power. We understand in each case that power carries potential; it suggests the ability to accomplish something. In Scruton's terms, power is "the ability to achieve whatever effect is desired, whether or not in the face of opposition."[9] We can read about varieties, types, and kinds of power, but usually they are named for the strategies used to produce effects, or to influence. The exercise of sufficient coercive power, for example, will usually influence the recipient to behave in ways that closely resemble what the power holder intends.

Influence is viewed by some as a subset or a variety of power. Considered that way, influence might be thought of as a relatively mild display of power. If we were to think of types and degrees of power as lying along a continuum from little to much, probably we would place influence somewhat closer to little power than to much power. That understanding of the word influence is a less-than-useful conception. It can lead us into semantic traps and unproductive discussions such as a debate about whether something we have observed is a case of influence or an example of some other variety of power. In fact, we can distinguish between power and influence at a more fundamental level.

When we leave the discussion of power and begin to speak of influence, we move from thinking about potential and promise to examining realization and fact. We accept that power exists. We believe that someone possesses power and perhaps holds more or less of it than someone else. We visualize and measure power, though, on the basis of evidence – its effects. In the case of politics in organizations, we measure power by its effects on people and groups – by evidence of influence. Unless the exercise of power results in changes in the recipient's behavior or in actions that shape an outcome, this power exists only in the realm of ideas and beliefs. In many cases that will be sufficient: we do not always want to see proof by way of a demonstration. We might say that the proof of the power is in the influence, or in the demonstrated effect. Used as a noun, *influence* is the result or the effect of power. If an action is successful, power will be credited with having influenced the individual or group.

Assertion 4.3: To discuss power without influence is to debate a non sequitur.

In this book, I will use *influence* most often as a verb. Hence, we will examine various processes of influencing. I will part company with some other writers and will use the term *influence* to include all activities that result in change in the behavior of others or that accomplish a desired result. In other words, I will use the term generically. That immediately raises a moral question regarding the exercise of power. We will consider a wide range of influencing strategies and stances, all of which we need to recognize but some of which we might consider illegitimate, unethical, or even just unacceptable for our own use. Once we move beyond definition and understanding to action, both our choices of influencing behaviors and our response to those behaviors in others will reflect the nature and quality of our leadership. They will identify its moral base.

THE NATURE OF INFLUENCE

My decision to use the term *influence* in this book primarily as a verb will simplify our discussion throughout the remainder of this chapter. Where it is useful to do so we can describe a particular means of successfully exercising influence in the pursuit of a goal as evidence of a particular type or form of power. We can read about varieties, types, and kinds of power, but typically they are named for the strategies used to produce effects. I seldom use the term *power* except where the nature of the influence is clear or can be made clear in the context.

We will consider some key terms in this section that will be useful in our reading, in our discussion with colleagues, and in our practice in the political context of the workplace or service setting. Each of these terms has been defined by other writers. Each is an element of the vocabulary we typically use to describe behavior in organizations when interests and resources are the focus of our efforts and activity. None is inherently either right or wrong in all circumstances. However, in the organizational contexts with which we are familiar, some influencing strategies are widely considered to be acceptable, even desirable. Others, though commonly practiced, clearly are considered by many to be inappropriate or unacceptable. The valuing begins when individuals in formal or informal leadership positions contemplate decisions and when others assess the legitimacy of those leaders' actions. The most powerful and useful thinking and discussion that might arise among leaders who use this book as a tool for professional growth will be about their own processes of weighing, choosing, and acting – the 'hard stuff' of leadership. For the moment, though, our interest is in clarifying meaning to facilitate our thinking and discussion.

Understanding Interests

It is difficult to develop a plausible schema of influencing behaviors or to place influencing strategies on a continuum. Although the polar concepts of freedom and control are useful they are not singular in their application. One risk of preparing and studying a list of terms for definition is that we will mask meaning with a simplicity that hides the complexities of human interaction. Until we understand interests, context, and circumstance, the potential for misreading the influencing behaviors and strategies of others remains high.

Although our interests often differ, they sometimes lie comfortably adjacent to the interests of others. In other circumstances, though our priorities differ, we can engage in joint effort around points of agreement.

Adjacent Interests. As individuals, as groups within the organization, or as a whole organization, our interests differ. While our interests will not always be complementary they will not always create a conflict situation. Sometimes they will simply exist side by side with the interests of others. This is especially the case when there are adequate resources to permit differing interests to be recognized without competition and conflict. In the case of a community centre with a dedicated theater, for example, conflict between singers and actors over practice and performance space and time can sometimes be minimized, although we soon realize that the others certainly are interested players. The interests of one party often overlap with those of another, creating both complementarity and the possibility of conflict.

From time to time, our particular and personal interests will differ from those of others in our organization. Even though that fact alone will not necessarily create conflict, we may form a temporary alliance with other individuals or groups to pursue a particular common interest. Sometimes during such interactions we will find the expression *a state of flux* to be more descriptive than the idea of *a steady state*.

Temporary Alliances. Often the outcome of a conflict will be a temporary resolution. Both circumstances and our perspectives may change, depending on the issue and its surrounding circumstances. In many cases both alliances and resolutions will be temporary. That does not necessarily mean that if a group's active membership changes from one problem or issue to the next, conflicts have arisen to cause that change. In the case of temporary alliances, we draw alongside others on the basis of our priorities and preferences, although depending on the matter at hand, that may not always occur with the same people. Also, while the first category suggested a situation of no conflict between differing interests, temporary alliances often acknowledge conflicting interests but agree for the moment to exclude that from the debate in favor of a component of common purpose. Afonso suggests that

> People's cooperation, in the achievement of the same organizational goals, does not correspond necessarily to organizational cohesiveness and shared values. On the contrary, it could be no more than a specific convergence of disparate interests and strategies. In any occasion, organizational life is characterized by conflict and cooperation, representing divergence or convergence with regard to the clear or implicit interests, motivations and ongoing strategies of the organizations' actors.[10]

Assertion 4.4: When things are politically complex, predicting the outcomes of events is a bit like predicting the path water will follow between stones on a beach.

Contextual Change. We could describe contextual change as shifts in circumstances, situations, factors, or considerations. Contextual change will affect the status and character of the other realities described above. With that in mind, we will proceed with the definitional task on the assumption that it is useful when dealing with a list of related terms to identify a set of plausible categories (Figure 4.1). These categories will enable us to organize our thinking and develop helpful descriptions without forcing narrow, prescriptive definitions. I have identified two domains of interest: **organizational** and **personal**. Within the personal domain two further distinctions have been made **high freedom** and **low freedom**. I acknowledge two things from the outset. First, this is not an inclusive list; these are simply working definitions of a few terms commonly used in considering the demonstration of power in interpersonal and organizational life. Second, these terms or variations of them are used by other writers. My aim here, while recognizing the contributions of others, is to define selected terms in ways that will be particularly useful to those who lead in the micropolitical context of organizations, in particular, to the readers of this book.

Organizational Domain

Authority

Expertise

Reward Control

Personal Domain

High Freedom	**High Control**
Charisma	Manipulative Persuasion
Rational Persuasion	Coercion
Inducement	Force

Figure 4.1 Varieties of Power

The Organizational Domain

Leaders are responsible to ensure that organizational ends are met. They must ensure that the organization accomplishes its purposes or, depending on the nature of the leader's task, that some designated subset of those ends is achieved. It is a truism to say that not all ends will be accomplished to everyone's satisfaction. In fact, some ends may not be accomplished at all. Sometimes there will be conflict between and among competing organizational ends and between those ends and the interests of various individuals or groups in and around the organization. It is also reasonable to observe that despite the best of intent, available resources in many cases will be insufficient to accomplish all that we want to do. We must make choices and we must live with the outcomes of our choices.

The tasks of choosing, deciding, and allocating are leadership tasks carried out in a political milieu. They are not always the responsibility of a single leader but they are always leadership tasks. They are both process and outcome – choosing leads to a choice, deciding produces a decision, and allocating results in an allocation. Hodgkinson speaks of resource scarcity as a primary fact of economic life, suggesting that "consciousness of this underlies all administrative decisions and establishes a criterion of choice wherein one seeks the largest result or pay-off for any given application of resources."[11] Through the processes we choose, the ways in which influencing is carried out become broadly significant to the outcomes.

I have identified one domain of influencing as the **organizational** domain, because each element represents the organization's legitimization, or at least its official recognition, of a particular influencing opportunity. The first is position-related, the second is person-related, and the third is policy-related. Although our focus will usually be on the behavior of designated leaders, these attributes and activities will characterize many members of the organization at various times.

Authority. Authority is granted as a function of position or mandate. We can distinguish authority from power as "a relation *de jure* and not necessarily *de facto*; authority is a right to act, rather than a power to act."[12] In those terms, authority is the 'I/we may', while power is the 'I/we can'. However, in the terms I have used, the phrase *power of* is perhaps more helpful for describing influencing processes. If we speak about the power of authority, we mean that someone has been sanctioned or given the right to act. A question arises, though, when we speak of perceived authority and ascribed authority. If one is sanctioned to exercise authority, does that person actually possess authority? At this point, our emphasis on using the word *influence* as a verb is helpful, since that leads us directly to a focus on outcomes. In other words, if one's choices and subsequent actions are influenced by the perception that someone else has the right to decide and to act, it is accurate and reasonable to refer to that as **authority** or as the **power of authority**. Whether there really is a sanctioned right to influence or simply a perception that the right exists is a separate and equally important question.

That question arises because there is another dimension to the term. Although one may have been granted authority by law, contract, or job description, that represents only one side of the equation. Authority requires explicit recognition and response in the form of influenced behavior. Law or contract may not always be sufficient to elicit support, cooperation, participation, or even compliance from others. We might describe a circumstance in which one possesses designated authority but is unable to act authoritatively. Leadership demands both. The leadership challenge lies in the matching of perceived reality with actual reality as well as in the ability to influence behavior after authority has been granted.

Assertion 4.5: The authority to act is only a casual acquaintance of the ability to lead.

Expertise. The power of expertise provides opportunity to influence because one has particular skill or knowledge. Expertise is a significant source of influence but it is conceptually more difficult than the idea of authority. Expertise is validated when it is recognized by others, and the criteria may vary among the perceivers. When we must license someone, we strive to develop and apply what we call objective criteria and usually we keep a formal record of these criteria. However, we might continue to disagree on whether someone actually is expert, even though he or she is licensed, credentialed, or certified.

When we appoint or elect a person to a position, we will usually determine first to our satisfaction that he or she has or will be able to develop the necessary expertise. One important factor in that process is our determination that the individual's expertise will be acknowledged by those who have an interest in the particular activities in which he or she is engaged. We depend on that acknowledgement as a key indicator of one's ability to lead. Particularly when we realize our own lack of a certain expertise or when we recognize another person as an expert among experts, we will rely on our confidence in that person's ability to act and to lead us as we act. The leadership possibility in this case lies in the credible and accepted demonstration of expertise.

Reward Control. In various ways, and to a greater or lesser degree depending on organization and position, the authority of office usually includes the ability to grant or to withhold something perceived by another as having value or as being desirable. The reward may be salary, promotion, a bigger share of the budget, or the opportunity to take a day off work. The term implies both an earned right to the reward and another's authority to grant it. The process becomes complicated, however, if it is not defined by precise criteria and by a formula- or policy-based approach for making the reward-granting decision. Unfortunately, that is often the case. For reward control to be useful in any situation, both giver and receiver must hold two beliefs: that the reward has value and that the recipient is entitled to receive it. The leadership possibility lies in the defining, in the deciding, and in the awarding.

It is not only designated leaders that have opportunities to influence. Even if there is a lack of designated authority or reward control, expertise is located throughout an organization. One of the puzzling mysteries of organizational life is that we have only recently begun to give explicit recognition to this reality. All too often individuals who seek to influence others fail to recognize that whether their desire to lead springs from confidence in their own expertise, from willingness to serve, or from a desire for the organization's success, or whether it is simply a masked search for power, it is a desire held not only by designated organizational leaders. It is shared, as are capabilities and expertise, by others throughout the organization – in it and around it. The leadership opportunity lies in recognizing and acting on that reality.

The Personal Domain: High Freedom

When we move to the personal domain the shared nature of influence potential becomes evident. Powers of charisma, persuasion, inducement, coercion, force, and dominance are not restricted to designated leaders, although those people may be expected to show evidence of some of these attributes while not displaying others as strongly. Leaders are frequently selected at least partly because of their records in regard to some of these influencing behaviors.

Charisma. Sometimes referred to as personal power, **charisma** rests in the qualities of the individual, particularly in her or his publicly obvious qualities. The charismatic leader attracts others and inspires them to join in the effort, not necessarily for its merits or substance, but always because of the personality and style of the leader. Much has been written about charismatic leaders, both those who have enlightened and those who have darkened our world. For the leader, the important moral question has to do with the worth of the effort and with our valuing of the people involved. Where that question has been settled positively, charismatic leadership in some cases can enhance the ability of a team to accomplish the goal.

Rational Persuasion. The idea of persuasion raises immediately the question of truth-telling. In debate, dialogue, and other efforts to persuade, the substance of the case is information – the data or the facts. The leader's presentation and use of the facts carries important implications for others' judgments of her or his credibility. Where the leader presents and utilizes data in a manner that neither omits nor adds, and where the effort is to use the data in ways that will strengthen the decision making process, persuasion can be said to be *rational*. Consistent with other activities, the nature of efforts to persuade will often paint an important piece of the leadership picture. I will deal with nonrational or manipulative persuasion below as an example of low freedom/high control behavior.

Inducement. I will differentiate between reward control and inducement by using the latter to describe situations of lesser certainty. The individual retains a high degree of control over her or his course of action, because the inducement often is about prospect as much as or more than about reality. It remains for the individual to determine whether the prospect has sufficient likelihood of becoming reality, whether in fact it already is a reality, and whether the inducement is to some thing or some state of affairs she or he desires.

The Personal Domain: Low Freedom

Manipulative Persuasion. The idea of rational persuasion suggests that the individual has a full array of factual information to use in decision making. In other words, one's consent to participate is informed. Inducement may deal less with an already-established reality than with plans and hopes. For an action to be characterized properly as inducement, the individual's independence must be preserved by ensuring a solid basis of fact and an honest presentation of hoped-for outcomes. **Manipulative persuasion** precludes that possibility.

When the intent is to mislead, perhaps by presenting a partial picture, by distorting facts, or by adding inappropriate or untrue data, the effort to persuade is *manipulative* in nature. The word is almost always used pejoratively, although its origins do not necessarily imply that connotation. In that respect, perhaps **contrived** is a more useful term. However we express it, and whatever words we use, manipulative persuasion is not about candor or full disclosure. It represents an instrumentalist view of others as means or in many cases as barriers to be overcome, rather than as ends in themselves. Goodin has suggested that manipulation

> is not a means of 'overcoming resistance.' Rather, it is a means of undermining resistance... The concept of manipulation, then, is circumscribed in these two ways: it is power exercised (1) deceptively and (2) against the putative [presumed] will of its subjects. Each of these aspects is morally objectionable in its own right. Together, they guarantee that manipulation constitutes the evil core of the concept of 'power.'[13]

Moral philosopher Sissela Bok has treated this subject extensively, beginning with the meaning of the word **lying**. Bok begins her argument by asserting that "the moral question of whether you are lying or not is not settled by establishing the truth or falsity of what you say. In order to settle this question, we must know whether you intend your statement to mislead."[14] The question of how she or he will seek to influence stands as a constant at the front of the leader's thinking and choosing. Always our efforts to persuade will present us with the ends-means dilemma. Bok goes on to suggest that

> we must single out, therefore, from the countless ways in which we blunder misinformed through life, that which is done with the *intention to mislead*; and from the countless partial stabs at truth, those which are intended to be truthful. Only if this distinction is clear will it be possible to ask the moral question with rigor. And it is to this question alone – the intentional manipulation of information – that the court addresses itself in its request for "the truth, the whole truth, and nothing but the truth."[15]

Coercion. When our strategy is to persuade another person by manipulative means, a significant immediate risk to the persuader, short of loss of confidence and trust, is that the other person will ascertain the facts and will not comply. Assuming that to be the case, the individual retains a degree of autonomy – she or he has the right to decide on the basis of the new knowledge and the value she or he assigns to that knowledge.

Coercion, on the other hand, is less about making informed decisions freely. Manipulative persuasion rises or falls on the strength of its supporting arguments. It risks the possibility that those arguments or the supporting data will prove not to be valid. Coercion, on the other hand, implies that there will be consequences for noncompliance. Although one's decision is not unilaterally limited, noncompliance may carry undesirable consequences and the supporting data may become a lesser consideration. Scruton has defined coercion as

> any force or threat of force which reduces the freedom of an action, so that, in performing it, an agent acts less freely than he might have done, although not unintentionally. (You can be forced to do something which you do not do intentionally, but coercion is essentially a constraining of intentional action).... This reflects a distinction that we need to make, between forces which interfere with freedom by removing it, and those which merely narrow the range of autonomous choice.[16]

Force. Other words could be included among the terms we will use when discussing the topic of politics, particularly in reference to power: dominance, training, or conditioning, to mention just three. However, for our purpose, to facilitate discussion and study with the goal of building understanding, this functional definition list is probably complete with a clear conception of the term **force**. In some respects, our discussion of these terms has moved along a continuum of autonomy, choice, and control over one's own decisions. We reach the end of that journey with **force** – the final narrowing of the individual's range of freedom. Scruton asserts the following: "To force someone to do something involves making alternatives sufficiently undesirable to him that [he] will do what one desires. In other words the active idea of force is that of deliberately restricting available courses of action."[17]

POWER AND THE MORAL CHARACTER OF LEADERSHIP

As a leader in the political milieu of an organization, one must ask and answer several fundamental questions about the matter of power, one's own power, that of others, and the interaction between those dimensions. Each question highlights a dilemma:

- The **priority** dilemma: What and whose ends are to be accomplished?
- The **influence** dilemma: How will power be used in this circumstance?
- The **means** dilemma: Are these means consistent with my values?
- The **effectiveness** dilemma: Will the necessary end(s) be accomplished by the proposed course of action?

There are other basic questions; I encourage readers to add to the list. I have presented these four questions as dilemmas rather than simply as choices because often a struggle is implied. That struggle surrounds ideas such as integrity and consistency. Earlier in this book, we examined the idea of thoughtfulness. Complexities arise with every opportunity for action. The questioning process systematically applied is one way we can discipline ourselves towards becoming more thoughtful.

The Priority Dilemma

What ends are to be accomplished and whose ends are those? In response to this question, the leader's primary responsibility is to the organization. Yet that responsibility is not singular. It carries real opportunities for choice and an accompanying obligation not to lose sight of the person. How will we balance our mandated occupational and professional responsibility to the organization with our fundamental human responsibility to the individuals within it? The answer will depend on our values in relation to each. It is important to note at this point that in addition to lengthening this list of questions we can begin a new discussion around each. The perplexities are real and usually there will be a mixed response to each question in the list above. In fact the answer can often be found and expressed not simply in 'either/or' terms, but more usefully as 'and also.' The leadership challenge is to meet the needs and interests of individuals and groups as legitimate ends in themselves as we seek also to achieve organizational goals.

The Influence Dilemma

How might power be used in this circumstance? Inevitably, this question will be answered in terms of possibilities, legitimacy, acceptability, and appropriateness. What works is not always acceptable, and what seems acceptable may not always be the better alternative. For the leader, the choices and possibilities are always complex. We are committed by the fact of our employment or appointment to achieve the ends and purposes of our organization. The means we choose must include those most effective in the circumstances. The matching reality is that the means available to us are not always supportive of the growth of people in our organizations. That is a fact of life. The leadership challenge is to balance our choices of method with an approach to complex circumstances that recognizes the moral nature of making choices and resource allocation processes.

The Means Dilemma

Are the means I am proposing to use consistent with my values? On some occasions, urgency is the enemy of reflection and ethical choice. Pragmatism is sometimes its co-conspirator against thoughtfulness. We cannot always be sure, particularly in pressured circumstances, that all of our choices have arisen from a reliably grounded approach to leadership in the political context of our organizations. We are not always sure that our values will reliably inform us after the fact as to whether we have made good or bad choices. Sometimes we will not want to hear that commentary, even when it comes privately from confidants or personally from ourselves. That alone is sufficient argument to support advance thoughtfulness of the kind that guides us to choices that not only will stand up to scrutiny but also will invite it.

We will not always make the best choices from among available alternatives. We will usually hear promptly from those around us when we do not. Our poorer choices, provided they are not our regular pattern, will allow us to learn for the next time how to avoid painful recurrences. If we can ensure that even our errors will reflect a set of values acceptable both to ourselves and to those for whose lives we accept some responsibility, in most cases our fellow workers will 'cut us some slack'. Our competence will usually be judged not primarily by single events, even when those are problematic, but by the prevailing patterns of action that characterize our work and identify our character.

The Effectiveness Dilemma

Will the necessary end(s) be accomplished by the proposed course of action? I have left this question to the last, not because of its priority, but because the previous questions can all too easily be given less-than-careful consideration in the quest for simplicity and closure. This fourth question restores the perspective. It calls for actions based on thoughtful reflection – it calls for praxis. In the final analysis our actions must count for something. In the organizational context, that 'something' is the achievement of results, both those expected of us and those we expect of ourselves. In many cases, the answer to the effectiveness dilemma will be seen as an acceptable and complete basis for judging the quality of our power.

For the leader, a hierarchy of prioritized ends is to be planned for, anticipated, and welcomed. There is seldom only a single end to be achieved. Leadership takes place in a context. Often the essential fact of achieving organizational ends will best be expressed in terms of inclusiveness and multiplicity. Despite the fact that we often describe and record our action in terms of the substantive ends we are seeking to achieve, the doing of the work must reflect something far more complex and thought-demanding. The reality of scarce resources, and the expectation that our leadership will play a part both in allocating value and in reconciling diverse interests, demand that we be skilled in understanding power and ethical in exercising influence.

Organization or Individual?
A Perennial Dilemma?

Leaders can founder on the rocks of ineffectiveness because of their failure to address the organization/individual challenge – which set of interests will be served and when do our choices exclude or diminish other interests? We often couch the discussion within the oppositions between nomothetic versus idiographic or initiating structure versus consideration, but that does little to address the problem of how we will reconcile inevitable conflicts between organizational and personal ends. The difficulty becomes more perplexing when our personal interests are in conflict with those of others or of the organization. While it can sometimes be argued that the origins of the difficulty lie elsewhere, leaders must deal with present circumstance, sometimes without the luxury of being able to speculate about the origins of the problem. Our values and, consequently, our basic beliefs about the people with whom we work (a subset of the way we view people generally) shape our choices. Our choices in turn guide our practice. Throughout this book, I argue for a level of leader thoughtfulness that will lead us to walk a useful path toward strengthening practice. For this discussion, let us assume that one can be thoroughly and simultaneously committed to both the achievement of organizational ends and the development of people. To the extent that we believe this to be a valid premise, we will have disciplined ourselves to engage in a continuous search for ways to accomplish our dual mission.

The nature of our social service enterprises can predispose us to problems of achievement and accountability even when our intent is the best. Some realities of the not-for-profit enterprise as a type of organization may serve as a useful example. Newman and Wallender, writing in the mid-1970s of a world that has changed much since then, captured a still persistent difficulty in their early discussion of the constraining characteristics of these enterprises:

> Service is intangible and hard to measure... planning focus tends to shift from results to resources. There is no net "bottom line." Instead, much of the planning deals with performance of activities which presumably will create desirable results.... The implicit assumption is that assigned resources will be used for proper activities which in turn will produce desired results.[18]

The authors relate this reality to the probability of politics, which they cast in negative terms:

> Ambiguous operating objectives create opportunities for internal politics. When fuzzy objectives are combined with planning in terms of resources only, operating executives have considerable leeway in what they actually do.... Such leeway makes possible political maneuvering for personal ends.[19]

If through lack of clarity about measurability of results the stage is set for unhelpful political practice, it is also set with an open trapdoor for the 'thoughtless' and the unwary. If we are not clear about ends, if we cannot agree on them or perhaps even discuss them, we will naturally focus on means. However, Newman and Wallender were speaking of 'the dark side' of politics in organizations, and while that must be recognized as an unwelcome reality, it need not be a defining characteristic of our leadership.

> **Assertion 4.6: The matter of whose ends are to be served through leadership has a mandatory single answer – the organization's ends – and a range of supplementary answers. For the leader, the unitary answer is unavoidable; the supplementary answers cluster around it and beg to replace it.**
>
> **Assertion 4.7: The single answer contains a dual focus – collective and individual purpose. Both are legitimate ends.**
>
> **Assertion 4.8: Seeking to clarify foggy organizational ends and find evidence of their achievement is a fundamental leadership challenge, but the opportunity to take refuge in the fog is often more inviting.**
>
> **Assertion 4.9: Politics practiced in the fog displays only an apparition of leadership.**

Understanding that the primary leadership task involves attaining organizational ends frees the leader for the parallel pursuit of complementary goals and for a focus on the human dimension of the enterprise. It is not simply a question of whose aims *must* be achieved – the answer to that question is clear. It is also a question of what our remaining priorities will be and how we will achieve those aims. Our discussion is less useful when we view the choice and selection process as a dilemma or as an automatic choice between organization and individual. That implies a simple 'either/or' choice, and in the main, that will not be the case. We will not always be able to say 'both/and,' but if our efforts are characterized by that quest, we will not be surprised when we experience success.

We might view this organization/individual challenge along a continuum with one term at either end. The domain between the extremities is the domain of leadership, power, and influence. It is also therefore the domain of politics. At one extreme or the other only one set of ends can be satisfied. At any point between we can describe a 'more or less' degree of ends attainment and interest satisfaction.

In some circumstances, the individual does not enjoy a place on the continuum. That is unfortunate. When it occurs, it demands honest reflection by the leader, but the conclusion may be that no error of ethics or practice has been made; there simply was no way to satisfy a particular personal agenda or set of interests. In other circumstances, the organization is omitted from the continuum. That indicates a serious failure of leadership. In a few ideal and elusive circumstances, both organizational and individual ends can be fully attained. That is usually a serendipitous leadership occurrence, though we can often achieve a measure of success in both directions. In every instance, there will be politics, because in each instance interests will vary. That will lead to competition, sometimes conflict, and the need for resolution. For the leader, that resolution must include achieving the required ends. When we seek refuge in avoidance or move to one end of the continuum, we fail to meet the leadership challenge. In each circumstance, we can usefully ask, "Is there an inherent and unavoidable conflict in this case between the ends of the organization and those of its people?" The further challenge is to seek sound, ethical reasons to answer "No" because we have found ways to work along the continuum.

The Power of Transparent Leadership

In the reality of organizational life to 'tell all' is not always possible or wise. However, transparency is an important objective. It is reasonable to hope that transparency will characterize our practice of leadership as a general way of acting, even though in the sense of full disclosure not every instance of leadership practice will be or should be transparent. Not all things can or should be discussed and debated in the public arena. Our concern here, though, is with the extent to which motive, value, and ethic can be revealed through the way in which the leadership effort is conducted.

> **Assertion 4.10: The quality of leadership will be measured by its apparent openness and transparency. For those who are the focus of leadership practice, the difficult word is *apparent*. We are selective in our willingness to be manipulated.**

When people are positive about leaders we often hear those leaders described in terms such as "He or she has no hidden agendas" or "You always know where you stand," or "What you see is what you get." Transparency in the sense described here has little to do with confidentiality and much to do with confidence and consistency, with wisdom and judgment. The essential transparency is that associated with ends. We are more likely to be confident that our interests will be considered when we believe that a supportable set of mandated interests is being pursued, when we know what those interests are, and when we understand the costs their satisfaction carries.

We are familiar with the definition of **transparent** as something easily seen through. In the sphere of human activity, we often apply the term to a character or to a scheme, implying that despite devious motive or subterfuge, one can easily 'see through it', that somehow we have discovered the truth that lies just beyond. That is not the way I use the term here. Rather, transparency carries connotations of openness and frankness. It speaks of leadership practice that is free of dishonesty and negative manipulation.

Must the leader always tell all? Or, *may* he or she tell all? Clearly, some things may not be discussed in all settings, with all parties, or at particular times. There are issues of both confidentiality and appropriateness, the first a policy issue and the second an ethical matter. Clearly some decisions surrounding openness are moral decisions relating to the consequences both ways. One perspective would suggest that total honesty does not necessarily mean total disclosure. In other words, the courtroom standard

'The truth, the whole truth, and nothing but the truth,' will not always apply to leadership practice, at least in respect to 'the whole truth'. At every turn the leader is confronted with the moral character of his or her activity. Often there are few markers to point the direction, especially when we must decide whether or not it is appropriate to tell.

I have mentioned this example because of its pervasiveness in the practice of leadership. Judgments about the quality of our leadership and within that about our political behavior will often be made on the basis of what we disclose and how and to whom we disclose it. Bok has raised the level of the debate by suggesting that "truth and truthfulness are not identical, any more than falsity and falsehood."[20] The first term in each pair describes an incident, the second an ethic. **Truth** and **falsity** speak of data; **truthfulness** and **falsehood** speak of the use of that data. In regard to leadership transparency, our concern is with an ethic that includes truthfulness. For the leader searching for a course of action in a political context, the single issue (the effort to distinguish truth from falsity) will remain difficult, but the ethic (truthfulness vs. falsehood) can guide our action. In other words, though the data regarding which we tell the truth may itself be a falsity, we may not realize that. In reference to the choice of falsehood over truthfulness, Bok offers a definition of lying as "an intentionally deceptive message in the form of a statement."[21] Beyond and above that simple definition, she suggests that

> the whole truth *is* out of reach. But this fact has little to do with our choices about whether to lie or to speak honestly, about what to say and what to hold back. These choices can be set forth, compared, evaluated. And when they are, even rudimentary distinctions can give guidance.... The moral question of whether you are lying or not is not *settled* by establishing the truth or falsity of what you say. In order to settle this question, we must know whether you *intend your statement to mislead*.[22]

It is both a reality and a challenge of leadership in the political context of organizations that few roads are easy to walk. Leadership observed will be leadership analyzed, questioned, and judged. Not all of the conclusions reached about its worth will lie within the leader's sphere of influence. In a sense, life for the leader who seeks transparency and openness as a way of being becomes harder and more complex rather than easier and less complicated. On the other hand, we live in a world in which we will give less ground than before to leadership that sees people, though they are not equipment or money, as simply instruments nonetheless. In response to that leadership, the people we work with "can quit, walk away, or sabotage the organization... [because] The follower not only has power. He has ultimate power."[23] We expect, we even demand, that human leadership will be humane in quality. Otherwise we will walk away if we can or seek other recourse if we cannot. Transparency in leadership carries risks however; not all contests will be settled in its favor.

The leader makes many choices, but the choice of whether to hold power is not one of those choices. Greenfield asserts leadership "is a matter of will and power: of bending others to one's will and of being bent in turn by others."[24] We are mandated to accomplish goals through people. We must seek to influence others in particular directions. For the leader whose context is the political reality of an organization, the issue is not one of power alone but of the ways in which he or she will utilize that power to influence others. We will use power effectively among our colleagues when we step away from its conventional 'dark side' definition to embrace and celebrate its use in ways that move organizations and their members farther and more usefully than otherwise would have been the case. Galbraith's words sum up the dilemma perfectly: "There can be suffering, indignity, and unhappiness from the exercise of power. There can, as well, be suffering, indignity, and unhappiness from the absence of its exercise."[25] Leadership and leaders make a difference.

WORKING WITH THE REALITY OF POWER

I have presented definitions of several terms that are key to our understanding of the political dimension of organizational life. It is important, though, to be clear on the purpose of this effort. It is common to read about politics in organizations and to hear the topic discussed in terms of counsel and advice about how to win at the game. The presence of winners guarantees that in the reality of human experience, often there will be losers. A Machiavellian perspective would explore the possibilities of exploiting that fact. It would be easy, though somewhat naive and perhaps even manipulative, to suggest that my intent in this chapter has been simply to inform and clarify. To remain consistent in using the terms as we have defined them here, such an assertion would be an example of manipulative persuasion. Clarifying definitions is merely a means to an end; the end is to ensure quality leadership in politically challenging organizational environments. Throughout this discussion, and particularly through the later reinforcing value of the critical incidents and case studies, my aim is to provoke the reader and encourage praxis. My aim is to encourage thoughtfulness rather than thoughtlessness in the sense either of intellectual laziness or of suspect leadership behavior.

There is power within organizations. There is power wherever humans work in relationship to accomplish purpose. That power will be evident in its influencing effects. The reality of politics in the work setting is sufficiently self-evident that we can move on to the profoundly moral question facing our leaders: how might our behavior, day-to-day and over the long haul, shape and be shaped by the reality that characterizes our working relationships? In particular, how will we view and relate to individuals and groups with whom we interact? The choices, decisions, and actions of those individuals and groups are the focus of the Chapter 5.

END NOTES

1. Galbraith, *Anatomy of Power*, 11,13.
2. Hodgkinson, *Educational Leadership*, 153.
3. Crick, *In Defence of Politics*, 4.
4. Ibid.
5. Galbraith, *Anatomy of Power*, 12.
6. Dahl & Stinebrickner, *Modern Political Analysis*, 12.
7. Ibid.
8. Roger Scruton, *A Dictionary of Political Thought* (London: Pan Books, 1983), 224.
9. Ibid., 366.
10. Natarcia Afonso, "Key Players and Groups in Schools as Learning Organizations," *Proceedings from the DELSO Project 2001*, http://www.progettodeslo.it/documents/Natercio.pdf
11. Hodgkinson, *Educational Leadership*, 103.
12. Dahl & Stinebrickner, *Modern Political Analysis*, 40-41.
13. Robert E. Goodin, *Manipulatory Politics* (New Haven, CT: Yale University Press, 1980), 8.
14. Sissela Bok, *Lying: Moral Choice in Public and Private Life* (New York: Vintage, 1989), 6.
15. Ibid., 8.
16. Scruton, *Dictionary of Political Thought*, 70.
17. Ibid., 174.
18. William Newman & Harvey Wallender, "Managing Not-for-profit Enterprises," *Academy of Management Review*, January 1978, 28.
19. Sissela Bok, *Lying*, 6.
20. Ibid., 6.
21. Ibid., 15.
22. Ibid., 4.
23. Christopher Hodgkinson, *Educational Leadership*, 80-81.
24. Thomas Greenfield in Christopher Hodgkinson, *Administrative Philosophy*, 8.
25. John Galbraith, *Anatomy of Power*, 188.

Chapter 5 — Actors and Agendas: The Human Face of Organizations

What we see when we turn to the political conversion of demands into supports is not [a] simple, clean process....but a divisive, difficult, and often messy struggle among conflicting groups.[1]

In the first four chapters of this book we engaged in some sense-making about politics in organizations. All too often, though, that exercise of thought and reflection is far removed from the messy struggle of organizational life. We cannot always enjoy the luxury of standing back, whether alone or with colleagues, to decode what we see around us and reflect on what we will do. However, if we want our leadership to be effective and trusted, the kind of thoughtfulness we discussed in Chapter 4 is critically important.

Leadership is in some ways a personal venture. It is not a solitary quest. Almost always leadership will be both strengthened and fully realized as a joint pursuit carried out in collaborative endeavor. In the daily reality of leadership in the political context of organizations, there is less tolerance today than there was yesterday for solo ventures by those we might once have seen as stars or heroic leaders.

In the best of worlds, we can imagine we might experience much mutuality and joint endeavor. In reality we usually find ourselves acknowledging multiple conflicting voices; we hope that to a reasonable degree they can be harmonized. The leadership challenge is to hear the voices, to understand the messages they convey, and to work toward ends that will balance the needs and interests of individuals and groups with those of the organization. We understand that in this venture we must sometimes be satisfied simply with the fact that we have made the effort. Differing interests carry at least the possibility that not all can be satisfied.

Assertion 5.1: Interests and preferences are the raw material of agendas. Both actors and audiences have agendas.

Traditionally many organizations have regarded members and supporters as onlookers or outsiders. Those descriptors, though persistent, are not always seen as valid or acceptable by many involved in social enterprises. As the model suggests, we can think inclusively of actors and audiences as all of the individuals and groups who are interested in the outcome of an organization's decisions and who prefer a particular value action or set of value actions as the outcome. In other words, whether or not they choose to become actively involved in the decision process, whether they aspire to be participants or wish to remain onlookers, audiences have an interest in the outcomes.

Assertion 5.2: The line between actors and onlookers is more likely to be a negotiated temporary accommodation than a fixed permanent boundary.

Assertion 5.3: Having a part to play and a place on the stage is more likely than before to be seen by all parties as an interest-based right.

Assertion 5.4: Values and beliefs, though they may not be discussed, play a significant role in determining one's ability and desire or determination to move between onlooker and actor status.

When we use the term **actor** or the word **agenda** in reference to life in organizations we are likely to attach negative connotations. To be identified as an actor in a social situation suggests that there is a degree of masking or cover up, that our acting is less than sincere and honest, or perhaps that our motives should be questioned. For our purposes it is more accurate to suggest that an actor is someone who participates in the action as opposed to being someone who is not involved. The term *actor* simply differentiates that individual or group from the *audience*. Both are interested in the outcome of the action; both have reasons for being there to work or to watch. All understand that their choice of involvement, whether as a member of the cast or as an onlooker, carries both opportunities and costs. Both actors and audiences are aware of and reliant on the other – it is a symbiotic relationship. Whether one is an actor or an audience member, she or he will have an *agenda*, a set of objectives determined by interests. At the broadest level of objective actors and audiences often share interests, but our more particular interests differentiate our personal agendas from those of others. We will observe or act different parts in different plays depending on our preferences.

UNDERSTANDING AGENDAS

Just as we are cautious when we hear someone described as an actor, we often attach negative significance to the word *agenda*. We are inclined to think first of hidden or private agendas, and that usually implies less-than-full disclosure. While in this book we will acknowledge that there are dubious agendas and bad actors, the goal of deepening our understanding will require us to take a broader view. It will be useful at the outset to develop a typology of agendas, a set of categories and descriptors that will allow us to discuss the subject usefully. Such a typology, as outlined in Figure 5.1, is multidimensional. It deals with the status or type of agenda, the extent to which access to that agenda is open, and the degree to which the agenda can be discussed among the parties involved or affected.

> **Assertion 5.5: Only typologies contain 'pure' agenda types. In practice, agendas usually are multiple, mixed, and simultaneous in occurrence.**

A weakness of any typology is that its usefulness for action is restricted by the fact that its purpose is usually descriptive and categorical in nature. The richness and the frustration of human behavior lie in human complexity and in the immediacy of real-world action, not in models. Our models, though, can help us understand action. Examining a description such as that presented in Figure 5.1 will be useful in our search for ways to translate information into knowledge and use that knowledge to strengthen our understanding and skill. Beyond that the helpfulness of our models will depend on our capacity to see agendas as rich and complex components of the scene.

Human agendas are more likely to be multiple than singular. They are more likely to be complex than simple. Usually, they will exist in a variety of types within a given situation, even within a single actor. With that in mind, we will step back from the complexity for a moment and consider the matter of agendas in step-wise fashion as though the categories were discrete.

> **Assertion 5.6: Soon after we have developed a useful classification scheme we will probably discover that it is less inclusive and tidy than we would have preferred.**

The Public Agenda

In Figure 5.1, I have identified agendas according to **status**, **access**, and **discussability**. We are most familiar with the first category, the public agenda. It is usually the only type written down for general reading, as in the meeting agenda, an artifact with which most of us are more familiar than we would prefer. Written or not, a public agenda, whether organizational or individual, is available and communicated, at least to the relevant actor(s) and audience group(s). Access is open to all who are involved in the decision process or who might be affected by its outcomes. We often refer to them as stakeholders.

Status	Access	Discussable
Public	Evident/available	Open
Private/Personal	Limited availability	Restricted
Hidden/Secret	Unavailable/undisclosed	Inferable

Figure 5.1 A typology of agendas

When we speak of the public agendas of individuals the details will not always be written, but the primary criteria of accessibility – **declared**, **evident**, and **available**, will have been met. In terms of discussability, the agenda is open. It is simplistic, though, to suggest that by definition this category will apply as a pure type – that simply may not be the case. It is not always the norm, nor is it always the better alternative. When the agenda is less than public the leadership challenge is to ascertain that fact and to understand why. When the leader's own agenda is being considered, the moral imperative is to ask "why?" for answers that can guide our actions. We realize that not all agendas are, can be, or should be public agendas, but at least our reasons for that choice should be open to scrutiny.

When our agendas are **public**, openness will often mean that those not directly involved – disinterested parties, according to our definition – may choose to declare their views, or to define themselves as interested. We will usually accept that with little or no concern. In fact, we will often invite and encourage their participation. However, as the horizontal line in Figure 5.1 indicates, we can distinguish the public, open agenda from both other types.

The Private/Personal Agenda

In the private case, the agenda will not be shared with everyone who might express interest or even with all who might have a legitimate stake in the matter at hand. The moral question – "why not public?" – presents itself. It may be asked not only by the agenda-setter(s) but also by others, some of whom are included in the discussion and others who are not.

The fact that there are private agendas does not imply that by definition these are unfair or that they lack justification. In some instances, they are essential. The private agenda, like the public agenda, is declared, evident, and available, but only on a limited basis. Without sitting on too fine a semantic line, we might suggest that the difference between the first two categories does not lie primarily in whether there is broad knowledge of the components of the agenda. Rather it may lie in the extent to which the agenda can be discussed in a broader context. In the case of the private learning agenda of a colleague group, membership in the informed group is limited. Sometimes that is for reasons of confidentiality. Sometimes the reasons are practical or logistical, and sometimes confidentiality is required for ethical reasons. In the case of the hidden/secret agenda, though, only the owner of the agenda knows what it is and why it has an audience of one. The issue is not whether there should be private or secret agendas. For leaders, the moral basis of our choices and the routes we take to arrive at decisions are primary indicators of the quality of our leadership practice.

The Hidden/Secret Agenda

The decision to maintain and operate from a **hidden** or a **secret agenda** rests solely with the agenda-setter. In this instance, the reflective leader is acutely aware of the presence or absence of both affirmation and dissent and, as a result, with the legitimacy of his or her leadership base. Values, principles, and practices that will determine the nature and quality of our actions on behalf of our organizations and the people whose lives will be affected by our choices move to the fore. We reach the high ground in decisions about our secret agendas when we raise the same questions that others ask when they challenge the legitimacy of our agendas. The simple "why?" question may test whether there is a greater good to be served by moving toward openness, or whether it is simply more convenient, or less hassle, or more economical of time and effort to limit the opportunity for involvement, in this case to oneself alone. In the case of the hidden/secret agenda, the pursuit is a solitary one by definition; sometimes that is legitimate. Our hidden/secret agendas can only be inferred by others because to disclose their existence will move them in toward public view or at least to private agenda status. The leader who has an agenda that cannot be shared may stand alone. If his or her decisions are ethical ones, that will not always and necessarily be a lonely stance nor will it be illegitimate.

We may understand that the interests and preferences of an individual or a group grow out of and are shaped by values held. However the efforts we make to discover those values will not always yield rich data. We can comprehend interests more readily as they are displayed in agendas, even though we know that the origins may exist one or two steps back from the actual discussion. The challenge is to ensure that where necessary and where possible, agendas and interests will be clear and evident. That is a difficult challenge in some instances.

Moore, speaking of parties involved in a dispute, has identified four types of obstacles to identifying interests: awareness, intent, commitment, and approach. He suggests that

> this lack of clarity occurs because parties (1) often do not know what their genuine interests are, (2) are pursuing a strategy of hiding their interests on the assumption that they will gain more from a settlement if their genuine goals are obscured from the scrutiny of other parties, (3) have adhered so strongly to a particular position that meets their interests that the interest itself becomes obscured and equated with the position and can no longer be seen as a separate entity, or (4) are unaware of procedures for exploring interests.[2]

The practice of leadership is at best a complex business. We have identified a typology of agendas and some of their characteristics. However, on reading Moore, it appears that although we might infer an agenda to be secret or deliberately hidden, that may not actually be the case. Moore suggests that while an agenda may appear to be secret, it might actually be legitimately available for examination and debate. Only the second type in Moore's list suggests the active maintenance of secrecy; the others indicate that work is required to identify, clarify, and locate the interest-produced agenda. Our most productive work in regard to agendas probably will be done as we seek to identify interests. If we set that as our before-action priority, we will be less likely to obscure interests by focusing on positions. To recap:

- Identifying public agendas appears to be a reasonably concrete task, although it will not always be easy. As we move in the direction of the hidden/secret agenda the task becomes a much greater challenge, particularly if we require a common interpretation.
- Interests and preferences create agendas. Understanding the former will be helpful in understanding the latter.

- Given the political character of organizations it is reasonable to assume that interest, preferences, and agendas exist universally. That says nothing about the quality of the leadership being practiced.

Assertion 5.7: Identifying interests, preferences, and agendas is the preliminary task; leadership has to do with what happens after that.

ORIGINS OF AGENDAS

Leaders in a political context must be **interested in the interests of interests**. Leaders must know the actors – the interested groups and individuals to whom she or he must relate – and the nature and substance of the interests they represent. That places agenda identification in perspective, although knowing the agenda is useful for developing our response only to the extent that we understand what drives it.

Every setting includes a range of actors. In the case of our organizations and companies, the actors are many. There is little value in developing a list that begins with clients or customers and ends with the broader interests of the community at large. It will be more useful to identify a set of criteria that will help us to identify interests by looking at their possible origins (Figure 5.2). Like the list mentioned above, no set of

	Origin	
FORMAL	GROUNDED	UNIQUE
Statutory	Role/Office	Emergency
Policy	Accepted practice	Assertion/Demand
Contractual	Precedent	Extra-situational

	Level of Legitimization	
Societal or Organizational	Organizational or Group	Group or Individual

Figure 5.2 Origins of interests, legitimization of agendas

criteria will be exhaustive or universally applicable. However, it may be helpful for discussion and analysis – the work of sense-making. I have identified three categories of origin: **formal, grounded,** and **unique**.

Formal Origins

Statutory Provisions: The existence of an interest is legitimized by federal or provincial/state legislation. We are most familiar with these as acts or bills.

Policy Provisions: As to level, policy is a generic term. The same authorities that enact provincial/state policy through the statutory provisions of legislation may also authorize by statute the creation and implementation of specific policies at the local level. We generally refer to these as being within the legitimate policy role of a local authority, such as a hospital board.

Contractual Provisions: Leaders are familiar with the formal origins of interests and agendas. Most often these will be found in contracts or agreements that specify the parties. These contractual arrangements stipulate terms and conditions and implementation procedures. In addition to the fact that they must be legitimized either at a broad societal level or within an organization, most contractual mechanisms share several characteristics. Almost always the origin is documented, the parameters are specified, and it is clear who is affected by the contract. We know who has a legitimate interest in the existence and provisions of the policy. In addition there are specified procedures and guidelines for action – rules to regulate behavior. Regulations exist to ensure that specified results are attained or that conditions are met; there are guidelines for resolution and redress when they are not. Formality and documentation, though, will not in themselves ensure that interests are achieved. Certainly they will not eliminate the possibility of conflicting or competing interests.

Grounded Origins

Documentation may still exist when we move to the second cluster of origins, but we begin to contemplate greater variation in what is done and the manner of practice. While there may not be broad societal concern with or support for these interests, they must be legitimized at least by the organizations or groups involved and affected. The president of a union local has rights and responsibilities – interests to pursue – that arise from the role. Our experience, though, tells us that there are wide variations in style and practice among presidents. Repetition of practices until they become patterns creates powerful organizational and social norms. Especially in the absence of guiding policy, prior instances provide a common-sense basis for asserting that the same should happen again, perhaps always. Elements of this cluster include the following.

Role or Office: The origin of an interest and therefore of its pursuit as an agenda lies in an individual's position or group membership. By-laws or other structural guidelines will provide for members and officers, and membership in one of those groups will carry specified rights and responsibilities.

Accepted Practice: In this case an interest is widely recognized through a history of accepted practice. At its strongest, that history will provide a documented pattern or at least a set of examples of effectiveness or results achievement. At its weakest, there may be simply a passive, inertial acceptance of current practice because "it's always been done that way."

Precedent: This source or origin of an agenda-expressed interest differs from the previous case in that it does not require a pattern of repeated similar practice and response, simply prior occurrence. Proponents assert that previous instances have created a precedent and that they therefore legitimize the interest and a particular course of action. Opponents may assert regarding a matter, sometimes even in advance, that "this cannot be considered a precedent." That is legitimate if we define the word narrowly as simply preceding in time, but generally we understand precedent to be an acceptable source of guidance for subsequent action.

Unique Origins

The opportunity for debate and differing interpretation, which usually is open even in cases of tight legislation, contract, or policy, is broadened by the second category – grounded origins. However, there remains opportunity for considered discussion and a full range of legitimate activities. Those may include negotiation, compromise, mediation, and a range of other strategies for pursuing our interests. That will not be the case in some **unique** circumstances. The origin lies in the situation itself in this case, in the stance of an individual or group, or outside the authority or control of the actors involved. That applies also in situations where the circumstance is not likely to recur. In these situations, debate is likely to be narrowed rather than broadened, either because circumstances preclude broadening it or because people act to prevent that from happening.

Emergency. In some cases urgent interests are expressed because of an immediate and imperative need created by the situation. A key criterion in this case, particularly if others are expected to join in or respond to some proposed action, is that they agree on the existence of a genuine emergency. In these cases, we are more likely to abandon our own interests, or at least to set them aside for the moment, to address the compelling need or urgent situation. We also are likely to show a reluctance to respond again after an experience of someone 'crying wolf', or asserting an emergency where none exists.

Assertion or Demand. In this case, shared perceptions are not a requirement – there is a unitary insistence by the proponent(s) that the interest is legitimate and that the resulting action agenda is essential. The action itself may be solitary, carried out by the proponent alone. If that is not the case, the proponent will need to back her or his assertion and demand actual power to achieve the desired result. At least she or he must be able to persuade others to join in the effort.

Extra-situational. Enacting a decision to accept, to support, or to oppose an interest that is alleged to originate from a higher principle or authority is always challenging. Sometimes it is impossible. Refuting a position or a proposal becomes more difficult if its origin lies outside our shared terms of reference or generally accepted knowledge. In some cases, the origin of the interest and the source of the values behind it may be not only extra-situational, but also extra-rational.[3] That is not to suggest that it is irrational. It may be a matter of faith or belief that cannot be communicated clearly or compellingly.

WORKING WITH INTERESTS AND PREFERENCES

I have focused on identifying the origin of interests and agendas, suggesting that values drive interests and preferences and that these in turn shape and drive our agendas. Because we are people and because we work in human organizations we are often inclined to personalize agendas and value them according to their sources – the people and groups who are advancing them. Leaders, though, stand on higher ground when their efforts are to achieve organizational ends and when they operate from a perspective that also values the people involved. For that reason, it will be helpful to consider some assertions that might assist us to remain focused on the effort to identify and understand agendas.

Assertion 5.8: It is useful to assume a continuum from values through interests and preferences to agendas, and to gain understanding of as much of that continuum as is relevant to the particular situation.

Assertion 5.9: In a context where not all agendas can be achieved, we will gain the best early yield by seeking to identify interests.

Assertion 5.10: Identifying interests as a basis for agendas can offer protection against personalizing issues and focusing on positions, either of which can restrict one's capacity for leadership action.

The leadership task begins when we seek to build a knowledge base with regard to a particular topic, supported in that effort by our study and understanding of politics in organizations. Leadership calls for clear understanding of both the larger case – the interests and preferences that characterize and accompany the enterprise – and the specific instance – the organization or region that is the leader's primary frame of reference.

In terms of the conceptual framework presented in Chapter 2, it is important to note that interests and preferences are intrinsic to the political process. They may appear at any point, even before we have identified a decision focus. Leaders are challenged to be proactive rather than reactive; to the extent that we have the background of training and experience and the prerequisite mindset and attitudes, we can accomplish this. However, few of us are exceptionally gifted at accurately foreseeing and predicting the future. The science of meteorology provides a good example. Weather prediction gets better as the measuring sticks improve, but our knowledge that in the end it is an educated best guess and a set of probabilities prompts us to leave an umbrella in the car in case it rains. The decision focus will not always originate with us, nor is that necessarily a criterion for leadership or a measure of our initiative. What counts is that we rely on something more than "It looks like a fine day" rather than simply deciding to fly over the mountains with someone we accept to be a pilot because she or he is wearing a uniform with a wing design on the shoulder.

In many cases, interests and preferences will be the first and primary factors in identifying and shaping a decision focus. A review of a hospital's staff in-service program, for example, may be triggered by the interest of a union in ensuring control over professional development initiatives. It may equally be sparked by a board's concern over financial pressures and a resulting study of ways to economize. Usually, there will be multiple interests and multiple agendas developed as expressions of those interests. To be proactive does not demand that one be 'first on the scene' or the originator of the idea but that the action response is marked by initiative and focused energy.

> **Assertion 5.11: Where there are interests, there will be demands for action in regard to agendas.**

Our interests provide the substantive decision focus for our action demands – we want to achieve our goals. We embark on a process that initially seems linear, sequential, and neat. The reality is that it is likely to become nonlinear, recursive, and messy. The leadership challenge is to make a difference in the course of events by recognizing and dealing expertly with the complex elements of political activity in our organizations. We express our interests as preferences for a specific course of action, one that if taken will lead to goal achievement.

In an in-service example, a union's preference stated as a demand may be that it be allowed to control funding for its members' professional growth activities. After all, those members are responsible for the direct provision of quality service to clients. If that assignment of authority seems unlikely, a second-level preference stated as an alternative might be to have substantial employee representation on the committee screening applications for in-service training grants. It is conceivable that an organization's board, which is not bound by the norms of its employees' professional group, might be interested only in shaving as much as possible from the operating budget, even if that interest is shaped and forced primarily by the priorities of government at a higher level. Whatever the course of debate, interested parties will seek to influence outcomes by expressing their own interests, those of their organizations, or those of their clients. Each will demand a meaningful and substantial part in determining value actions. Each will be bound by constraints and pressures and each will have a conception of the desired outcome. Each will be aware of important actors and audiences and their interests and preferences. Each will need a repertoire of knowledge and skill to support the effort to influence. In other words, each will be called upon to lead.

SPECIAL CASE: DETERMINED PURSUIT OF A SINGLE INTEREST

We expect energy and initiative from leaders. We expect that they will show zeal in pursuing and protecting our interests. We know also that throughout history great zeal has produced both significant social progress and substantial human pain. Where we have benefited, often it has been because of the positive energy of **zealousness** – earnestness or fervor;

hearty and persistent endeavor. Where there is suffering and when we meet insurmountable obstacles, that is often partly because of **zealotry** – extreme partisanship or fanaticism. The fact of zealotry's existence as the counterpoint to zealousness on the political landscape places it on the working agenda of the reflective leader, sometimes at the margin and sometimes at the core of activity.

> **Assertion 5.12: Zealotry without apparent power is like a lion without apparent teeth – things change when the lion opens its mouth.**

Interests drive agendas. It may be difficult to offer a useful definition of a special interest, but we are familiar with what we call single interests. Often we describe their proponents as *single-issue people*. However, not all of these people are necessarily zealots. The descriptor *zealot* describes a designated category of interest representation, with at least enough significance to warrant a closer look.

Single-issue people often move into view when they run for office aided by their supporters on the basis of their single interest. They appear in the conversations of boards and councils when they come repeatedly before those groups with the same request as before. They may discourage others from membership, participation, and even meeting attendance because today's story is simply yesterday's tale retold and no one wants to hear it again. Those attributes alone suggest that a brief exploration of the sometimes fine line between zealousness and zealotry is worthwhile. To sharpen the focus we will move in this analysis toward the zealot and her or his behavior. Taken alone, some of the zealot's attributes represent reasonable, even admirable, behavior. Those attributes are not owned solely by the zealots among us, nor are they necessarily evidence of zealotry. I propose several attributes as a set of assertions for your consideration and response:

1. Zealots are often singularly but narrowly well informed on their issue.
2. Zealots know the literature, cases, and precedents relevant to their interest, and they are well aware of settings in which they assert that it has previously been satisfied.
3. "Relevant literature" is drawn selectively from a carefully controlled pool of resources. The zealot will hold a tight rein on the list of acceptable data. Full and open inquiry is unlikely. Challenge is resisted.
4. The zealot may have a special set of norms not widely shared for determining the acceptability of tactics to be employed in pursuing the interest.

5. Except where the zealot chooses tactics outside the mainstream of general acceptability, stance and presentation quickly become familiar and predictable.
6. For the zealot, the agenda takes precedence over the person, although that may be denied by asserting that the proposed action is 'for your benefit'.
7. Relying on rational persuasion to convince a zealot is ineffective. The zealot's position is immovable even though it may appear to be open to discussion.
8. Zealots often refer to higher principles or authorities but the language of their script may be unfamiliar to most of us.
9. Although the zealot's affiliations may be tenuous, small in number, or elusive from discovery and conversation, that may say nothing about the power of the individual or group.
10. The 'wannabee' and the 'rent-a-crowd' enjoy being alongside the zealot; that is not always welcomed by the zealot.
11. In many instances zealots are faced by other zealots. Only the vocabulary changes.
12. Debate on the zealot's home turf is always won by the zealot, at least in his or her view.

One might ask why we would focus on such a marginal category. My purpose here is not to offer a new term for inclusion in the lexicon of politics in organizations, but to call attention to one often difficult point on the continuum of human behavior in a political context. Second, I am not reporting here the results of research or suggesting the early stages of theory development. I am simply offering you a list of observations from experience to stimulate discussion. If it seems worthwhile, add to the list, delete from it, or modify it to make it more functional. Third, understanding life at the margins has value for our work nearer the center. I have painted the zealot in relatively stark terms as a special case in point. Our decisions about responding to zealots will be influenced by whether or not we believe that the lion has teeth.

Stepping back from the special case of the zealot, it is useful to consider what Pross has termed **issue-oriented groups** as the first step in a developmental progression that extends through fledgling and mature groups to what he has called institutionalized groups.[4] Given the terms in which I have discussed zealotry one might suggest that developmentally it is a category prior to the issue-oriented group. The question, though, is whether a group founded on zealotry would follow the same sequence as those Pross has identified. His comments about issue-oriented groups are informative, though writing today he might reconsider his assertion of "little experience of the policy process":

> They allow their concern with the resolution of one or two issues to dominate both their internal affairs and their relations with government, with the public, and with other groups. They spring up where there is strong feeling about particular issues and tend to be led by people who have little experience of the policy process. The magnitude of the issue is of little consequence for the long-term evolution of the group. Nor does it matter whether the group's concern is with material benefits or is ideologically or attitudinally based. As long as the group is concerned with one issue to the exclusion of all others, that concern will dominate the group's organizational arrangements.[5]

One might infer that issue-oriented groups are the first cousins of zealotry. However, Pross places them on the other side of the boundary, noting that "many groups concerned with preventing action of a particular kind can achieve their objectives through techniques that institutional groups consider crude and self-defeating," and that

> they frequently serve important functions in the political system.... Because they can develop extremely quickly and are unencumbered by institutional structures, they are excellent vehicles for generating immediate public reaction to specific issues... they can indulge in forms of political communication that institutional groups are reluctant to use.[6]

While undoubtedly there are zealots among the members of some issue-oriented groups, those groups often serve a vital social and political purpose. One could equally posit the existence of zealots within any interest-based group.

A Challenge for Leaders: Whose Interests?

Except when we are concerned that the lion may have real teeth, we often disregard zealots. On occasion, though, we place the zealous in the same space as the zealot. This error is unfortunate for leadership because the energy required for a focus solely on actors draws attention away from the plot, away from the interests at stake. Again, the call to leadership demands we walk on higher ground. We take for granted that there will be interests. If we accept that not all of them can be satisfied, choice is a necessity and competition and conflict can be anticipated and faced. That reality presents an exciting challenge to some. Some view it as an uncomfortable necessity and others class it as 'avoid at all costs'. Speaking more specifically of his observation of school principals, Sarason has offered a comment that probably applies to most organizations that have at least two people occupying positions with similar terms of reference:

> First, the knowledge on the part of the [leader] that what he or she wants to do may and will encounter frustrating obstacles frequently serves as justification for staying near the lower limits of the scope of the role. Second, the [leader's] actual knowledge of the characteristics of the system is frequently incomplete and faulty to the degree that his or her conception or picture of what the system will permit or tolerate leads ... to a passive rather than an active role. Third, and perhaps most important, the range in practices ... within the same system is sufficiently great so as to suggest that the system permits and tolerates passivity and activity, conformity and boldness, dullness and excitement, incompetency and competency ... One has ... to take account of the variations in the ways in which individuals conceive of the system.[7]

For Sarason, leadership as political activity is well within "the scope of the role." With that in mind it is reasonable to suggest that as part of the leader's reflective activity it would be worthwhile to examine Sarason's observations as a self-assessment. Given not only the degree of change in organizational life since Sarason wrote in the early 1980s but also the ever-turbulent and often unpredictable character of today's organizations, leadership demands performance near the upper limits of the "scope of the role." For today's leader, that means addressing the reality of conflict in responding to demands for support and in allocating shares of scarce resources. We will turn in the next chapter to a discussion of those issues.

END NOTES

1. Wirt & Kirst, *Schools in Conflict*, 61-62.
2. Christopher Moore, *The Mediation Process: Practical Strategies for Resolving Conflict* (San Francisco: Jossey-Bass, 1986), 187.
3. Hodgkinson, *Educational Leadership*, 96ff.
4. Paul Pross, *Group Politics and Public Policy* (Toronto: Oxford University Press, 1986), 117-119.
5. Ibid., 117.
6. Ibid., 118.
7. Seymour Sarason, *The Culture of the School and the Problem of Change*, 2nd ed. (Berkeley: McCutchan, 1982), 171.

CHAPTER 6 — INTERFACE TURBULENCE: CONFLICT AS LEADERSHIP OPPORTUNITY

Conflict is an omnipresent phenomenon in human interaction. Conflicts can lead to productive and positive change or to the destruction and degradation of relationships.[1]

Omnipresent is a characteristic we would ascribe to someone or something we believe to be present everywhere. **Ubiquitous**, meaning present everywhere at the same time and often encountered, adds another dimension to the definition. Both words are relevant to our discussions about conflict. Both in its omnipresence and in its ubiquity, conflict has something in common with another human condition – stress – although there is at least one important difference. Stress needs only one subject, although it can be aided and strengthened (or worsened) by the involvement of others. Conflict on the other hand demands two or more people. An assumption associated with conflict is that interests will differ from person to person and among groups. The idea of conflict presumes that not all interests will be satisfied. Few leaders thrive on or welcome conflict, but we understand both its reality and the fact that we will have to deal with it, if not today, then probably tomorrow .

Assertion 6.1: The reality of politics is one first principle of organizational life, measured by its ubiquity. The reality of conflict is another.

Previously I defined politics in organizations as activity surrounding demands for support of values and interests and authoritative response to demand. If that is the context, and if it includes the preconditions noted above – two or more people, differing interests, and scarce resources – there will be conflict. This should not be unusual or surprising. Conflict will not always be overtly expressed or even clearly evident. It will not always require special action; often it will be addressed successfully. We walk an uncertain path, though, when we assume, perhaps because we are not comfortable considering the alternative, that a particular situation is free of conflict. If our circumstances are at all complex, we will probably express that view infrequently and usually for a shorter rather than a longer time. We are surrounded, nonetheless, by events and circumstances that suggest not everyone understands either the reality of conflict or its characteristics.

A Perspective on Conflict

It is important to our discussion in this chapter that we agree on at least an elemental idea of what constitutes conflict. We might think of conflict as a struggle, a state of opposition, or a clashing of opposed interests. We tend to move toward the third part of that definition because we see conflict as an activity, an event, or a state of affairs. We view it as a situation that is stronger and more pressing than a simple statement of disagreement. However, when we adopt the narrower view we also narrow our options by overlooking the process component. To call a situation *a state of opposition* carries at least the possibility that change could occur through dialogue and negotiation; *clashing* is more suggestive of a final win/lose outcome. Conflict has roots and origins; that fact makes it developmental rather than spontaneous. For leaders, in fact for anyone who must deal with conflict, including each of us, the concern for resolution begins with a search for the roots and origins of the conflict. We usually want to understand what we are facing.

Earlier we noted the importance of leaders' perceptiveness or the ability to know what we are seeing when we see it. In the case of conflict, the initial leadership challenge is to see the situation clearly and understand its nuances and implications. Beyond that, most of us would agree that the challenge is to spot conflict in the early stages and not be caught by surprise. We have dealt with the fact that conflict is not an uncommon occurrence and we realize that it stands among the more troublesome realities we face. We cannot always identify conflict in the early stages but developing our ability to do that seems a reasonable target.

We often refer facetiously to '20/20 hindsight'. Our retrospective view of a conflict situation is often more precise than our prospective view. The challenge is to develop our capacity to anticipate, or at least our ability to identify the signs of emerging conflict and circumstances that are likely to lead to conflict. If that is our goal and if our intent is to be proactive rather than reactive, our focus on resolving conflict will begin in the early stages. Our learning agendas will originate there also.

Though it is often tragic, it is not uncommon to hear news of railway accidents, sometimes involving hazardous chemicals and perhaps loss of life. We are even more attuned to reports of airplane crashes because they almost always carry a human cost. We relate most immediately to the actual event – the collision or the crash – because that is what we see on the screen or in newspaper pictures. The event itself is certainly an example of conflict, or in the terms used above, a clashing of opposed interests. For the investigator, though, the journey begins much earlier, and the intent is to prevent similar occurrences. If that effort is successful, changes in air traffic control procedures or train routing practices will deal with situations of potential conflict much closer to their origins – conditions which if they are not altered probably will lead to more collisions.

If two trains on the same track are moving toward each other at a high rate of speed, at what point does that constitute a conflict? Our perspectives will differ widely depending on whether our task is to set signals, to be an alert engineer, to rescue victims, to protect the environment from pollution, to clear the tracks, or to prevent future incidents. In each case, there is the possibility of conflict and, thus, leadership action will be required in all elements of the situation. Early recognition of the possibility of conflict is a key ingredient in preventing its occurrence, although that will not always be possible, and in assessing the possibility of resolution.

Our example illustrates the point that early identification of conflict potential is important. But it falls short in some respects. It is highly unlikely that to place an east-bound and a west-bound train on the same track and the same schedule will ever be seen as standard practice. We are unlikely to accept collisions as a routine 'cost of doing business' or to ever agree that our main task as simply to clean up the mess. In the pattern of interactions that is organizational life, though, when there are differing interests and limited resources we recognize that inevitably there will be collisions. The leadership challenge is to build alternate tracks where possible, to adjust speeds and schedules, and sometimes just to clean up the inevitable mess with tomorrow in mind.

Whatever analogies and examples we use to clarify our conceptions of conflict, it seems clear that prevention where possible, amelioration where practical, and resolution where required usually will be a collaborative rather than an individual enterprise. It may also be the case that the results of our collective efforts, although they may be temporary, will offer a stronger and more durable option than any of our separate and individual efforts. If we accept that conflict is inevitable, we are free to question its origins and to examine it from other perspectives: How might we recognize conflict in the early stages? How can we minimize both its occurrence and its impact? How might we utilize conflict in the accomplishment of legitimate ends? How can we ensure that as far as possible our organizations and the people in and around them will be strengthened rather than weakened by the experience of conflict?

The Possibility of Resolution

The concepts and definitions in this book rest on the assumption that there is a close and important two-way link between understanding and behavior. The terms in which we view and understand conflict will affect and be affected by the ways in which we address it. For that reason, it is important that we search for a degree of precision in the vocabulary we use to present concepts that are important components of our repertoire of skills and knowledge.

It is legitimate to ask, "Can conflict really be resolved?" It is less than useful to respond with a categorical answer, because the question is complex. When we speak of resolution, we suggest that the problem has been solved, explained, or settled. However, other questions lurk behind that assumption: In whose mind? Do all agree? Is everyone fully satisfied or have some simply agreed to proceed in the manner proposed? Often the difficulty is that the answers are not sufficient to satisfy us. In many cases, the problem arises when a quest for understanding has not answered the prior question: What is the nature of this particular conflict? Moore has offered a helpful schema that he calls the **sphere of conflict**. He suggests five basic types of conflict: data, interest, relationship, structural, and value conflicts. Moore offers both a perspective on the causes of various types of conflict and suggestions for intervention strategies as part of the process of addressing conflict.[2] Extending that idea, Fisher, Kopelman, and Schneider have suggested that

> when one is faced with any conflict, we believe it is more useful to think about a good process for handling a flow of problems than to think about "solving" a particular problem once and for all. In fluid and turbulent times, it is better to think in terms of coping with conflicts than resolving them.
>
> Understanding our task as conflict management rather than conflict resolution is a paradigm shift – away from a conception of conflict and negotiation that stresses static substantive solutions and toward an approach that stresses the power of process. Rarely is a conflict intractable simply

because no one has a good idea of how things ought to be.... In most cases the difficulty lies not in the lack of potential substantive options but in the failure to design, negotiate, and pursue a process that moves us forward from where we are now to where we would like to be.[3]

For this discussion, rather than speaking of **resolution** we might suggest that the task of leadership is to **address** conflict, to direct attention to it and deal with it effectively. Addressing conflict in some cases will lead to a solution or to resolution. In other cases, we will choose an acceptable compromise from among less-than-desirable alternatives. This is perhaps a more useful vocabulary. The term *address* is more supportive of ideas such as process and mutuality than is either of the terms *manage* or *resolve*; it suggests a process rather than a set of discrete actions. To suggest that we will *address* issues also admits to the possibility that not all conflicts will be resolved to the point that we arrive at fully and finally acceptable answers. In fact, "Conflict cannot be eliminated from organizations; it is an essential, necessary and healthy part of their life. The leader has not so much to solve value conflict as to resolve it, continuously." The notion here is that leaders will be engaged constantly in addressing conflict. Conflict itself is a legitimate part of the normal and expected state of human affairs. The leadership challenge throughout this book is to ensure that our engagements with conflict will be principled engagements with a dual focus – the welfare of both our organizations and the people who work in them.

THE PLACE OF DIFFERENCE AND DISSENT

A newspaper editorial cartoon depicted the members of a board with their arms connected by ropes and pulleys to a cord hanging in front of the board's chairperson. The message was clear – the members of the board or at least its chair had placed a high premium on unanimity in decision making. The community on the other hand, or at least the newspaper's editorial cartoonist, was calling that value into question. The unasked second question was perhaps: What does unanimity signify? That query might open the door to a consequential third question – Why do we value and strive for unanimity? The answer might lead us to a clearer analysis of the purpose of the conflict-related debate and discussion leading to decisions and action.

Principled dissent is an important component of decision making around resource allocation and, therefore, of politics in organizations. Assume for the moment that our involvement in a group, whether that is for work, service, or social purposes, is an expression of our values and interests. Assume also that while these values and interests will overlap to a degree with the values and interests of others in the group, usually there will not be an exact match. In fact, the congruency may be minimal, just enough for us to accept that our membership in the group contributes sufficiently to our own agenda for us to continue participating. In this circumstance, particularly if the group has multiple decisions to make and especially if it will have a life that extends beyond immediate circumstances, unanimity may be an elusive target. Even if we achieve it, simple unanimity does not necessarily indicate full or lasting agreement.

Assertion 6.2: Unanimity may demonstrate only that when the vote was taken, no one formally registered a contrary opinion.

Even when unanimity is gained, it is likely that some in the group will question its validity. We are familiar with scenarios in which candidates run for community office on the basis of a stated platform and are elected through the efforts of like-minded people. To the extent that a candidate's platform represents the vision that he or she will bring to the board or council table, we understand that the presence of multiple board members will mean the presence of multiple individual visions. The challenge facing the board is to develop a clear sense of corporate direction that not only will reflect those personal visions but also will carry the support of the board as a whole and of its important reference communities. In these circumstances, negotiated agreement may be more meaningful than a unanimous vote. As one chief executive officer observed, "We always try to work for a win-win situation. We try to help the [board members] to ... expand their vision without feeling that they are letting go of their own cherished goals."[5]

If the emphasis of a group's activity is on discussion and debate leading to decisions and value actions, and if that activity reflects the assumptions articulated above, we will use such words as *vigorous*, *lively* and *spirited* to describe our best examples, and *acrimonious*, *bitter*, and *angry* to describe the worst we have observed. The leadership challenge is to ensure that both organization and people move in ways that will lead each toward development rather than toward dysfunction (Figure 6.1).

Assertion 6.3: Healthy debate will be marked by difference, divergence, disagreement, and dissent – the end is development.

Depending on workplace processes and the groups and decisions in which we are involved, we will work within a variety of frameworks for decision making and action: voting, consensus, authorized decision, and

```
DISCUSSION  ←――――――――→  DECISIONS

Difference                Dispute

Divergence                Discord

Disagreement              Disharmony

Dissent                   Disunity
   │                         │
   │         Outcomes        │
   ▼          and            ▼
Development ←――――  ――――→ Dysfunction
            Relations
```

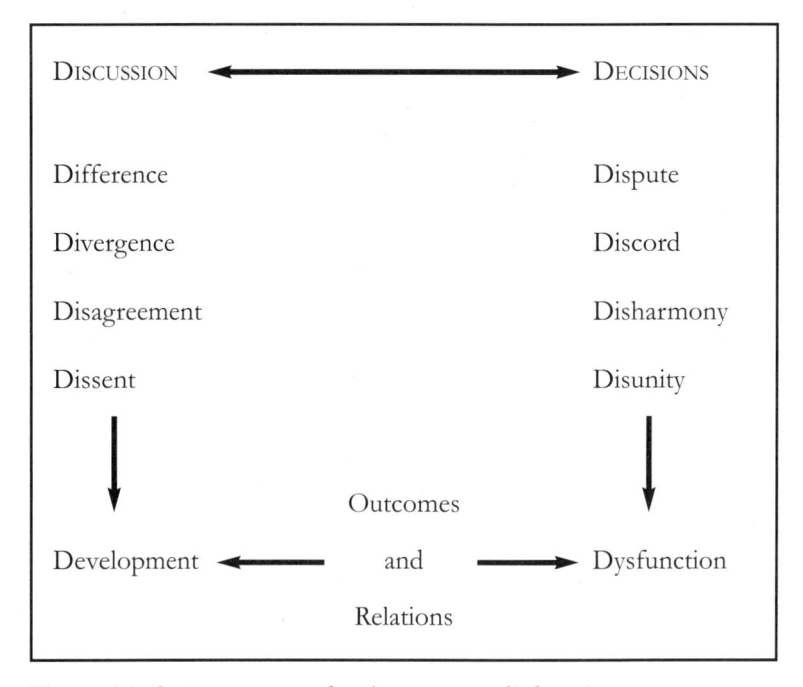

Figure 6.1 Steps to group development or disfunction

perhaps other strategies. We can recall instances where discussion that might be described as a ferment of ideas was provoked by one group member who saw things differently, or where our best arguments failed to persuade everyone. Either despite or because of that, worthwhile decisions were made. The issue is not whether there is a range and diversity of views within the group – almost always that will be the case – but whether we will value that range and diversity to the point of ensuring that it is encouraged and heard, even sought out and stimulated.

For leaders the concern is simultaneously with destination and journey, with outcome and process. Because that is the case, we take the higher ground when we seek to ensure a climate in which difference is respected, divergence is valued, disagreement is explored, and dissent is legitimized. At the same time, both leaders and groups understand that these processes and stances must contribute to the legitimate interests of organization and person. This will be a perennial challenge. From time to time it will raise difficult and troubling questions about the locus of our primary responsibility.

Committees and boards provide useful examples of the role of dissent. Because they are comprised of humans with legitimate interests they offer contexts in which decisions play an officially acknowledged role and the processes of decision making are formally identified. Without suggesting that the group contexts in which we work will lead in a given circumstance to a single statement of position, it is reasonable to consider that Carver's useful counsel to boards may also be useful counsel in other group and committee contexts. We might simply substitute **group** wherever the word **board** appears:

> Whatever the agenda content, the central interpersonal challenge to the board is to convert divergent viewpoints into a single official view. It is as important for the board to have multiple minds as it is for it to have a single voice. To weaken the multiplicity of viewpoints would be to rob the board of its richness of wisdom. To weaken the unity of voice would be to rob the board of its opportunity for effectiveness. On many issues, the board must elicit as much divergence as possible and resolve it into a single position.[6]

Whatever our group and whatever its style, structures, processes, and intended outcomes, the legitimate end of the dialogue we have considered is **development** (Figure 6.1). We will not always satisfy all interests of the organization, of leader(s), or of individual group members. The issue is one of both destination and journey. Development will be marked both by progress toward the destination and by the character of the journey. The extent to which we meet the challenge will be measured in terms of both **outcomes** – what we accomplish within and for the organization, and **relations** – the quality of the effort and its impact on people within the organization and its key reference communities.

> **Assertion 6.4: Unhealthy debate will be marked by dispute, discord, disharmony, and disunity – the end is dysfunction.**

Even a cursory examination of the list in the assertion above will suggest that dialogue and debate can take on a different character, one that will negatively affect both outcomes and relations. Where the debate is marked by an unhealthy interpersonal component or by a lack of respect characterized behaviorally in any of a number of ways, we will not address conflict with development as the likely outcome. In these cases, both the quality of outcomes measured by what we accomplish on behalf of the group and the quality of relationships measured by the impact of the effort on the people involved will be affected in ways that move us away from development and toward **dysfunction**.

Not all of our activities in groups and organizations, whether they are channeled positively or negatively, will be marked by vigor and energy. There will be times and circumstances, perhaps more often than we would prefer, when the effort is marked by apathy or reluctance. Our focus here, however, is on circumstances in which values held strongly and interests assigned priority are expressed through stated preferences and in agendas. That, more than apathy and reluctance, will offer us both the promise of accomplishment and the likelihood of conflict.

IDENTIFYING POSITIONS AND INTERESTS

Much has been written about the distinction between positions and interests and about the relative merits of interest-based bargaining over positional bargaining in situations of conflict or negotiation. For more detailed and focused reading on that subject, I would draw your attention to works which have that as a primary emphasis. For the purposes of this book, though, it is important to realize that "people routinely engage in positional bargaining. Each side takes a position, argues for it, and makes concessions to reach a compromise."[7] We know also that compromises are not always made and that the choice and acceptance of a final position often determines the eventual outcome of a conflict situation.

The identification of positions frequently stands in front of and blocks the identification of interests, both in sequence of presentation and in ease of discovery. By definition, **position** implies a place occupied or a stance taken. Positions are often problematic because of their fixed and unitary nature. We stand in one place as opposed to standing in another; we demand a four percent salary increase as opposed to a two percent increase; we are or we are not willing to grant access through our private property. We often say, "I know her position on that matter." We often assess the perceived usefulness or futility of further dialogue on the basis of our perception of another's position on the matter.

Assertion 6.5: Positions are evidence of interests. Interests may be displayed, discoverable, hidden, or secret, but they exist.

The difficulty with a positional stance is that it invites reaction rather than response. It offers few opportunities to achieve goals except within the tight confines of a position taken on the issue at hand. Yet positions are attractive because they are concrete. Responding to my four percent salary demand is a much simpler task than the challenge of understanding the complex set of interests that stands behind it – my educational plans, my desire for a newer car, or my need to ensure that the grocery budget will provide food for my family. I am interested in improving my education, in having reliable transportation, and in ensuring a healthy family – translating these interests into a specific salary demand or a position may or may not accomplish those purposes. It will not accomplish an answer to the question of whether there are other ways to achieve the same goals. My positional demand precludes the possibility that dialogue with others might lead to new questions with better answers or to a more thoughtful expression of my interests.

The primary difference between interests and positions lies in the fact that while interests offer the possibility of alternative paths to the same end, positions do not. A "No Trespassers" sign might have been placed on the fence by a property owner who simply wants to protect wildlife on the property, but it says much more than that. Not only the poacher but also the photographer and the picnicker are excluded, along with the possibility that the owner's enjoyment of the scenery might be enhanced through sharing it with visitors. The possibility exists, of course, that the "No Trespassers" notice does not really represent a firm and final stance, but most of us are not likely to wander through the woods to find out. Once we get to know the owner though, we may discover what led to the posting of the sign and whether there are any legitimate alternative possibilities. Perhaps we will become friends and discover what interests led the owner to post the sign.

A further difference is that positions usually are evident. Allowing for preferences in timing and tactic, it is usually to the position-taker's advantage to communicate his or her position. All the same if the stance is truly positional, that communication is likely to be characterized as information rather than discussion; it is likely to be announced rather than negotiated. Position-holders are more like tightrope walkers than hikers; there is little prospect of discussion about choosing a better path or a new destination, and it will not always be possible to turn back.

Assertion 6.6: Focusing on interests allows for the possibility of principled dialogue about the merits of positions.

It will not always be possible, nor will it always be desirable, to satisfy a demand. However, the effort is more likely to be principled when we focus on interests rather than positions. The possibility of dialogue is opened; interests can be discussed with the aim of developing an understanding and appreciation of positions. Dialogue and discussion rather than monologue and assertion might increase the likelihood that a better way can be found. The leadership challenge is to participate in principled dialogue about interests rather than simply reacting to statements of position. Time and the pressure of circumstances are our enemies in that endeavor. Our allies are the thoughtfulness and reflection that increase the likelihood we will know what we *SEE* when we *See* what we *see*.

ADDRESSING CONFLICT: SEEING AND READING

A healthy organization demands thoughtful, reflective leaders. It is strengthened when those attributes are shared widely among its members. The second essential component is the outcome of that reflection and deliberation – action. This book is about action of a particular order; action with a moral character or, in other words, action that reflects an ethical stance. The next two chapters have praxis – action guided and enhanced by reflection – as their particular focus. Chapter 7 examines the demand for leaders to make choices, reach decisions, and attain outcomes. Chapter 8 considers the moral and ethical foundations of leadership.

We know that one requirement for success in the political realm is astuteness, the ability to see clearly and to read capably. Another is the capacity to filter data through one's screen of competence and values before deciding and acting. The initial requirement is to *see* in the sense that we will understand the full range of data that is part of the scene before us. We might think of seeing as the beginning of a continuum that with additional insight extends to include the ability to *read* interests and agendas. We can understand neither unless we have available to us a full range of relevant data. Again, urgency and the pressure of circumstances, often expressed as a demand for immediate and simultaneous action on multiple fronts, can affect our ability to see by robbing us of the time and energy needed for thought and reflection.

Earlier we discussed *seeing* at three levels. At the first level, we are presented with the set of circumstances and data facing us immediately and in a specific situation. We may be discussing a motion at a meeting, an appointment with a determined delegation, or an altercation between two clients. At this level, the leadership challenge is to *see* as we gather data, both that which is presented and that which we gather through questions and discussion, to ensure a complete and accurate picture. At the second level, we add to that store of knowledge by beginning to *See* with a perspective developed through our own internal questioning: Is this an isolated example? If not, how is it similar to other cases and how do those differ? Beyond the immediate circumstance, are there patterns to observe? Finally, as we develop more sophisticated ways of looking, as we develop frameworks for analysis and are able to categorize, we begin to *SEE* the larger picture of events. We develop frameworks for thought, decision, and action on this and future occasions.

During that progression, leaders apply their backgrounds of training, experience, knowledge, and insight – their wisdom – in the manner that we have described as *reading*. Our ability to read will vary both situationally and personally. For the leader, the ability to read is a fundamental measure of capability and competence:

> Reading a situation incorrectly can prompt behavior from others which hooks inappropriate behavior in oneself, setting up a downward spiral as loss of confidence prompts more and more self-orientated behavior. And in this condition our 'reading' focuses on interpretations which satisfy that behavior... our perceptive reading of the situation is abandoned. Later on, out of the heat, everything looks different and we wonder how we behaved as we did – we are being 'wise after the event.'[8]

This post-event clarity of vision usually is hardest on the individual leader. Our efforts to analyze in retrospect and to learn from the situations we have experienced are carried out with the primary goal of avoiding repetition. At least we do not want to repeat our mistakes. It is a reality of leadership in the political milieu of organizational life, though, that there will not always be the opportunity to benefit from analyzing our 'reading difficulties'. The work of leadership demands that those who accept the responsibility of influencing also understand it, that they carry it out ethically and skillfully, and that they share power and equip others to use it. It demands also that each of us, often in concert with others, ensures that the decisions we make or in which we participate make a positive difference in the lives of organizations and individuals.

END NOTES

1. Moore, *The Mediation Process*, 297.
2. Ibid., 27.
3. Roger Fisher, Elizabeth Kopelman, & Andrea Schneider, *Beyond Machiavelli: Tools for Coping with Conflict* (New York: Penguin,1994), 4-5.
4. Hodgkinson, *Educational Leadership*, 76.
5. Peter Drucker, *Managing the Nonprofit Organization: Principles and Practices* (New York: Harper Collins, 1990), 176.
6. John Carver, *Boards that Make a Difference* (San Francisco: Jossey-Bass, 1990), 186.
7. Roger Fisher and William Ury, *Getting to Yes: Negotiating Agreement Without Giving In* (New York: Penguin, 1981), 3.
8. Simon Baddeley, "Political sensitivity in public managers," *Local Government Studies* 15, no. 2, (1989).

Chapter 7 — Evidence of Leadership:
Choices, Decisions, and Outcomes

One can allow, or not allow, one's leadership to be swayed by values deriving from hedonism, ambition or careerism, or by the prejudices and affinities one has for colleagues and peers. Each day and each hour provides the occasion for value judgments, and each choice has a determining effect on value options for the future.[1]

Finally we must choose, understanding what our choosing implies about politics, power, and influence – about leadership itself. We must make decisions and we must assign value with ends in mind. In the best of circumstances and practices, the path toward our choices will be a path of teamwork and collaborative effort. Our choices can be complicated, though, by the fact that in the rich and politically complex settings that mark our organizations we are seldom faced with a forced choice between a pair of options. We cannot simply pick one of two alternative possibilities, say to each other with a clear sense of closure, "That is that," and move on in linear fashion to the next decision. The work of leadership is not simply the task of crossing off completed items on a 'To Do' list, though that will characterize some of its associated managerial tasks and sometimes will occupy more of our work day than we might prefer.

Political leadership of the kind we have considered throughout this book recognizes that often our work will expose us to vigorous competition for recognition and satisfaction of interests. It will be measured most often by resource allocation decisions – Who gets what and how much? Or perhaps more to the point, Who gets little or nothing and why? Referring back to our original definition, there are two components to the political equation, demands for support of values and interests and authoritative response to those demands. Leadership offers that authoritative response.

Decisions Avoided or Delayed and the Search for Consensus

Occasionally the best decision is no decision at all. Unfortunately, that is often the desperate refuge of the procrastinator rather than the wise choice of the reflective practitioner. A nondecision is actually a decision. A common rationalization and sometimes a valid reason for our nondecisions is that if we just wait and do nothing the problematic circumstance will go away. The interests might sort themselves out without our involvement. Perhaps other initiatives will resolve the matter or other issues will surface to take its place. When that is a rationalization, we will often assert in advance that in this or that particular circumstance inaction is the better choice. When it is a valid reason and a workable strategy, we are more likely to assess the results thoughtfully after the fact as we reflect on our practice. If we simply avoid deciding, we may find ourselves forced to address the issue in a more complex and troublesome form as a result of our flawed decision to do nothing.

The reality is that circumstances and issues do not always resolve themselves. Sometimes there is simply insufficient time. The pressure of time and the complications introduced by competing issues and emerging realities demand action rather than inaction or delay. Persistent inaction is the excuse of the procrastinator, the home of the confused and frightened. Reflective leaders examine the array of decision demands facing them, recognizing that where it seems premature to act immediately, the better initial response may be "Not yet" rather than "Not at all."

Conventional wisdom about leadership suggests that to obtain consensus about decisions, and therefore about resource allocation decisions, is a worthy goal. There is some support in the literature for that assertion. It follows that to seek consensus is a worthwhile leadership activity. That reality demands clarity and accuracy – knowing what we mean when we speak of consensus. It is equally important that those who we hope will arrive at consensus will share our view of its meaning and implications. We may be frustrated unnecessarily in our search if we have not agreed on what consensus means and how we will know it when we see it.

It is seldom the case in most of the places of our lives that we will literally be 'of one mind'. The more we explore and debate our perspectives on issues, the more we discover both similarities and dissimilarities in our thinking. We will differ in our perspectives and opinions as we discuss an issue, and often our end position will be that we still differ. We will disagree, and often the resting point of our argument will be one that disagrees with a colleague's resting point. We will dissent, and at the end of the day, we may decide to register that dissent, perhaps in the form of a contrary vote. That ensures richness in our dialogue. The leadership challenge is to reach the point where we can move ahead toward common targets in unified fashion even when unanimity escapes us. We might ask, "For the greater good, will we agree to and support this as our chosen course of action? Can we choose it as our best corporate alternative even though some might have preferred another way?" Often there will be a substantial difference between consensus and unanimity; skilled leaders can work with both realities.

I noted previously that unanimity may simply be a situation in which no one formally registers a dissenting vote. If we have achieved consensus we may still hold our dissenting view but we will have agreed to join the group's effort to achieve a common or majority goal. True consensus will not always permit simple unanimity in which it is common practice to let a vote pass simply because we have chosen inertia over disagreement. True consensus demands a higher commitment. Consensus is less likely than unanimity to permit individual inaction because consensus is a 'we' rather than a 'they' decision. If we are committed to the principle that where we decide by a vote the majority will rule, we can even describe that as consensus. In those cases, we have agreed in advance to be bound by a group decision made that way.

Some of the conceptual clarity we need regarding consensus might be found in the origins of the term itself. Its root is contained in *sentio*, the Latin word for *I feel*, in regard to a group gathered to make decisions. It speaks of prevailing opinion, the sense or feeling of the meeting. Consensus implies that the group has reached general agreement or commonality of opinion about the overall goal or end. The logical extension is to suggest that when we reach consensus, we have given our consent. We have agreed to the proposed course of action as the appropriate choice, and we will stand in support of the direction chosen by the group.

A group's consensus does not necessarily imply unanimity of view about a substantive issue. In fact, the more complex the issue, the less likely the group's consensus also represents unanimity. However, true consensus does express agreement on the substantive issue, on the next course of action, or on both. Consensus may be about substance, about the goal or about the target. It may also be about process. Consensus can often be reached in a context of differing views that may continue to be held among group members. It is a commitment to join in common action, not necessarily to hold or adopt a common belief or viewpoint.

For each group member, including the leader, the challenge is to extend consent and endorsement beyond the verbal to include action in support of the consensual decision. For the leader in particular, the challenge is to *sense* consensus, to have a feel for it, to recognize the moment and the opportunity for a consensus-rich decision. It is equally challenging to realize that consensus is not the universal best target. We will not always reach consensus. Finally, though some would rather avoid the fact, we must decide and act anyway.

Assertion 7.1: Procrastination and indecision may wear a common mask – the unfinished search for consensus.

The Reality of Forced Choice

Whether a decision is a choice between two competing alternatives or among several plausible possibilities, whether it is a 'clean' decision or a compromise, leaders must choose. In a context of sharply limited fiscal resources, for example, the choice may be to allocate little to many, somewhat more to a few, everything to one, or nothing to some. The reality is that all roads, whether the trail of procrastination, the path of indecision, or the highway of consensus, lead to decision. Leaders must act and they must mobilize others to join the action.

The point of this brief section is that leadership demands decision and choice. In the worst circumstances, choice will be demanded of all but unemployed former leaders. The leadership demand is that we choose thoughtfully in advance of being forced to choose immediately and less carefully. Our actions and those of our organizations are more likely then to stand on a credible base. That will require determined work in a context of scarce resources, conflicting interests, and perhaps intense competition. The work of leadership will be marked by constraints and tight boundaries, by the presence and participation of both invited and uninvited actors and audiences, and by competition and conflict. It will involve unanticipated events, shifts, and changes. Even the ends may shift; that may confront participants with the need to revisit and reaffirm the organization's basic purpose and mission. But leaders must act.

Working within Tight Boundaries

To a considerable extent boundaries and constraints are matters of perspective. One writer's *influence* is another's *power* and one leader's *constraint* is another's *challenge*. A testable boundary for one may be a difficult hurdle for some and an insurmountable barrier for others.

Recognizing that there will be specific, definable boundaries that exist as real factors it will be useful to consider the *perspective dimension*, or what we might call one's *opportunity index*. At least to some extent, and perhaps more rather than less, constraints and parameters are pictures that we paint in our minds. Writing of Chicago schools in the 1980s (and perhaps his assertions might apply equally well today, in other jurisdictions, and to other organizational leaders), Seymour Sarason expressed dismay at what he observed among school principals. We might speak more generally of leaders:

> there are [leaders] who act as if *they* are primarily in control of their destiny, and there are those who act as if what they have been, are, and will be largely a function of external conditions and forces over which they have had or will have little control ... One's actions are mediated not only by how one views "locus of control," but by a set of values as well ... An important factor shaping [one's] view of his or her role and the system is, in part at least, determined by the degree to which the [leader] feels he or she rather than external factors will govern the course of action.[2]

Sarason's observations probably apply equally well to other settings and circumstances. Our actions are guided by our perceptions not only of what is possible but also of what is allowable.

When we consider the leader's view of surrounding circumstances and boundary conditions we are confronted with the matter of values and motivations. From these, most often when they are combined, negotiated, and conciliated, emerge the shape of an organizational mission that will guide action. We will treat constraints as factors to be addressed rather than as automatic stopping points. The leadership challenge is to stay focused in a way that sees, for example, an announced percentage budget reduction as a challenge to determine how the need to satisfy varying interests can be translated according to their importance to the larger goal.

Assertion 7.2: When we are faced with tight constraints, it is often more tempting to decry the limits than to explore the boundaries. The former is not leadership.

Not all boundaries present exciting opportunities. In fact, constraints are often more likely to distract leaders from vital agendas than to encourage them to press on vigorously. In a time of restraint or a shifting tide of public opinion, seizing the moment to review one's personal opportunity index is an important reflective challenge. That is essential if leaders are to mobilize others in pursuit of goals. In fact our reflection may lead us to see problematic situations from another angle, from a new perspective. To accomplish that we may need to step back from a willing acceptance of the idea that the problem is what has been presented to us in favor of a better rethinking of the circumstance. Schon argues for a reframing of our professional practice from a **problem solving** to a **problem setting** mode:

> In real-world practice, problems do not present themselves to the practitioner as givens. They must be constructed from the materials of problematic situations which are puzzling, troubling, and uncertain. In order to convert a problematic situation to a problem, a practitioner must do a certain kind of work.... must make sense of an uncertain situation that initially makes no sense... When we set the problem, we select what we will treat as the "things" of the situation, we set the boundaries of our attention to it, and we impose upon it a coherence which allows us to say what is wrong and in what directions the situation needs to be changed. The problem is a setting in which, interactively, we name the things to which we will attend and frame the context in which we will attend to them.[3]

That shift in perspective is more than semantic. When we think of a problem situation rather than a problem, our view is broader, our awareness of multiple elements and factors is deeper, and our approach is more usefully to seek a satisfying answer rather than simply to find a solution. We create a new circumstance that is likely to be different from the one initially offered. That provides opportunity to consider the fact that addressing leadership challenges will require a degree of political awareness and skill.

MANY ACTORS AND AUDIENCES

Who *owns* the organization? Some standing outside might prefer to ask, "Who *think* they own it or who *act as though* they own it?" The actor-audience debate in answer to those questions has often produced more heat than light. As with power, proprietary interest or ownership is not a subject we can discuss dispassionately if we are part of the cast or a member of an enthusiastic audience.

We sometimes observe that, in regard to our social service organizations, everyone is an expert. We all profess to have been there or at least in a similar place. We all have memory-created impressions that we have come to label as expertise. Many of us have been patients and we have visited our friends in hospital. Most of us have opinions about hospital food. Hospitals and schools are part of the common experience of most of us; each institution touches us personally because it affects the wellbeing of our children and the health of our families.

That complicates the political reality of life in both schools and hospitals because it broadens the range of differing interests demanding to be served. The question of ownership can no longer be answered with the traditional responses of yesterday. Often it seems there are new rules suggesting that questions of ownership and its accompanying rights are best settled by assertion and claim – by establishing 'turf'.

In the minds of many the turf debate has been settled unfortunately and unfairly in favor of groups other than their own. We often speak of groups on the 'outside' in terms that imply incursion and intrusion, and they may refer to us by speaking of locked doors guarding property that we do not own. We will not find a final answer to the question of ownership because it has no single answer. It will be a more fruitful quest to inquire who has legitimate interests, what those interests are, and how they can be prioritized and addressed. Sarason has proposed a political principle to suggest that in many cases the base of legitimate interest is quite broad: "When you are going to be affected, directly or indirectly, by a decision, you should stand in *some* relationship to the decision making process."[4] The leadership challenge is to define the character of that relationship in ways that will withstand scrutiny and create opportunities to strengthen our organizations.

URGENCY, IMPORTANCE, AND THE SUDDEN TURN OF EVENTS

The realities of power, influence, politics, and leadership itself are tied tightly to the fact that interests are not singular. Because that is the case, there will be competition for favor and preferential treatment and, in the most challenging circumstances, there will be outright conflict. With that as a starting point and a given, the task of leadership is to determine priorities and establish a course of action. The calls are many and loud.

> **Assertion 7.3: The illusion of importance is most easily created in the spotlight of urgency.**
>
> **Assertion 7.4: Despite appearance and assertion, not all that is urgent is important, and not all that is important is urgent.**

Assertion 7.5: Prioritizing includes learning that some things can't wait, some things can wait, some things must wait, and some things just don't matter.

There is a seemingly endless list of urgent items for the organizational leader. Many of those items are legitimate and almost all have energetic supporters. Regardless of the substantive content of the matter at hand, most things can be related in some way to the core dimension of the organization's mandate – patients and surgery, students and learning, or clients and services. The challenge is to establish both proximity and priority, and that will demand the political skills of leadership. Included in the challenge is the task of understanding that seldom will there be an undisputed list of priorities. Sooner or later, whether through establishing a list, assigning funds or personnel, or simply agreeing on a course of action, authoritative decisions must be made. For the leader, awareness of one's own and the other's values and interests, and a perception of the locus of control – who has the responsibility and the power to act? – provide direction for the task.

We live in a world in flux. Our only certainty may be uncertainty and today's uncertainty may differ from yesterday's. Our favorite current maxims express the view that change is occurring rapidly, even exponentially, and certainly faster than ever before. Determining what will happen tomorrow, unless we are fortune-tellers with a record of undisputed accuracy, is a matter of assessing probabilities. There will be surprises. Some of our surprises, particularly those of a fiscal variety, have underscored the fact that we are experiencing fundamental social and economic shifts. We feel those changes acutely, not only at the local level but also as symptoms and small examples of the larger issue:

> Crises always come packaged in economic terms first. And economically our schools, our health care systems, our government agencies, our private businesses and industries are under enormous pressure. They are all getting smaller as fast as they can... None of this is news. In fact, we are weary of hearing about it. The problem with all the emphasis on economics is that economics is not the real problem. If we keep describing the problem as one of economics and the need for more money, it will lead us to the same actions that created the problem in the first place.[5]

Urgent circumstances and seemingly uncontrollable events demand action. Leaders are often measured in terms of their response time. We can easily overlook the call for reflection, the call to reframe, the call to set the problem in terms we can understand and handle. We do not often have time to step back and consider where we will go next in leisurely fashion. On those occasions, our most potent antidote against the tyranny of the urgent is the assurance that we can turn toward both our own base of value-driven action and our organization's mission and fundamental purposes. From that base, leaders can decide and act.

A Vision for Action

This book is not about articulating an organization's mission or developing its strategic plan. It addresses questions that both precede and surround the planning function. Those are questions of how, in the organization's everyday human setting, its plans can be carried out. They examine the moral character of leadership. I have assumed in this book that fundamental goals and directions have been clarified. If they have not, the exercise of power and the realization of influence must first be focused on the tasks of goal definition and accomplishment by the organization on behalf of those it serves. That raises profound moral questions. In some cases, we may believe we have purged those dilemmas from the business of goal development. We cannot accomplish that, however, where the task of interaction is concerned. To move an organization toward goal achievement is a deeply human and a deeply political task. We will not easily escape its moral dimension.

Many of the settings in which organizational leaders work are characterized by an erosion of broad consensus. They are also marked by a new and perplexing plurality of interests and agendas. They are also marked by a broader conception of who holds a legitimate stake in the futures of the organization and the clients whose interests must be served. Those who accept the challenge of leadership will be watched closely. They will be tested and challenged both by circumstances and by people who consider themselves to be more than a merely interested bystanders. In that context, John Milton's observation "They also serve who only stand and wait"[6] is less likely to apply than "They also lead who first desire to serve."

END NOTES

1 Hodgkinson, *Educational Leadership*, 93.
2 Sarason, *The Culture of the School*, 172, 174.
3 Donald Schon, *The Reflective Practitioner*, 40.
4 Seymour Sarason, *Parental Involvement and the Political Principle* (San Francisco: Jossey-Bass, 1995), 7.
5 Peter Block, *Stewardship: Choosing Service over Self-Interest* (San Francisco: Berret-Koehler, 1993), 4.
6 John Milton, "Sonnet 19," in *The Sonnets of Milton*, ed. Mark Pattison (New York: D. Appleton and Co, 1889), www.luminarium.org/sevenlit/milton/sonnet19.htm

CHAPTER 8 — VITAL ENGAGEMENT:
PRINCIPLED LEADERSHIP AT THE INTERFACE

The role of the leader is crucial ... there are two aspects: the outer and the inner. The outer aspect calls for monitoring, investigation, searching and observation of the various subcultures within the organization ... the shifting patterns of informal organization ... intelligence gathering ... The inner aspect refers to a parallel searching, monitoring, investigation and observation of the leader's own values, internal conflicts, philosophy and ideology. The question always to be asked is "Where do I stand?", "What does this mean to me?"[1]

THE PLACE OF VALUES

We all hold values. Logically we will seek opportunities to promote our values, at least when their recognition by others seems important. As value-holders, we demand what we consider our fair share of scarce resources. In the context of politics in organizations, that demand is always for support, usually identified as favorable or 'right' decisions and optimum or 'fair' allocation of resources. Generally we expect that our value-based demands will be recognized and accepted in the organization's decision making processes and activities; we negotiate with that end in mind. Wirt and Kirst have suggested that "the essence of a political act is the struggle of a group to ensure ... authoritative support for its values."[2]

It is important to be clear that we are using the word **value** in two different ways (Figure 8.1). At the point of demand, a value held (V_H) is brought to the attention of others, or communicated (V_C) and proposed as a legitimate candidate for recognition (V_P). In other words, the value held is promoted as being worthy of tangible support. Decisions about whether to allocate a share of a resource, or all of it for that matter, follow and are identifiable evidence of a prior or accompanying decision or set of

```
V_H  ———————▶  V_C/V_P  ———————▶  V_V

Value           Value              Value
held            communicated/      valued
                promoted           (supported)
```

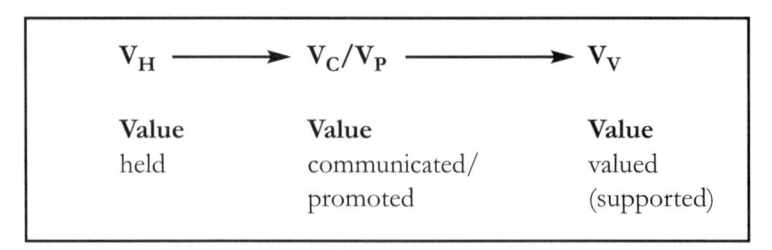

Figure 8.1 Values and the political process

decisions to grant support to a value-based demand. As outlined in Figure 8.1, a decision is made to ascribe value (V_V) to a particular value held (V_H). In our decisions and subsequent actions, we demonstrate that we value (V_V) certain values (V_P) and, as a result, that we probably do not value other values (V_H) to the same extent. In the example cited earlier in the book, a school board's decision to offer a requested second language program will be evidence of authoritative support for the value attached to it by its proponents.

Previously we examined the concept of allocation of value through the distribution of scarce resources. Our first thought in response to the word is usually to think of tangible resources – 'the stuff' that includes facilities, equipment, and supplies. We have redefined *personnel* more broadly as *human resources*, and we sometimes say that "our people are our best resource." We understand that time is a resource and we often speak of time spent usefully as "an investment of time." Few of us avoid the pressure of insufficient time; we recognize it is a scarce resource. We understand that time is both fixed in quantity and subject to priority decisions, that is, to valuing. In the political context, decisions made and actions taken to allocate resources are acknowledgments of the relative value we have attached to a demand. In that sense, we might define resources broadly as whatever is subject to demand that exceeds available supply. Often in addition to the challenge of finite supply we will acknowledge that a value faces competition with other demands for a share of the resource.

Assertion 8.1: Values rise to the surface as competition for scarce resources.

With varying degrees of enthusiasm, most of us have come to understand that politics is a fact of organizational life. Despite that realization, not all leaders have taken further steps to understand and approach politics in ways that will retrieve it from the dark side of organizational life. Because of what we read and sometimes see in practice, some have come to regard politics of all varieties as an art of deception, manipulation, and raw power that leaves victims in its wake and in the trails of its smug practitioners. We believe also that the realities of human conduct and organizational practice ensure that this brand of politics will have a very long life. We are probably correct for the most part in that assessment. We hold little admiration for many we see as politically skilled. We reluctantly acknowledge their ability to accomplish what they set out to do despite knowing that their accomplishments may carry a heavy human cost.

Sooner or later, wherever at least two people have gathered to accomplish a purpose, leadership will emerge. In fact, the best leadership will often emerge in the activity of defining purposes we intend to accomplish. Equally, where leadership emerges, there will be politics. For most of us, the concept of leadership is not at issue. Though we will insist on the right to accept, reject, or moderate the leadership that affects our lives, within the bounds of our own definitions we are prepared to accept leadership as an idea and potentially as a reality. That allows for the possibility that the leadership we experience or offer can be good leadership in whatever terms we define *good*. By definition it can also be bad leadership in whatever terms we define *bad*. A similar case can be made for politics, provided we are prepared to revisit our traditional and perhaps flawed definitions and understandings. The argument in this book is that politics will be defined by its practice. That includes the possibility that our politics can enhance our leadership.

> **Assertion 8.2: The presence of at least two people and the active participation of at least one of them, promises there will be leadership activity. Where there is leadership there will be politics.**
>
> **Assertion 8.3: The companionship of leadership and politics is not 'a bad thing' by definition.**

Leadership in organizations, whether carried out collaboratively or in solitary fashion, is about ensuring the movement of people toward ends. Where leadership activity occurs, there will be interaction, difference, and complementarity. In the usual case, there will be competition and conflict. We will therefore find politics. The requirements of leadership ensure that there will be **power** demonstrated as **influence** (two other terms we often have difficulty reconciling). As for leadership itself, the character of its accompanying politics will be determined by motivations, by ends, and certainly by practice.

There is a valid case to be made for asserting that politics in organizations can be more noble than ignoble. The extent to which that is true in a given situation will be determined in large part by the credibility of leaders and their leadership. We will seek those whose leadership is firmly grounded in values and commitments that we can observe and support.

GROUNDED LEADERSHIP: FOUNDATION FOR CREDIBILITY

Few aspects of life and leadership are easy. Life in organizations is complicated by politics and in that milieu we are sometimes vulnerable to thoughtlessness. This is not the lack of care or concern for others around us that we find unacceptable in leaders, but it is equally damaging. By *thoughtlessness* I mean a lack of reflection and reflection-based action – **praxis** – that marks each of us on occasion and some of us more frequently. Thoughtlessness as a pattern is not a legitimate option for leaders, though we understand its reality and expect its periodic recurrence. The thoughtfulness of reflection and careful analysis followed by action offers a plausible leadership alternative. We must be clear about what that implies and how we will achieve thoughtfulness.

In the excerpt that begins this chapter, Hodgkinson refers to two dimensions of leadership, the **outer aspect** and the **inner aspect**. We are concerned with the interface of the internal and external worlds of leaders. We seek a level of thoughtfulness that ensures competent understanding of the political character of organizational life and competent leadership practice.

> **Assertion 8.4: The demonstration of leadership in political behavior is influenced by the nature and degree of leaders' prior and continuing thoughtfulness.**
>
> **Assertion 8.5: Multiple events and actors, timelines, and surprising developments, aided sometimes by assured technical competence, are the natural and persistent opponents of thoughtfulness.**

The word **pragmatic** is often used to describe political behavior of the kind we disparage. If we are honest with ourselves, though, sometimes our criticism arises because the interests served by that pragmatism are not our own or those we advocate on behalf of others. We generally assign to pragmatism a moral character that goes beyond the merely and neutrally practical. Pragmatism can be destructive of **praxis**, which demands, as Hodgkinson describes it, that the end or union between ethics and action be considered a priori in advance of action. In the realm of morals it is not enough to proceed backwards into the future, forever seeking to remedy the ill effects of our actions after the event. That is mere pragmatics. Ethics requires commitment in advance.[3]

If that is the case, Hodgkinson's prior statement that "Values, morals, and ethics are the very stuff of leadership and administrative life" offers a useful descriptor of grounded leadership, albeit at this point without the specifics he offers elsewhere.[4]

There are many invitations to pragmatism of the variety that has colored our view of political activity in organizations. The ends-means conflict that goes to the heart of our view of others frequently is resolved pragmatically. We know through experience that many of our decisions must be made when we do not have all of the relevant information at hand. We do the best we can in the circumstances given the pressures of time and circumstance. We offer plausible justification for proceeding to some of our decisions without all parties at the table because often there is good reason to proceed rather than to wait. In a spirit of compromise, we have overlooked some agendas carrying greater moral weight to accomplish those we prefer. We know that sometimes we have stepped back from a higher order of leadership action. In short, day-to-day practice requires a degree of pragmatism. The character of our pragmatics will be shaped by the grounding of our practice.

Grounded leadership does nothing to simplify the issues faced by leaders. Rather it recognizes and accepts complexity, uncertainty, and challenge as realities. Paved or unpaved, two roads of sharp grade are both steep, but the climb might offer the hiker a choice of routes and vistas. The leadership challenge even when we must take the less desirable route is to be equipped for both climbs and for both descents. Grounded leadership is not about making easy choices. It is about understanding the implications of each choice and its significance for ourselves and others. It is about proceeding from a thoughtful base, a base that ensures reflection before it guides action.

For many years the study of leadership has provided us with an array of examples and possible perspectives. We have passed through the study of traits, debated the role of education and training, explored leader behavior, learned that situations affect the practice of leadership, and described types of leaders. In the process, we have learned much of value, confirmed some things that we already suspected, and discarded some that has proven irrelevant or unworkable. Many of us have suspected that the concept of leadership is actually too complex and elusive to be captured and displayed as a single exhibit.

The purpose of this book is not to debate the current status of the quest for leadership knowledge and understanding or the state of theory development. It is not to review and categorize the results of what we might consider the best of research in an effort to discover or to restate what leaders 'should do'. It is simply to offer a perspective on the character of the essentially political and potentially honorable work that leaders do, to propose an analytical and value-focused view of that work, and to suggest what that might mean for the journey. To extend the previous analogy, we might suggest that the first signpost on the road marked "Leadership" will alert us to the possibility of "Rough Pavement Ahead."

LEADERSHIP AS SERVICE, LEADERS AS SERVANTS

On July 6th, 1996, the Victoria Times-Colonist reported that the Alaska cruise ship *Golden Princess* had suffered a fire that disabled it just off the west coast and 100 kilometers from its next port of call. The vessel was in the process of making a hard starboard turn when the fire broke out; the rudder had jammed in the maximum turning position. No one was injured, the fire was extinguished quickly, and the *Golden Princess* was towed to port in Victoria, BC. The last 100 kilometers of the trip were lengthened by hours because of the locked rudder. Progress was agonizingly slow as the vessel was towed to port against the enormous resistance of the locked rudder. The ship arrived some fourteen hours late and unable to leave port as planned. The city was suddenly called to play host to several hundred vacationers and crew members who had anticipated spending their time differently. The vacationers' brief excitement and fear were replaced for some by the novelty of adventure, for others by frustration and disappointment because the cruise had been cut short.

The marine analogy of a rudder is used frequently to describe aspects of life in organizations, institutions, societies, even countries. We typically use it in specific instances of concern, sometimes using phrases such as rudderless, off course, or without a rudder. Our concern in this book is with leaders and leadership in the political context of organizations. The analogy though flawed, as are all analogies, can be useful. Particularly, where political activity is strong and turbulent, leadership demands a rudder and that rudder must be functional. The term **grounded** is a useful companion to the idea of a rudder. Both terms convey the notion of providing a direction for leadership; both by definition suggest that leadership will be characterized by focus and constancy.

Conceptions of leadership are plentiful; each is received warmly by the particular audience for whom its ideas resonate. The vocabulary of leadership is marked by terms such as transformational, charismatic, and laissez-faire, some of which have been clearly articulated while others remain ill-defined. Each is used to capture a particular perspective. In some respects, the challenge of describing a particular view of leadership is like asking people to define the term *democracy*. While use of the word is common to people of widely differing political persuasions, congruence of interpretation and shared understanding are elusive. We all *know* what democracy means until we discuss it with others who see it differently. From that point on, the success of our joint efforts will depend on dialogue marked by a reasonable degree of shared understanding of terms we use. This discussion focuses on ensuring our ability to apply that test to a particular conception, **servant leadership**, as one rudder-like source of leadership grounding.

We are more familiar with the idea of **service** than that of **servant**. Because of that and because we usually consider the latter a demeaning term we tend not to use the word *servant*. For one thing, few of us have or plan to have servants in a society that strives for equity, and we recognize the unacceptability of the idea usually connoted by the word *servant*. On the other hand, we think and talk quite comfortably about service. The air force pilot speaks of being *in the service*. We undertake in-*service* training, and meals on those days are prepared and presented by people who work in *service* occupations. Some of us belong to *service* clubs, many of which clearly perform leadership functions within our communities. Many of our organizations would find it extremely difficult to fulfill their social mandates without the support of a high level of *service* from volunteers.

Those understandings of service are easy enough. We are willing to describe both work and workers in some respects as service and to accept the respect often granted to those who serve. We cannot function effectively without their support. But there is an essential difference between doing service *for* and being servant *to* the organization's mission and its people. The difference does not always sit with us comfortably. Moving from the external performance criterion of **doing** to the internal motivating criterion of **being** brings us closer to the notion of servant as 'devoted helper', to which we might add, of another or of a community. That concept is unfamiliar, even foreign to our thinking, and the leadership implications are staggering. Interestingly, some of the leaders for whom we reserve the highest regard, fit and are described in terms of that definition – they are devoted helpers of others and of a community. In this case, the community is our organization.

Assertion 8.6: We understand the concept of service more easily, and we can accept it more readily, than the idea of servant.

The concept of service is more about both individual *and* community rather than being either individual *or* community. When we use the word *or,* the definition of *service* blocks the necessary conceptual bridge from individual to community and from outer to inner. It is the inclusive *and* rather than the exclusive *or* that describes servant. We can only move to a full understanding of the idea when we see a servant *being* and therefore *doing*. For the servant, priority is assigned to the job of building people as an integral component of goal achievement and mission accomplishment. For the servant, it is not a matter of choosing between the welfare of the individual and the goals of the organization; it is about achieving the one as we accomplish the other.

The leadership literature has addressed the ever-present individual/organization dichotomy. We have described it as idiographic/nomothetic and we have written about the dual significance of initiating structure and consideration. Most of us know that we respond to one of those leadership demands with greater insight, skill, and energy than to the other. We know also that leadership in a human context is more complex than that. It cannot be easily divided and wrapped in two neat packages of people and things. We understand its complexity. And we debate and struggle with choices and decisions that must be made with the greater good in mind. For leaders, the challenge is a double one – to identify that greater good in complex and difficult circumstances and to choose, usually between multiple and competing 'goods'. Why complicate the matter further by introducing the concept of servant leader?

It is important to understand what we can about the origins and implications of the ideas we choose to consider and debate before we accept and endorse those ideas. The idea of servant leadership is no exception. Whether we choose to embrace the notion or to turn away from the idea in favor of other possibilities, it will be helpful at least to understand the concept and know the reasons for our choice.

The concept of servant leadership was developed and articulated over many years of reflective practice by Robert Greenleaf, who described his background of training and experience, some major influences that shaped his thinking, and a provocative, even revolutionary concept, in his early book *Servant Leadership*.[5] That work has been extended and expanded in Greenleaf's later works and in the many ideas, materials, and programs developed through the Indiana, USA Center that carries his name.[6] The concept of servant leadership is a vigorous and challenging idea, one that invites reflection of a sort that will lead us either toward it or away from it. I will summarize the process with some of Greenleaf's own grounding statements about the servant leader perspective:

- The great leader is seen as servant first, and that simple fact is seen as the key.
- Leadership ... something given, or assumed, that could be taken away ... servant nature ... not bestowed, not assumed, and not to be taken away.
- But if one is servant, either leader or follower, one is always searching, listening, expecting that a better wheel for these times is in the making.
- A new moral principle is emerging which holds that the only authority deserving one's allegiance is that which is freely and knowingly granted by the led to the leader in response to, and in proportion to, the clearly evident servant stature of the leader. Those who choose to follow this principle will not casually accept the authority of existing institutions. Rather, they will freely respond only to individuals who are chosen as leaders because they are proven and trusted as servants. To the extent that this principle prevails in the future, the only viable institutions will be those that are predominantly servant-led.
- It begins with the natural feeling that one wants to serve, to serve first. Then conscious choice brings one to aspire to lead.
- The difference manifests itself in the care taken by the servant-first to make sure that other people's highest priority needs are being served.
- The natural servant, the one who is *servant first*, is more likely to persevere and refine a particular hypothesis on what serves another's highest priority needs than is the person who is *leader first* and who later serves out of promptings of conscience or in conformity with normative expectations.[7]

On the surface, the idea of servant leadership might look like a walk back down the road of history to the era of human relations. That time was a puzzling interlude between the idea of people as extensions of the machine and the notion that people are themselves resources. Both of those perspectives saw people as means to an end. In fact, a strong case can be made to suggest that whether scientific management, human relations, human resources, or another of the myriad variations that we have seen and that continue to emerge, people typically are seen as means to one organizational end or another. To focus our discussion simply on the nobility or merit of the material end is to adjourn the debate prematurely. A fundamental ends-means perspective on leadership is proposed, a choice that does not make the idea of servant leadership simply a 'soft' alternative that de-emphasizes the 'hard' stuff of organizational goal achievement.

> **Assertion 8.7: For servant leaders, the choice that recognizes the person as the ultimate end of effort also ensures that high priority and unrelenting effort will be directed toward accomplishing the organization's goals.**

Several of the excerpts I list have been cited by others who have commented on or extended Greenleaf's ideas. I have quoted from his original work to capture his presentation of the core ideas of servant-leadership, ideas that invite us to make a choice. They are markers for the development of one's basic view of leadership. Once we have identified a leadership perspective that we are confident is both defensible and our preferred guide for action we might describe ourselves as having 'a place to stand,' an ethos that will characterize our practice. Servant leadership as articulated by Greenleaf and developed further by others offers that grounding opportunity. It also demands a substantive answer to an important "why?" question that can be understood and addressed as a foundational raison d'etre – **stewardship**.

LEADERSHIP AS STEWARDSHIP

Whether our leadership is paid or voluntary, whether we work in a for-profit corporation or a service organization, we act in trust of interests beyond our own. To assert that we are not at all self-interested in that context is either duplicitous or naïve. To assert credibly that we subordinate our own interests to the service of others demands we substantiate our claim. For servant leaders the 'step beyond' is to establish that as we understand it and live it, leadership is stewardship.

The Oxford Dictionary defines a steward as a "person entrusted with management of another's property."[8] We might differentiate *steward* from *executor* in the common usage, because the work of the latter begins post mortem. Stewardship, on the other hand, implies a living set of interests, whether organizational or individual. Stewardship is akin to the concept of trusteeship. Stewards and trustees hold in care the interests of another; they act on behalf of the other to accomplish the other's interests. Stewardship "asks us to be deeply accountable for the outcomes of an institution."[9] Sergiovanni, in the concluding section of *Moral Leadership*, suggests that

> stewardship represents primarily an act of trust, whereby people and institutions entrust a leader with certain obligations and duties to fulfill and perform on their behalf.... stewardship involves placing oneself in service to ideas and ideals and to others who are committed to their fulfillment.[10]

It might be argued that concepts such as stewardship and servant-leadership are 'mushy', that they lack the rigor we require for successful pursuit of business interests or competent oversight of people in organizations. Even among proponents of a different and presumably better approach the terminology is sometimes 'fuzzy'. Block, for example, has suggested that "the alternative to leadership is stewardship."[11]

I suggest that if we have a clear foundational understanding of leadership as the movement of people toward ends the discussion will be sharpened considerably. Having addressed the basic "what?" question, we are free to consider "how?" Our missteps, when they demonstrate that we have lost sight of or have not pursued the "what," will be fundamental missteps of leadership. Effective leadership demands success along both axes. Both effective servant leadership and competent stewardship demonstrate compellingly that we understand both task and technique, that we are skilled and determined about both substance and process.

Pressures and the Grounded Leader

What does this discussion of the ideas of Robert Greenleaf and the notion of stewardship have to do with our work as twenty-first-century organizational leaders? What does it have to do with the political character of leadership? We might open a discussion about those questions with brief restatements of some basic points we have considered:

- Organizations are constructed to achieve ends.
- People are the primary achievers of organizational ends.
- Leadership is about mobilization to achieve ends.
- Power and influence are integral to mobilization and achievement.

- The continuing presence of power and influence can be observed as politics.
- Leadership includes politics.
- The character of our political activity will be determined by our resolution of the ends-means dilemma as it relates to the people with whom we work.

That list carries none of the qualifiers and includes none of the background discussion contained in these chapters. However, it leads logically to a basic question: How will we work with people? Our response will determine and be determined by the fundamental perspectives and attitudes we bring to the practice of leadership. Our responses will be shaped and developed to the extent that we engage with the task as thoughtful, reflective leaders.

The question raised by some who decline the call to leadership, by those who turn away in favor of another direction, is often, "Who needs it?" The question is often self-answered with details of *it*, which we sometimes describe as hassles or grief. The point is that if we accept and move to implement the third statement above, acknowledging that leadership is about mobilization to achieve ends, we will begin to realize that one essential element of the question and its answers is the fact of pressure, even for grounded leaders.

There is a further consideration. The presence of pressure introduces the appealing idea of making decisions quickly, even if it only enables us to move on and deal with the next set of pressures. Fast action, though, often includes traps for the unwary. The decision demands with which leaders are confronted present provocative and often troubling questions. The challenge for the grounded leader is to respond with integrity, with a wholeness that includes and moves well beyond simple honesty.

Stephen Carter suggests that "one cannot have integrity without being honest (although ... the matter gets complicated), but one can certainly be honest and yet have little integrity."[12] He proposes three components of integrity: "discerning what is right and wrong; acting on what you have discerned, even at personal cost; and saying openly that you are acting on your understanding of right and wrong."[13] The flesh on the bones of those three components – discernment, direction, and declaration – will differ between leaders and among different pressure-filled situations. The right in one situation may not be the right in another, especially because our choices have impact. In the sense in which I have used the term in this book, Carter presents an argument for thoughtfulness, for praxis.

It would be difficult to find a leader unfamiliar with the reality of pressure in life with others in an organization. Grounding will not eliminate pressure. The leader who works from a thoughtful perspective still leads, and inevitably that brings pressure. Clarity of vision will not remove pressure from the leader's work. In fact awareness of the present gap between our vision and our reality may increase the pressure. The exemplary leaders studied by Warren Bennis knew pressure but had achieved "fortunate mastery over present confusion – in contrast to those who simply react, throw up their hands, and live in a perpetual state of 'present shock'."[14] The grounded nature of their leadership was reflected in Bennis' comment that "we trust people who are predictable, whose positions are known and who keep at it; leaders who are trusted make themselves known, make their positions clear."[15] They were grounded leaders, able to process, interpret, and be proactive in addressing pressures as a result of their personal clarity about the basis and direction of their leadership, clarity about their 'place to stand'.

Grounded Leadership as a Guide for Action

The primary purpose of this concluding chapter of Part I is to encourage you toward personal reflection about leadership – toward praxis. Unless we are engaging solely in a casual, detached look at the phenomenon, studying leadership will lead us directly and inexorably to the personal, to an encounter with some of our most fundamental beliefs and attitudes about ourselves and about others. It will lead to reflection and thoughtfulness. My premise is that thought-guided, reflective leadership action will be more effective and more sustained than will its alternatives. It will be strengthened rather than weakened by the passage of time and events. We might be guided in our quest to lead in this way by a series of questions to stimulate reflection:

- Do I want to lead others?
- If my answer is "Yes," what will be my credible response to the person who, on hearing my answer, asks "Why?"
- What is it about my leadership that might cause another person to respond, "Yes, and I will be there too, to follow or to lead with you."?
- How will people's lives be affected by my leadership?
- How will this organization be changed and helped to succeed by my leadership?

In a context where pressure is the norm, the leader faces at least four tyrannies that simply will not leave. The first is the tyranny of the urgent and its frequent triumph over the important. The second is the tyranny of incomplete information in competition with the demand for prompt decision. Third, leaders face the tyranny of the plausibly expedient and more convenient over the knowledge that consideration is needed. Finally, we face the tyranny of resource scarcity over the desire to satisfy. For some those circumstances will be enough to cause them to turn away from leadership, especially when they realize that leadership involves political activity. Whether we will turn toward the challenge of leadership or away from it, doing that thoughtfully and deciding from a grounded perspective and position will lend quality to our decision and a quiet assurance that we are in the right place.

Conclusion

Individuals called upon to lead are also expected to be broadly competent, able to complete the task and able to do that with the support and enthusiastic participation of others in the organization. They are called to be conceptually competent people who know what they see when they see it and who know what they do when they do it. They will be competent in choosing a path that values and seeks to build others, people who are able to 'stay the course' until the job is done, and people who are clearly competent in character.

The challenge at hand is serious and important – to build community confidence in the organizations we have built to serve our needs. We must ensure that those communities will see in their institutions a competent response to today's challenges that is developed with the future in mind. Further, on the basis of what they see in organizations led with competence, our communities will understand that there is more to follow, more of that same level of quality.

The circumstances of challenge are persistent, even unremitting. They become more pressing as we seek options and answers. The German poet Rainer Rilke poses for us a compelling option for leaders:

> Most people have . . . turned their solutions toward what is easy and toward the easiest side of what is easy; but it is clear that we must trust in what is difficult; everything alive trusts in it. . . . We know little, but that we must trust in what is difficult is a certainty that will never abandon us.[16]

End Notes

1. Hodgkinson, *Educational Leadership*, 82.
2. Wirt & Kirst, *Schools in Conflict*, 1-2.
3. Hodgkinson, *Educational Leadership*, 50.
4. Ibid., 1.
5. Robert Greenleaf, *Servant Leadership* (New York: Paulist, 1977).
6. http://www.greenleaf.org/
7. Ibid., 8-14.
8. Concise Oxford Dictionary (London: Oxford University Press, 1976), 1128.
9. Block, *Stewardship*, 18.
10. Thomas Sergiovanni, *Moral Leadership: Getting to the Heart of School Improvement* (San Francisco: Jossey-Bass, 1992), 139.
11. Block, *Stewardship*, 18.
12. Stephen Carter, "The Insufficiency of Honesty," *The Atlantic Monthly*, February 1996, 74.
13. Ibid.
14. Warren Bennis & Bert Nanus, *Leaders: The Strategies for Taking Charge* (New York: Harper & Row, 1985), 21.
15. Ibid.
16. Rainer Rilke, "Letter 7 (Rome, May 14, 1904), *Letters to a Young Poet*, http://www.sfgoth.com/~immanis/rilke/letter7.html

Assertions

Throughout the book I have inserted contextually relevant assertions to draw attention to nearby points of discussion. The intent of these statements is to encourage focused thought regarding the items presented, to support the reader's written reflections, and to stimulate discussion among colleagues at strategic points. I have also recorded the assertions here as a simple list to encourage a further round of reflection and discussion outside their immediate textual surround.

The assertions provide learning opportunities. Each can be challenged, extended, or developed further as part of a discussion among colleagues engaged together in learning activities. The text itself will be strengthened when learners incorporate their own sets of assertions developed as a result of reading and thinking. I encourage you to do that.

Chapter 1 — Fire on the mountain:
The reality of politics in organizational life

1.1 Leadership and politics are inextricably bound, and that is reasonable.

1.2 Politically skilled, humane leadership is not an oxymoron.

1.3 The fact of scarce resources is an ever-present organizational reality. Wisdom in searching out reasonable ways of sharing resources is a leadership imperative. Effectiveness in implementing resource allocation decisions is a political skill.

1.4 Economic theory and political theory are working partners in the leadership enterprise, whether or not our leadership actions are overtly financial in character.

Chapter 2 — Mapping the ground:
Making sense of organizational life

2.1 Understanding of constraints facing the parties remains incomplete unless those parties hold a common data base. Even then, holding common data does not necessarily ensure common interpretation and understanding, let alone agreement.

2.2 Analysis of a constraint will remain incomplete until we have gained some understanding of why it is seen as a limiting factor.

2.3 Values are most likely to be revealed by evidential indicators, not by being announced or claimed.

2.4 We can spot preferences, and we can often elicit interests, but values are a more complex and elusive target.

2.5 Uncovering interests is important to understanding preferences, but the process may be difficult and our conclusions sometimes uncertain.

2.6 Preferences are more likely to be flexible and open to alternative possibilities than are interests.

2.7 Knowing what is to be decided is prerequisite to further action.

2.8 Even to agree about what must be decided is likely sometimes to be difficult.

2.9 When we believe that agreement exists, it is probably worthwhile to check carefully that our perception is shared.

2.10 The decision reached may address the initial decision statement, or it may not – circumstances and preferences change.

2.11 Organizational decisions provide some indication of values, but the moral heart of leadership is most clearly visible in the influencing patterns and processes that lead to those decisions being implemented.

2.12 In most resource allocation decisions, chances are good that someone will perceive inequity.

2.13 To avoid viewing shaping and decisions as wins and losses is a perpetual leadership challenge.

2.14 The values revealed by a decision will be perceived differently. There may be as many views on what the decision means as there are people offering comment.

2.15 Time pressures and the tyranny of the urgent can threaten one's ability to see outcome implications.

2.16 A selective tendency of decision makers to ignore outcome implications, even obvious ones, is to be expected as a possibility, perhaps even a frequent occurrence.

2.17 There is not necessarily any correspondence between the perceived importance of a realized implication and its actual effects.

Chapter 3 — Who will lead? Context and capability

3.1 Organizations require leadership to accomplish purpose. Considering how to ensure that outcome creates a context for deciding structure and appointing personnel.

Chapter 4 — Purpose in mind: Power as a condition of leadership

4.1 A leader without power has no influence. To deny having power is to misrepresent leadership.

4.2 A leader without influence has no power. To avoid influencing is to decline leadership.

4.3 To discuss power without influence is to debate a non sequitur.

4.4 When things are politically complex, predicting the outcomes of events is a bit like predicting the path water will follow between stones on a beach.

4.5 The authority to act is only a casual acquaintance of the ability to lead.

4.6 The matter of whose ends are to be served through leadership has a mandatory single answer – the organization's ends – and a range of supplementary answers. For the leader, the unitary answer is unavoidable; the supplementary answers cluster around it and beg to replace it.

4.7 The single answer contains a dual focus – collective and individual purpose. Both are legitimate ends.

4.8 Seeking to clarify foggy organizational ends and find evidence of their achievement is a fundamental leadership challenge, but the opportunity to take refuge in the fog is often more inviting.

4.9 Politics practiced in the fog displays only an apparition of leadership.

4.10 The quality of leadership will be measured by its apparent openness and transparency. For those who are the focus of leadership practice, the difficult word is *apparent*. We are selective in our willingness to be manipulated.

Chapter 5 — Actors and agendas: The human face of organizations

5.1 Interests and preferences are the raw material of agendas. Both actors and audiences have agendas.

5.2 The line between actors and onlookers is more likely to be a negotiated temporary accommodation than a fixed permanent boundary.

5.3 Having a part to play and a place on the stage is more likely than before to be seen by all parties as an interest-based right.

5.4 Values and beliefs, though they may not be discussed, play a significant role in determining one's ability and desire or determination to move between onlooker and actor status.

5.5 Only typologies contain 'pure' agenda types. In practice, agendas usually are multiple, mixed, and simultaneous in occurrence.

5.6 Soon after we have developed a useful classification scheme we will probably discover that it is less inclusive and tidy than we would have preferred.

5.7 Identifying interests, preferences, and agendas is the preliminary task; leadership has to do with what happens after that.

5.8 It is useful to assume a continuum from values through interests and preferences to agendas, and to gain understanding of as much of that continuum as is relevant to the particular situation.

5.9 In a context where not all agendas can be achieved, we will gain the best early yield by seeking to identify interests.

5.10 Identifying interests as a basis for agendas can offer protection against personalizing issues and focusing on positions, either of which can restrict one's capacity for leadership action.

5.11 Where there are interests, there will be demands for action in regard to agendas.

5.12 Zealotry without apparent power is like a lion without apparent teeth – things change when the lion opens its mouth.

Chapter 6 — Interface turbulence: Conflict as leadership opportunity

6.1 The reality of politics is one first principle of organizational life, measured by its ubiquity. The reality of conflict is another.

6.2 Unanimity may demonstrate only that when the vote was taken, no one formally registered a contrary opinion.

6.3 Healthy debate will be marked by difference, divergence, disagreement, and dissent – the end is development.

6.4 Unhealthy debate will be marked by dispute, discord, disharmony, and disunity – the end is dysfunction.

6.5 Positions are evidence of interests. Interests may be displayed, discoverable, hidden, or secret, but they exist.

6.6 Focusing on interests allows for the possibility of principled dialogue about the merits of positions.

Chapter 7 — Evidence of leadership: Choices, decisions, outcomes

7.1 Procrastination and indecision may wear a common mask – the unfinished search for consensus.

7.2 When we are faced with tight constraints, it is often more tempting to decry the limits than to explore the boundaries. The former is not leadership.

7.3 The illusion of importance is most easily created in the spotlight of urgency.

7.4 Despite appearance and assertion, not all that is urgent is important, and not all that is important is urgent.

7.5 Prioritizing includes learning that some things can't wait, some things can wait, some things must wait, and some things just don't matter.

Chapter 8 — Vital engagement: Principled leadership at the interface

8.1 Values rise to the surface as competition for scarce resources.

8.2 The presence of at least two people and the active participation of at least one of them, promises there will be leadership activity. Where there is leadership there will be politics.

8.3 The companionship of leadership and politics is not 'a bad thing' by definition.

8.4 The demonstration of leadership in political behavior is influenced by the nature and degree of leaders' prior and continuing thoughtfulness.

8.5 Multiple events and actors, timelines, and surprising developments, aided sometimes by assured technical competence, are the natural and persistent opponents of thoughtfulness.

8.6 We understand the concept of service more easily, and we can accept it more readily, than the idea of servant.

8.7 For servant leaders, the choice that recognizes the person as the ultimate end of effort also ensures that high priority and unrelenting effort will be directed toward accomplishing the organization's goals.

PART II

LEADING AT THE INTERFACE

Using Scenarios for Learning

The critical incidents and case studies in this book are grounded in experience. However, they do not depict actual incidents or people. All names and places are fictional; any apparent resemblance to specific real individuals is unintended and coincidental. Group discussions about these and other stories will probably trigger accounts of similar circumstances from your own repertoire of experience. That can serve to validate the text, suggesting that the case examples and critical incidents written for this book do have connections to the real world of organizations and their leaders. I encourage you to use these scenarios, both critical incidents and case studies, as opportunities to explore your own real-life dilemmas through personal reflection and in discussion with your colleagues, and to add your own case studies and critical incidents. That exercise combined with group study of the book can offer a relevant professional development experience.

The Cast of Characters

I have introduced a variety of characters in the critical incidents and case studies. In some cases I have tried to employ humor in the selection and development of characters' names, often as a way of underlining some of their key characteristics. Where possible, I have chosen names that are not gender-specific. I have tried to develop each person as a complex, real character rather than simply a stereotypical place-filler. I did not seek a one-on-one experiential match between the book's themes and as many readers as possible. Rather, I tried to identify a cross-section of roles and characters we might reasonably expect to find among the populations of our organizations.

I have tried to write in gender-neutral language whenever possible. You will also note that most of the names I have chosen for the critical incidents and case studies tend to be typical of circumstances we often think of as Canadian, British, or American. That is deliberate rather than forgetful. In many cases the scenarios in this book create characters who, for the immediate purposes of that situation, are somewhat larger than life. I did not coin names as caricatures or in a manner that would suggest inappropriate or stereotypical reference to ethnic origin. We live in a multicultural country and in a world that is richer because of its diversity; my concern was to avoid diminishing that in any wa, hence my use of what for the most part might be termed 'mainstream' English and French names. Where the scenario includes an 'unforgettable' character I have sometimes chosen names invented specifically to depict that situation, for instance, the wealthy Morris Better.

The characters you will encounter, and you will meet most of them only once, provide reference points for both the case studies and the critical incidents. Often I have contrived to ensure that an individual's name will match that particular role or persona. My purpose in doing this was to facilitate discussion, attain some common understanding of the individual in focus, albeit at a surface level, and situate these characters in your memory.

Chapter 9 — The Demand of Critical Incidents

The term critical incident carries different connotations in various organizational settings. It will be helpful to identify the parameters of its use in the scenarios I developed for this book. To establish a scenario as a critical incident, one or more of the following four factors must be present in the mind of at least one of the parties involved: **urgency**, **importance**, **prominence**, and/or **complexity**. First, the incident is **urgent** because someone believes that it demands immediate attention – it cannot wait. Second, it is **important**; consequences are likely if it is not addressed. Third, it is **prominent**, or awkward; it cannot easily be ignored. Fourth, it is **complex**, even though it may appear quite simple. There may not be an easy answer; in all probability, sometimes there may be no satisfying answer at all. There can be great value, though, in considering the possibilities and examining the alternatives with colleagues whose experience may draw them to different conclusions and actions than those we might choose.

The challenge as you read the critical incidents is to assess the extent to which their brevity signifies simplicity and clear solution alternatives. In most cases, it will signify neither. The benefits of supporting individual reading and analysis with group study and discussion of the critical incident become clear. This is something of a luxury situation not always available to us in the pressure of the moment's circumstances. I have tried to develop and present scenarios that will carry relevance for a wide range of readers, stimulate discussion among colleagues, and extend and deepen the discussion by triggering awareness of similar circumstances.

You may wish to consider a two-pronged approach to utilizing the critical incidents as part of your professional learning program. Some readers will find it helpful to identify a particular critical incident with a point or principle presented somewhere in the book and to determine its relevance for and application to a scenario such as the one described. As part of that effort, it will also be helpful to analyze the critical incident to determine the extent to which it meets the four criteria presented above.

Finally, you and your colleagues may find it relevant to write some of your own critical incidents using real-life situations from your workplace or service organization setting. That process offers the additional benefit of being able to bring the collected wisdom and expertise of your colleagues to bear on situations that have real-world relevance for you.

Index to the Critical Incidents

All for One, One for All — 175
The mayor has a moral conflict regarding an upcoming Council decision.

Behind Closed Doors — 175
A donor's discovery of purchasing plans threatens to make life difficult for the CEO and the Board chair.

Best of Intentions — 176
A hospital CEO becomes involved in influencing a candidate for hospital board membership.

Black, White, or a Shade of Grey? — 176
An ethical dilemma over whether to acknowledge one's availability for a meeting.

Bus Stop? — 177
A principal decides whether to wait for a student who is late for the trip.

Challenging the System — 177
Parents want their daughter's support worker to move into the school system with her.

Chess or Chaucer? — 178
A chess club and a reading support project compete for a grant.

Coffee Time — 178
A staff member moves quickly to preserve an old pattern of relationship with the new president.

Don't Mess Around — 179
Staff members have no office access while the secretary is at lunch.

Health is the Issue — 179
A school principal is pressured to adopt an interest group's set of curriculum materials.

High Stakes — 180
A secretary wonders whether to point out an error to an unappreciative treasurer.

In the Oven — 180
A not-for-profit agency's president asks his assistant to sell an item to the staff group.

In the Oven – Goose Cooked — 181
Questions are asked when an internally purchased microwave breaks down.

Just Trying to Help 181
A board member wants to discuss the school superintendent's professional development.

Let's Get on with It 182
Pressure on the planning committee to select a keynote conference speaker.

Let's See the Files 182
A question of a board member's right of access to office files.

My People Elected Me 182
A town council and a single-issue council member confront each other's agendas.

No Easy Shots 183
Changes in community centre gym availability may cancel the choir's practice times.

Obstacle to Income 183
Complexities of decisions surrounding a proposed beverage contract.

Perfect Illustration 184
Session presenters decide whether to show a videotape clip.

Space Available 184
A police department must decide how to use available building space.

To Grant or Not to Grant 185
A social workers' union executive faces a decision over awarding an external grant.

Unexpected Fallout 185
Unresolved tensions from contract negotiations create difficulties with committee work.

What's Fair? 186
Conflict over the inclusion of professional development funds in a budget freeze.

ALL FOR ONE, ONE FOR ALL

Lon Jevity   Long-time Mayor of Valleyfield
Kent Advance   President, Valleyfield Chamber of Commerce

Lon Jevity's claim on a fourth term as Valleyfield's Mayor was not a done deal by any means. Lon realized that. The Chamber of Commerce was his best hope. They had the largest membership of any Chamber in the area and they had a broad reach into the community. In the Mayor's view, the Chamber could swing the election. Historically, the town's business people had been Lon's strong and vocal supporters. They knew he would usually exercise his considerable influence with Council to ensure business-friendly decisions. Now, though, the Chamber wanted Council to approve a gambling casino to bring economic prosperity to Valleyfield. Lon was personally opposed to casino gambling and Council was split on the issue – even the Mayor didn't know how the vote would go. His coffee meeting with Chamber President Kent Advance was unusually tense. Kent was all business: "What goes around comes around, Lon. The Chamber is counting on you to deliver this vote – after all, we've always delivered for you."

BEHIND CLOSED DOORS

Stan Fast   Executive Director, Metropolitan Hospital
Sheila Gree   Chair, Metropolitan Hospital Board
Wanda Keepit   Wealthy donor

Stan Fast, Executive Director of Metropolitan Hospital, is preparing a major capital equipment purchase. He has persuaded Sheila Gree, Board Chair, that it will be a good idea to refurnish both the Board Room and his own office as a quiet part of this purchase. After all, Stan mused, virtually all of the new money will be spent on major medical equipment, so what's the big deal? However, the scene is changing fast. Somehow Wanda Keepit has found out about the plan. She has come to meet with Stan. Wanda says that if Stan proceeds, she will withdraw her planned personal donation of six children's beds for the Pediatric Ward. Not only that, she threatens to reveal this "grossly extravagant squandering of funds" to the press. Wanda will not leave without an answer. However, Stan knows that Wanda's recent "fact-finding" junket to San Francisco with Kent Advance included a few side trips and other clearly personal costs they had included in their expense claims to the Hospital. Stan had approved the expenses, though he had doubts about some items. Now Stan thinks perhaps Wanda's 'unwarranted intrusion' into Hospital affairs might be neutralized by posing some strategic questions to her.

Best of Intentions

Leslie Munro   Parkside Memorial Hospital CEO
Martha Winters   Newly elected Board member of the hospital

Leslie Munro had thought Martha Winters would be an excellent addition to the Parkside Memorial Hospital Board (certainly better than one or two of the incumbents, Leslie had told her). Martha was flattered and she agreed to run (Leslie cautioned her not to say anything about their conversation). Martha won the public election, topping the polls. But she defeated an incumbent board member in the process who was very well regarded by the others. That had raised some hackles. Several weeks later, Martha confided to Leslie that another board member had been pressing her hard about what had made her decide to enter the race after having shown no previous interest. In the same conversation, Martha asked Leslie whether anything could be done to get her son a job at the hospital, saying that the CEO obviously seemed to have confidence in the Winters family.

Black, White or a Shade of Grey?

Robin Severs   President, Creekview Public Sector
                         Employees Federation (CPSEF)
Candice Weight   Member, CPSEF Executive

Candice had just hung up the phone. Tomorrow's ski trip was canceled due to poor conditions on the hill. Oh well, it would be an unexpected bonus to have a free day. Almost immediately, though, and even before Candice had erased the ski trip from her calendar, the phone rang again – it was Robin Severs. "Is there any way you can help me?" Robin pleaded, "I promised to represent the CPSEF at a meeting tomorrow, and I've got a horrible case of the flu. Is there any way you could take my place? There are some crucial decisions pending, and we really need to be represented." Candice thought quickly. Tomorrow was clear now because of the long-planned and now canceled trip, but that had just happened, and no one knew. What if Robin had called five minutes earlier? Candice had to say something.

Bus Stop

Terry Castwell　　　　Principal, Water's Edge Elementary School
Stan Weighten　　　　Student at Water's Edge

Everybody knew that the bus was scheduled to leave at 5:00 *sharp* Saturday morning for the ski trip – that had been stressed many times. They were all excited about the trip and everyone was there with lunches and equipment – except Stan Weighten. Just as the driver started the bus and Terry reached for the key to lock the office door, the phone on the desk rang. It had to be Stan, who lived a few kilometers from the school. Everyone else was on the bus ready to leave. The bus horn sounded, the phone rang a second time, and Terry looked at the key.

Challenging the System

Shelley Weller　　　　Student about to enter Elementary School
Mr. and Mrs. Weller　　Shelley's parents
Terry Castwell　　　　Principal, Whitewater Elementary School

Shelley Weller faced some severe physical challenges. The little girl was six years old and about to enter the school system. Arrangements for her transition from medical care at a provincial center into Whitewater Elementary were going smoothly until Shelley's parents were told they could not have their daughter's attendant simply become an employee of the school system in order to continue as the girl's support worker. The Wellers, incensed about what they call "bureaucratic insensitivity," told Terry Castwell that "this is a matter of principle," and that they intended to pursue the matter "as high as necessary."

Chess or Chaucer?

Wanda Bishop	Cook and chess enthusiast, on the staff of Memory Long Term Care Centre
Steven Planwell	Occupational Therapist at Memory Centre
David Fehr	President, Memory Centre Auxiliary Society (MCAS)

The requirements were clear – decision time had arrived. The Memory Centre Auxiliary Society (MCAS) would provide a $1,000 grant in support of a specified initiative proposed by a single staff member or a group, provided the application was signed as acceptable by the Centre Director. There were two signed proposals. The first was a detailed and thoroughly researched brief and interesting survey from Wanda Bishop, a part-time Centre cook who planned to introduce chess as a recreational program and promote it as a thinking skills course for residents. The second was a brief memo from Occupational Therapist Steven Planwell, who wanted MCAS to underwrite part of the costs involved in taking a group of residents to the Festival of Early English Literature in a nearby town. No Centre funds were available for either project, and David Fehr knew that the Auxiliary would look to their president for a recommendation.

Coffee Time

Pat Onnabach	Landmark Community College Facilities Officer

On your second day in your new position as President of Landmark Community College, Pat Onnabach arrives at your door with two mugs of coffee and asks if you have time for a break. When you say "yes," Pat passes one mug to you and sits down with the other in hand. You have a general discussion about Pat's recent visits to two College satellite campuses and resulting observations about the administrator of each building. Pat says that this coffee time used to be a regular feature of working with the former president, who had found it "most informative." Pat leaves after coffee. As you go to wash your cup, you overhear one of the other campus directors, who is at the main campus office for a meeting, say to another, "I see Pat doesn't waste any time getting to the head of the line. Nothing changes, I guess – looks like we're in for more of the same."

Don't Mess Around

The recreation centre staff has filed a complaint alleging that the general office is locked whenever the secretary is not there. As a result of this action, they say there are frequent occasions when staff members cannot have access to equipment or supplies. To complicate matters, the secretary is known to take a generous lunch break. Staff members have asked for keys, but the centre manager has stated that the office is the secretary's work area and that there have been frequent instances of a mess being left behind or items missing. The manager also expresses concern about security, since access can be gained to the staff lounge and the equipment storage area via the office. The complaint has come to you as the city's Manager of Recreation Services.

Health is the Issue

Stan Garden	Principal, Memorial Secondary School
Dr. Henry Wall	Local physician
Frank Speaker	Member of the provincial Legislative Assembly

When Frank Speaker said, "I have someone I'd like you to meet," Shawn's guard went up. They had been down this road before. Why hadn't Frank identified this *someone*? One thing was certain – this would be more than simply an introduction. The two arrived at the principal's office the next morning. Frank introduced Dr. Henry Wall, a local physician. The doctor produced a kit of teaching materials related to several health issues. He stated that they had been prepared by a colleague of his and were available in quantity for free distribution to classroom teachers. The doctor asked for Shawn's agreement to introduce the materials and promote their use. The kits, said the doctor, were endorsed by the Medical Society and carried the "enthusiastic support" of members of the school board. Dr. Wall indicated that he had a supply of the kits in his vehicle and was anxious to distribute all of them that day.

High Stakes

Weir Watson	Treasurer, Aspen City Legacy Society (ACLS)
Wanda Tell	Secretary, ACLS

Bingo had been good to the Aspen City Legacy Society. As a result, many other groups in town had received small grants from ACLS. Weir Watson, ACLS Treasurer, was always reluctant to part with a penny, but he was usually overruled by others with a clear commitment to building the community. Even with generous distribution of funds (Weir would say it was because of his care), the Council had always maintained a healthy six-figure bank balance.

Wanda Tell didn't know how the Council ever kept their finances straight, the reports were so confusing, but the Council executive never seemed to worry. Anyway, her job as secretary was simply to type and print the Treasurer's Report each month. Weir Watson had made that clear two months ago when Wanda had suggested some format changes to make the report clearer: "Just type it – I know what I'm doing," Weir had said. Yet Wanda could see a glaring error in the report in front of her now. If she said nothing and the mistake was not noticed, the Council would spend money they did not have, and Weir Watson would lose any chance of re-election. According to Weir, though, Wanda's job was clear – "Just type the report."

In the Oven

Will Tradeoff	President, Community Service Associates (CSA)

You are the vice-president of Community Service Associates, a small local not-for-profit agency. Agency President Will Tradeoff calls you into his office to plan for tomorrow's staff meeting. Will asks you to make a presentation on his behalf. He has been given a new microwave oven by his mother, who won it in a drugstore draw. His mother already has a good microwave and doesn't want to change it. Knowing that Will's microwave is older, she has passed the new one to him. Will has advertised his old oven for sale, but there have been no takers. The CSA staff committee has been planning to buy a microwave and Will is prepared to offer them a good deal.

In the Oven – Goose Cooked

Will Tradeoff   President, Community Service Associates (CSA)
Stan Firm   Senior staff member at CSA

For reasons he outlined at last week's staff meeting, Stan Firm, a technician on staff, was very critical of the decision to buy Will Tradeoff's microwave oven. However, the staff committee decided to purchase it. Will left for a retirement planning conference the day after providing the oven, which he had been keeping in a carton in his office. The next day, on first use, the oven broke, and the repair estimate was more than the price CSA had paid for the oven. Stan Firm and several others want a full refund and a CSA policy on this type of purchase. Will T. has left the matter in your hands, saying, "A deal is a deal."

Just Trying to Help

Robin Severs   President, Parkside Public Sector Employees Federation
Colin Allshots   Personnel Committee Chair, Parkside School Board

At a chance meeting with Robin Severs, Colin Allshots almost immediately began asking whether Robin had any helpful suggestions that could be passed on to Leslie Wingard, Superintendent of Schools to aid in Leslie's professional development. Colin said, "I have great respect for Leslie, but we all know we can improve." As the conversation progressed, the questions got more specific in reference to the Superintendent's leadership style and interpersonal relations. Robin's discomfort grew.

Let's Get on with It.

Pat Slater   Caseworkers' Association Professional Development Committee Chair

Time was of the essence. The Professional Development Committee had invited several potential annual conference keynote presenters to submit outlines. To date there had been just one response – "The best of them all, by far," Pat Slater said. Only three of the five Pro-D Committee members were able to attend the meeting Pat had called on short notice – a majority, clearly, but they usually proceeded with such matters on the basis of consensus. Pat pressed the other two members for a decision, arguing that they had to get on with their plans. Deadlines were looming, especially for printing. Pat argued that it seemed the other possible speakers were not interested.

Let's See the Files

A member of the hospital board has asked to see the files of senior staff expense claims for the past six months. The board member wants to make a copy for "study." The President and the Vice-President Finance are away, and you are Acting President. You cannot stall for time because this board member is leaving town tomorrow and wants to take the file copy.

My People Elected Me

Byrna Bridge   New councilor, Wind River Municipal Council

Byrna Bridge was going to add a new dimension to Council meetings. The new councilor had been asked by the mayor to chair the Zoning Committee. Byrna's surprising reply? "My people elected me to make sure you guys don't tear down the old Fitzpatrick House to make room for your rich friends to build condominiums. If you think you can divert me that easily, think again. And forget about putting me on any committees – I know what I have to do."

No Easy Shots

Terry Castwell   Manager, Jill Brown Community Centre
Jim Booker   Athletic director, Greenville Regional District
Phil Octave   Choir director, Greenville Children's Choir

Terry Castwell was between a rock and a hard place – the Friday morning phone call had done that. Excitement was high in Greenville about next week's community youth league volleyball tournament, which was to be held at the Westway Arena. Until today, that was. A maintenance problem meant that the tournament would have to be moved to another site. Except for the Jill Brown Centre, every facility in town was fully booked. Even there, Terry had reserved the only available gym time for the Greenville Children's Choir after school for the full week – next Friday would be their dress rehearsal. The phone call was from Jim Booker, who wanted to reserve the Jill Brown gym during that time slot all week so that the tournament wouldn't be disrupted. Jim reminded Terry that the Regional Board Chair's daughter was a star volleyball player. The trouble was, Phil Octave and the Children's Choir were stars too – the whole town knew that. The annual choir concert in the gym was a community highlight. Phil would not be impressed by any plan to change rehearsal arrangements. Terry promised to call Jim Booker with an answer by the end of the day.

Obstacle to Income

Shawn Merritt   Executive Director, Farmington Civic Centre
Morris Better   President, Better Vending

The Farmington Civic Centre (FCC) had always supported local business. Community loyalties ran high, and everyone was pleased with things as they were. Recently though, the big beverage companies had come on the scene. The FCC senior staff, whose budget was perennially in need of a better income stream, was anxious to pursue the potential of what some, perhaps euphemistically, called "corporate partnerships." Executive Director Shawn Merritt, always on the lookout for fund-raising possibilities, saw huge potential in doing things a different way. The topic was on the agenda of the next Civic Centre Board meeting for action. Surprisingly, the Board was anxious to explore the possibilities, probably as a way of relieving some budget pressure. Clearly, almost everyone was ready to move. That made the telephone message on Shawn's desk, "Call Morris Better at Better Vending as soon as possible," a bit troublesome. Clearly, any move toward the large corporations would mean more income for the Centre but less for Better Vending, their long-term local supplier. Morris was not likely to let that change happen easily.

Perfect Illustration

You and your colleague are presenting a professional development training series on personal financial planning. Your audience is the staff of a local not-for-profit organization. You are approaching the final session, a particularly important one. People have been encouraged to bring a friend. Last weekend, your colleague rented a feature video containing a five-minute segment that will add immensely to the usefulness of your presentation. You watch the clip together and agree that it is a 'must see'. The association will provide a video player and monitor. You have signed their waiver certifying that you either possess copyright on all materials or have a use agreement with the copyright holder. You have neither. Your colleague is anxious to show the clip. When you ask the association representative about the agreement you signed, the response is an unconcerned "That's pretty well just pro forma."

Space Available

Sergeant Walker	Semi-retired curator of the Waterpark Police Museum
Sergeant Driver	Officer in Charge, Community Detail

Waterpark Police Department was an anomaly in the area. While other departments were jammed for space, Waterpark P. D. had a spare building they had not used for two years, since the new office had been built. The town had no plans for the building. The new space meant that the Police Department was very well situated for the most part. The major focus of today's staff meeting was on possible uses of the building. One person with a definite proposal was the popular Sergeant Walker, curator of the widely known and award-winning Waterpark Police Museum. For five years, Walker had operated out of what he called a "cubbyhole" beside the cells. It was time for a change. For one thing, said Walker, it was a poor location for a facility that the public visited. Walker's point was that citizens with an interest in the PD's venerable history were not well served by being sent off to a substandard, almost forgotten space. The other contender was Sergeant Driver of the Community Detail, who was planning to introduce a Citizens' Patrol that not all members welcomed enthusiastically and that some certainly did not want using the main building. They needed to decide something now. After all, they had known since February that the building would be available for other uses, and City Council needed a recommendation soon.

To Grant or Not to Grant

Randy Frank	President, Mountainside Social Workers Federation (MSWF)
Ada Frend	MSWF Presidential candidate

Financially speaking, it had been a tough year. The Mountainside Social Workers Federation Mutual Aid Fund was empty and here was Ada Frend, the only challenger to President Randy Frank in next month's election for the MSWF presidency, asking once more for a grant to help a fledgling union in a developing country to get organized. Ada's timing left something to be desired, Randy thought. The membership had clearly said, at least informally, that enough was enough (at least, that was how Randy read it), but the executive did have the authority to levy special fees and allocate additional funds. They were split on the issue and Randy knew that on this executive vote the President would probably have to be the tie-breaker. Next week's agenda included "Mutual Aid Fund supplement proposal." Clearly, this was an election issue lurking in the wings.

Unexpected Fallout

Terry Winton	Director, Sunset Ridge Eldercare (SRE)
Sandy Seinhoff	SRE's Assistant Director

Negotiations were over at last. It had been a tough session, thought Terry Winton, Director of Sunset Ridge Eldercare's chain of retirement homes. Assistant Director Sandy Seinhoff had not negotiated before but had certainly learned a lot from being a member of the Board's team. The sessions had been tense at times; Sandy had made a few tactical errors that were only minimally harmful but had 'raised the temperature' of the meetings considerably. Maybe Sandy's style needed some work. Anyway, Sandy was back to regular work in staff development and training, yet not without some fallout. Some members of the staff development planning committee were declining to come to further meetings, saying that they had lost respect for the Assistant Director.

What's Fair?

Foster Wellbrook   CEO, Northridge Hospital

President Foster Wellbrook had it all: authority from the Northridge Hospital Board, undisputed financial expertise, and control of the purse – the discretionary portion of the budget at least. The Board's sudden decision was surprising: they placed a temporary freeze on non-essential spending pending a review of some 'puzzling irregularities' in the Accounting Department. The grievance was a surprise to Foster. Apparently some members of the Northridge Nursing Federation (NNF) were disturbed about the fact that professional development funds were included in the freeze. In Foster's view, one had to be even-handed, but he was unable to answer questions about the 'irregularities'. The NNF executive was not sympathetic – why should their members' ability to carry out their own growth plans be curtailed by something so obviously out of their control?

Chapter 10 — Learning through Case Study

The case studies relate to concepts developed in Part I. They are intended to provide a pause for thought and discussion, an opportunity to reflect on the material developed in the first eight chapters. While the initial focus of the case studies is usually on the analysis and application of that scenario in reference to a concept or set of concepts developed in Part I, almost always there is also a broader application to other elements and concepts. The items in this strand can be used both independently and with colleagues. They can be revisited for their applicability at various points throughout the book – several have more than one reference point. Additionally, what is particularly relevant for one reader may be less applicable for another, or the necessary relevance might be better established utilizing another scenario.

I have resisted the temptation to relate the critical incidents and case studies to specific pages or sections of the book. I believe that our paths to learning are often best charted in dialogue with our fellow learners. I encourage you to write and pose your own questions and to use the scenarios at various points throughout the book.

The case studies focus on a variety of situations. Primarily, but not exclusively, they relate to the not-for-profit sector. Some of the case studies address issues arising in school districts, though in almost every instance, the matter has broader applicability – the issues that arise in schools are often very similar to those we see elsewhere.

INDEX TO THE CASE STUDIES

Agreement for Tomorrow   191
Conclusions about a meeting of two friends create board-staff tensions.

Beyond all Expectations   193
Two parents propose their conception of what constitutes excellence, and others listen.

Blindsided Once, But Not Twice   196
A hospital's chief financial officer uses prior experience to shape his leadership style

Breaking up the Logjams   199
A new principal puzzles over underlying, undiscussed issues.

Cultured Minority   202
The culture of a college department affects the whole organization

Dodging the Real Issue   205
A retirement home residents' group decides to lobby the government about construction of a new facility.

Explosion at High Valley   207
Competitiveness, loss of prestige, and a science department head vacancy combine.

Firm Foundation   209
A large charitable foundation struggles to establish a path toward the future

Francais ou Anglais?   212
Parents collide over language programs.

Fun, Funds, and Friction   214
Parents differ in their views of fund-raising and parent-school interaction.

Let's be Fair About This   216
Everyone has differing views on what to do about a student's suspension.

Lobbying for Learning   219
Parents collide over the regular class inclusion of students with special needs.

Midnight Madness   221
Trustee proposes succession policy, although the superintendent has no plans to leave.

Office Parties   223
A property management firm's staff contends with a new manager

One Pocket to Another 225
A hospital board's personnel plans become suspect due to budgetary constraints.

Pressing Matters 227
A family-owned printing firm struggles to survive in a new world of business

Restoration Project 230
Organizational success rests on participant commitment to a civic project

Slippery Slopes 232
Tangled relationships and interests create problems for a school principal and her entrepreneurial spouse

Straight Goods 235
Bargaining session tensions lead to ethical questions

Takeover 237
New board policy on parent involvement creates possibilities and tensions.

Time for a Change? 239
Perceptions, norms, change, and the school's budget development process.

Us and Them 241
Confusion surrounds an interest group's real agenda.

What are Schools For? 243
Parents' effort to include community development as a major school purpose.

Agreement for Tomorrow

Wanda Rule	Mayor of Arborside
Robin Severs	President, Arborside Public Employees Federation (APEF)
Sandy Seinhoff	Assistant City Manager, Board negotiator
Weir Watson	Council member and Chair of the City's Negotiating Committee
Cara Goodbit	Council member
Mark Mywords	Council member, friend of Weir Watson

"Rethinking Human Resources" – Robin Severs reflected back on the series of events triggered by that phrase. Robin had been elected as the President of the Arborside Public Employees Federation (APEF) on the basis of a strong commitment as a professional engineer and a fine reputation for design capability and negotiating skill.

It had been a reasonable round of bargaining for the most part. Relations at the contract table during the current round of negotiations could almost be called cordial. Sandy Seinhoff, Assistant City Manager, was the City's staff negotiator. Although Sandy was a formidable bargaining opponent with every relevant fact at hand, fairness and honesty played an equal part. Sandy was also willing to share more data than others Robin had known, commenting, "There's no point trying to use information that the other side doesn't have, understand, or believe." Sandy and Robin were old friends from Works Department days, although they hadn't had much contact since starting their new jobs.

Weir Watson, Councilor and Chair of the City's Negotiating Committee, was another story. He was close-mouthed in the extreme, and anyone could see that he had little patience with Sandy's open style. Today's problem, though, was of a different order. Councilor Cara Goodbit had come back excited from a "Rethinking Human Resources" presentation at the recent Municipal Association conference, convinced that this was an initiative to be tried. The Council, under pressure from the community to improve employee relations, had responded enthusiastically, endorsed the Goodbit report, and directed central office staff to consult with the APEF and prepare a training series around that theme.

For Robin, that had created a dilemma. Cara Goodbit had discovered that the APEF President knew the keynote speaker for the first sequence, and had asked Robin to introduce the opening session. Robin had agreed. The program date, though, meant canceling a APEF bargaining committee meeting, and some committee members weren't overjoyed about that. Worse, whispers of "sellout" were circulating. Any excuse, thought Robin.

Robin realized that involvement in the program opening probably was not the best idea. However, the training program had seemed like the first break in the efforts of some of the City's best employees to start the process of re-thinking personnel relations in Arborside.

For the first time, the APEF President felt a deep conflict between union role and professional identity. Yet Robin had argued often and successfully that professionalism was seamless, that office and negotiating table were both part of the tapestry.

What bothered Robin now was there seemed to be no meeting point. There was no apparent willingness among some leaders of the local to address personal learning issues while, as an earlier negotiator had often said, "Dollars are on the table." Yet the APEF President was confident that on the whole the members were committed to exploring new ways of doing their work.

A red herring had floated into view, coaxed into action by Weir Watson. Robin Severs and Sandy Seinhoff, separately attending a movie, had bumped into each other on the way out, and had stopped for a drink together on their way home. Sandy had studied "Rethinking Human Resources." They had been asked to lead a session at the upcoming training course. For the first time since they had worked together, the friends spent two casual but invigorating hours exploring ideas about the personnel dimension of the City's operations. It was one of those chance meetings with good results – an opportunity to renew an old friendship and a somewhat forgotten mutual respect. It was an opportunity to set offices aside and talk about the human side of work life. The best part of it all was that bargaining didn't even enter the conversation.

At least it didn't until they were leaving. They passed a corner table and heard Weir Watson's voice – "Glad to see you're having a good time. It's interesting how much gets done behind the scenes." Neither of them mentioned it as they left, but both sensed trouble ahead.

Trouble wasn't long in coming. Weir Watson had been in the lounge with another Council member, Mark Mywords; the two of them lost no time in intimating to the other councilors that Sandy's ability to act on behalf of the City was compromised. Erring on the cautious side, new Mayor Wanda Rule had suggested that Sandy cancel the presentation at the staff training session 'to clear the air'. It seemed that no one was long on reflection.

Beyond all Expectations

Marge and Stan Overall	Owners of Overall Development Corporation (ODC)
Leslie Wingard	Parkside Superintendent of Schools
Terry Castwell	Principal, Water's Edge Elementary School
Lester Senter	Parkside school trustee
Una Laterall	Parkside school trustee

There was little doubt that Marge and Stan Overall had awakened Parkside. Leslie Wingard thought back to the first day they had arrived in town, ostensibly "just visiting the area," as they had said to Leslie while they stood in front of a real estate office with a map. It was an unusual place for tourists to stop, Leslie had reflected, but then maybe they were just comparing prices with values at home.

Clearly, they weren't. That was three years ago, and since then, signs for Overall Development Corporation had sprouted all over town. Their first project was the Four Peaks resort, and that had been welcomed by everyone. Four Peaks was nothing, though, compared with their second project, the ski hill. Leslie wondered why development in the area had only really started when these two whirlwinds of ideas, cash, and connections had arrived in Parkside.

Leslie's first meeting with the Overalls, like most meetings people had with them, had been like standing in front of a smorgasbord of exciting ideas, almost all worth pursuing. They had come to see Leslie (why the superintendent and not their area school principal, Leslie had wondered) about placing their children in school. Clearly, they had firm ideas about schooling as they did about almost everything. Challenge seemed to be the major thing. Both Marge and Stan were Olympic medalists in skiing. Leslie had come to know the couple since their arrival and had begun to realize the meaning of the term athletes used so often – *focus*. That explained a lot about the Overalls and their business success. They had established reputations as thoroughly honest and fair business people, which explained their easy acceptance in Parkside. They were equally recognized as expecting the same from others. A few local merchants had fallen by the wayside, no longer able to get contracts with Overall Development because they hadn't measured up to the company's standards. No doubt about it, ODC was a major business player in Parkside.

Marge and Stan themselves were major players, too. Terry Castwell, the principal of Water's Edge Elementary School, seemed no match for them. The Overalls had never held executive positions in anything, but they were always tireless workers at whatever they took on and they had clearly taken on Water's Edge Elementary School.

Their idea was simple – involve everyone, students, teachers, administrators, parents, and the community at large in developing a school that would stand second to none. The idea had appealed to Terry, partly because what some referred to as "The Indianapolis Team" sounded as though they were willing to contribute not only ideas but also their time and effort. The bonus, though, Terry hadn't expected. The three C's of the Overall team were cash, connections, and commitment. That had been a bonanza. On any measure of these three indicators Water's Edge Elementary School was reaping the benefits. The Overalls' rationale was clear – the best for my child's school. Terry had been glad their children were in the first and second years of school.

That was then, and this was now. With some chagrin, Terry remembered the Overalls' comments at their first meeting – "focus" and "second to none." That had meant that through Overalls' connections with a major supplier the Parkside Parents' Council had been able to equip a full computer classroom and sponsor teacher in-service to enable best use of the facility. It had also meant a critical look at a couple of other areas, though – physical education and sports, and general achievement.

The Overalls had unfolded their "three-point plan" to Terry over coffee one spring day. They wanted to start early, they had said, so that the school would be able to get some things rolling by fall. As always, they were clear and precise. They wanted top-level physical fitness among students, high academic achievement, and up-to-date knowledge and skills. It was the unpacking of those ideas that had become the problem. Top level physical fitness meant providing training in attitude development and focus, and Stan and Marge wanted to introduce a motivational program developed by one of their friends and used widely for athletic training. High academic achievement meant identifying the brightest and best and grooming them Olympic style. Up-to-date knowledge and skills meant computer literacy and an exposure to entrepreneurship and marketing.

The reason for the 'unveiling' over coffee was clear. Stan and Marge wanted the initiative to go ahead as a plan to be introduced before the end of school in June as a master plan for the coming year. They had left Terry a written summary of their ideas, and the three agreed to get together again in a week to "clarify and proceed."

There was little doubt about where the parents at Water's Edge Elementary school would come down on the Overalls' ideas – full support and "what's the matter with you?" to anyone who hesitated. They had seen the effect of the Stan and Marge and Overall Development on the community – nothing but good. They had heard the envious comments of parents whose children attended other schools. The parents were also aware of Trustee Lester Senter's initiative to get board policy established that would prevent one school from becoming better equipped than another. "Let's keep a level playing field," Lester had said. That was a poor analogy to use.

Anyway, next week's meeting with the Overalls was looming. On the surface, it seemed there was potential to develop broadly-based commitment to a comprehensive plan of school improvement. But Terry was troubled. Trustee Una Latterall had made reference to "Overall Elementary School," and Terry had wondered at the time whether she might be thinking of proposing a name change. Colleagues were backing away, too, it seemed – probably jealousy. Somehow Terry felt that there were issues buried in this somewhere. Those issues had to be identified fast.

Blindsided Once, But Not Twice

Leslie Trueman	President, Willow Grove Hospital (WGH)
Frank Ledger	Chief Financial Officer, WGH
Candy Evertrust	Comptroller, WGH
Stan Upright	Manager of Laboratory Services, WGH
Marion Stamp	President, Willow Grove Employees Union (WGHEU)

One thing Frank Ledger had much of was a lack of trust. Leslie had often thought privately that if the Chair of the Hospital Board died, Frank would withhold her last expense claim to make sure that she hadn't invited the undertaker to dinner at hospital expense. Frank's lack of trust in others was also well hidden, either because he knew that being obvious about it would cause problems, or because the dishonest could be lulled into a false sense of security that way.

It made life difficult, no doubt about that. Frank was widely seen as a highly competent financial officer. He was clearly that – he had a thorough grasp of the financial side of the Willow Grove Hospital operation. The budgeting process was flawless; Frank was frequently invited to present his systems to other organizations and to participate in operational reviews as a member, often the chair, of external teams.

Life in the Accounting Department, though, was not much fun for anyone. There was nothing you could put your finger on, yet it was a quiet, almost subdued place. If you happened to make a facetious comment about anything to do with irregularities in procedure, no one laughed. Memos from the Department office were full of detail – every 'i' dotted, people would say. The accounting staff was thoroughly competent because Frank knew how to pick them. Yet very few stayed long. Frank obviously trained people well, because when they left it was usually to a better job. Local businesses were always happy to hire one of Frank's former staff. Lately, the turnover had been so heavy that it seemed as though the hospital was functioning more as a training school for the financial industry.

Twice in the past month Candy Evertrust, the hospital comptroller, had made appointments to see Leslie Trueman, the hospital president. On both occasions she had cancelled at the last minute, blaming her heavy workload and the pressure of deadlines. Leslie was puzzled because it seemed that even casual hallway meetings were avoided. Candy had clearly decided that she didn't want to talk to Leslie after all.

It was Friday afternoon, and all of a sudden the cracks were beginning to appear. Candy had finally decided to meet with Leslie, but she had difficulty being specific about a problem she was having in her working relationship with Frank. She apologized for her earlier reluctance to meet, saying that since Frank was so highly regarded she was worried that her concerns would not be taken seriously.

It seemed that recently Frank had been questioning Candy closely about a number of operational procedures to the point she felt under investigation. She had asked Frank if there was a problem, but he had said, "Of course not – why would you think that?" To make things worse, Frank's questions seemed to be driving at something, but Candy said that she could not figure out what. Her only consolation, she said, was that others had previously reported the same kind of thing. Unfortunately, they had all left the hospital's employment.

After the meeting with Candy, Leslie looked at the mail. On top of the pile was a copy of a memo from Stan Upright, Manager of Laboratory Services. As far as Leslie was concerned, Stan was one of the straightest and most honest people on hospital staff. It was difficult to get a full picture from the memo, but one thing was clear. In a recent phone call to Stan, Frank Ledger had suggested that one of the laboratory's computers had disappeared from inventory and from the building. Leslie didn't know all the details, but dishonesty on Stan's part would certainly have to be proven before it would be believable!

Leslie decided to meet with Frank that afternoon and try to bring some things together. Frank's response revealed clearly for the first time a side of him that Leslie had long sensed but had never been able to put a finger on. Frank did not have a specific concern about Candy's work. In fact, there really was no basis for even questioning Stan about the 'missing' computer, let alone suggesting that one had disappeared.

Frank related a story about his own working past to Leslie in an effort to explain what he insisted was a legitimate operational strategy. Early in his working career, and in another city, Frank had been the victim of a financial scam carried out by a fellow employee. It was done so well that Frank had not sensed a thing until the day the police, sent by the auditors, had arrived at the office. At the time, Frank's immediate difficulty had been to convince the police that he had not in fact been part of the scheme.

From that incident, Frank said, he had learned his lesson well. Never again would anyone blindside him. He had developed a range of strategies, and his underlying method was to be pleasant to everyone and trust no one. He wasn't convinced by Leslie's suggestion that procedures, checks and safeguards were built into most systems to prevent wrongdoing. There was no substitute, Frank said, for what he called "a tiny measure of terror."

This was all new to Leslie, but it certainly made things fall into place. It was also true that Willow Grove's books had been 'squeaky clean' for as long as Frank had been in charge. That was small consolation, though. Stan Upright was incensed and planning to bring the matter up at the next department managers' meeting. When Leslie called him, he said that several other managers had similar complaints and that together, they were going to demand answers. He also warned Leslie that the Willow Grove Hospital Employees' Union (WHGEU) was getting into the act – something about allegations by Frank of impropriety regarding staff training funds and a meeting with Frank that Marion Stamp had called "nothing but innuendo, allegation and threat." The staff turnover problem must also be addressed. In addition to the human cost to people who left because they felt they were not trusted, the hospital simply could not afford repeated training and retraining.

One didn't need a problem like that to take home for the weekend, Leslie thought. On the plus side, Frank was thoroughly competent. His presence at Willow Grove was a major benefit to the hospital, and Frank himself had noted that in the past year alone, at least three hospitals and two private companies had tried to lure him away. It would be an uphill battle to convince the Board that anything about Frank Ledger's practice needed correcting. The way things had been going lately, it seemed just as likely that board members' eyebrows would be raised in Leslie's direction, not Frank's – and Leslie didn't need that.

Yet something would have to change. The managers were building a solid case. They would not be appeased simply by a suggestion that, after all, Frank was a thoroughly competent financial officer. As usual, sighed Leslie, it was the president who was at the centre of things. The president wanted to keep Frank, but things would have to change.

Breaking up the Logjams

Shawn Merritt	Principal, Memorial Secondary School
Faye Daway	Previous principal
Mark Harder	Former teacher, Memorial Secondary
Barry Hatchett	Student Council member
Ken Parsewell	French Department Head

Logjam – the word kept popping into Shawn Merritt's mind. Except it was actually plural – *logjams*, because there were several. Shawn had spent the early fall trying to come to grips with what was going on. Almost immediately after starting work, it became clear that nothing in the way of prior education or experience had been sufficient preparation for Memorial Secondary School.

It had been an unusual start, anyway, to be interviewed for the principalship while the students were still doing battle over Faye Daway's departure. The Board had told Faye in April that her contract would not be renewed for the fall. That night Faye had cleaned out her desk and left – left the country, many thought. That had puzzled the students, to say the least. They had known that something was about to happen (Board secrets didn't stay secret for long), and they had already begun to fight on behalf of their principal. The battle had come to an abrupt end, though, when Faye Daway disappeared.

Faye Daway had been principal at Memorial Secondary for the nine years before Shawn was appointed. It had been a stormy time interspersed with periods of relative calm, usually in the years after a significant staff turnover, which had happened twice. The first exodus of seven teachers had happened after the "standards battle." That group had argued long and loudly for a concerted effort to raise academic achievement levels. They were in the minority, though. No one in the community or within the school had ever expressed concern. In fact, people were often heard to say that Memorial was a great mix of athletic and academic prowess. It hadn't helped, either, that the group had been led by Mark Harder. His little study of the grade profiles of all the athletic team members hadn't helped his case. By the end of the year, "the magnificent seven" really had no choice but to leave. The next year had been quiet. Faye and some of the others had made sure that no one forgot – the number seven had appeared in almost everything sent out by the principal that year.

The second round of departures involved only four people, but no one had forgotten it. That was the year of "The Basketball Trip." The team was at its peak. They had won the provincial championship, and their reward was a trip to Hawaii. Fund raising had been easy – the kids were famous.

Hearing about it later, Shawn thought that the team members' fame must have gone to their heads – maybe to their coach's head, too. Anyway, some team members had stepped over the line more than once on the trip. The stories had grown bigger and bigger as time passed, but details of the actual events had remained the best kept public secret in town. Four of the teachers had complained to Faye Daway that her lack of action was inexcusable. They did their best to arouse others to action, but they met with a stone wall of resistance. No one was prepared to act on "nothing but rumors," as many called it. The four left at the end of the year. Anyway, all that was history. It was time to get on with life. But it was already the middle of October, and the logjams were showing no signs of breaking up. There were three of them: students, staff and parents.

The students were a puzzle. Shawn could understand their anger. They had wanted Faye Daway to stay on as principal. Clearly, they were not ready to forget. Yet no one would talk about Faye. Shawn wondered about the coolness of many of the students toward their new principal. Sometimes the temptation was to say to them, "Look, I wasn't part of all that. Why hold it against me?"

A few had been what Shawn called "cautiously positive, yet positively cautious." Barry Hatchett was one. Shawn had gotten to know Barry through his Student Council activities and had come to appreciate his strong commitment to the school. He had been helpful from the start; Shawn had appreciated his thoughtful approach. Barry always seemed to be listening closely to Shawn, but whenever the principal finished talking it seemed as though Barry was waiting for 'the other shoe to drop'.

It was clear that pulling this staff together was going to be a challenge. Except for a few, their attitudes seemed to suggest that they had written off school administrators as far as their relevance to the world of teaching was concerned. To Shawn it seemed that even though the new assignment had only begun in July, most of the teachers felt that it was only a matter of time until yet another principal moved on. It wasn't that they seemed to want that to happen, just that when it occurred, it would be a 'non-event' in their eyes. Even the planned new wing didn't seem to arouse their interest, although one teacher's comment had Shawn thinking that the project could be a catalyst. Ken Parsewell, head of the French department, had said, "If only we could clear the decks, I think people are just waiting to get on board."

Shawn was convinced that the students were the key to the parents. At the moment, though, the Parents' Advisory Council was struggling over its mandate. At least they had asked Shawn to help them work through that process with them. Curiously, though, they had a very short-term orientation. Shawn had suggested a couple of longer term projects, but the principal's proposal for a three-year computer acquisition program brought the puzzling response from their president, "Let's just deal with this year for now."

Not much ever kept Shawn Merritt awake at night, but this puzzle did. For the most part, things at Memorial Secondary looked pretty good, but the new principal was already beginning to realize that something was needed to break up the logjams, or clear the decks, whatever the analogy. Shawn needed to talk to someone with an informed outsider's view of the school.

Cultured Minority

Morris Bother	President, Barkley Community College
Adam Ant	Coordinator, Learning Support Services
Hy Standing	Vice-President, Programs
Marshall Power	union shop steward
Robin Time	inventory clerk

The Barkley Community College Education Office was a low, rambling rabbit warren of a building that hadn't met the institution's needs for a long time. The name was a misnomer – the building housed an assortment of offices, several of which had little or nothing to do with education. Both Morris and the previous president had tried repeatedly to get the College Board to look for a more suitable space for the curriculum development department, resource centre, and team meeting areas. However, when funding had been generous, the Board hadn't. In Morris' view, the window of opportunity hadn't just closed, it had been boarded up. Clearly, they would have to make do for the time being. Not that everyone was concerned – Adam Ant, for example, wanted no change at all from present circumstances.

The office included three aging portables out back. One of them housed the College Resources Centre, and that one was no problem. Those materials were going to be decentralized to their primary users throughout the College region, catalogued centrally, and made available for loan through an e-mail booking system. The second building housed the Accounting Department. There was a culture! Most of the time Morris was glad it was in a separate building. They had lots of space, too. On-line links to the Advanced Education and Skills Training Ministry, a strong move to electronic filing, and the shift of 30 boxes of dead files to a storage facility had turned the building into a roomy work area.

Morris had recently discovered the names that had been given to the clutter of buildings out back. The College Resource Centre was simply called "The CRC." The Accounting Department was referred to by its own name. Only one of the three buildings, the Community Education Office, was ever called "The Portable," even though they had all arrived at the same time and were virtually identical.

Morris knew that a major part of getting Barkley Community College up to full speed would be to get on with a plan of curriculum improvement, especially in the trades area. A new set of provincial competency-based curriculum had just been established, and the Ministry was moving strongly to that approach. In terms of allowing any amount of professional latitude, though, the program was a nightmare and instructors throughout the region were floundering and angry. Clearly, the task of selling the new approach would rest with the staff development personnel who made up the Portable Crew, or the PCs, as they fondly called themselves. They were not all fully committed to the idea of high energy and accomplishment, and that would have to change now.

Hy Standing was probably the one person who could take on the task of getting the PC moving. He had received several letters from instructors and one from the Union Executive wondering when serious support materials development and in-service training were going to begin. Even the fundamental notion of a competency-based program was new to many staff. Morris was certain Hy could handle the project. It was just a matter of developing an overall plan. Certainly the people in The Portable had the skills both to figure it out and to carry it out.

Some path-clearing would have to be done first. Around the College region, the Portable was referred to as "The Head Shed;" the word was that if the College needed a convenient resting place for you that was where you would be sent. That was unfair, Morris thought. Granted, a previous president had placed Lotta Slack out there years before, as Director of Energy Management. Except for Lotta, and she had retired some years ago, the staff had all been reasonably competent. Yet the myth persisted, perhaps because in her 'spare time', Lotta had been the PCs unofficial resident counselor and advisor. That role that had since been assumed by Robin Time.

One thing was clear. People who made it to The Portable, and for some that was a career goal, *did not* want to leave the place. Marshall Power was definitely the standard-bearer in that group. Marshall was full of creative ideas and wise enough to involve 'outsiders' in some of The Portable Crew's parties and events. Sometimes it seemed to Morris that they had one just about every week. Marshall was also the resident expert on College history – he could remember and vividly describe just about every milestone along its path.

The Portable had its own newsletter, "The Wagon Circle." At least it was rumored that they did – it was said to be a condition of continued acceptance as a PC member that no one from outside The Portable could ever see "The Circle." Anyway, it was probably harmless enough. As a matter of fact, Morris had come across a group of PCs engrossed in a paper that seemed to be drawing their rapt attention in a coffee shop until they spotted the President.

Tight was the word that came to mind. The PC's were all capable people with skills the College really needed. They were often in demand for secondment to Ministry teams and for consulting contracts. They were also highly regarded by one or two influential College Board members.

On the other side of it, some of the newer Board members had no time for the PCs, who they saw as a drain on the College's limited resources. The College Staff Union (CSU) shared that view, although they had to be careful because the PCs were dues-paying members. Interestingly, the focus was beginning to shift to Hy Standing. It was clear that in the minds of some onlookers, Hy had better make some changes out back or some people would begin to push for changes out front. Yet trying to crack that culture carried its own set of risks and challenges.

It all came to a head at a Board meeting. Hy had given a report about the new Competency-Based Trades Training program. There had been some probing questions from the floor, including several from the CSU representative. The outcome of the discussion was that Hy was directed by the Board to develop an implementation plan, a timeline and a budget. When he mentioned the staff in The Portable in response to a question about whether Centreville College had the necessary expertise, a Board member's comment said it all: "We need this work done now, not some time before retirement."

Several issues would have to be addressed. The first had to do with the problems caused by the culture of The Portable. Hy would need every bit of that staff's considerable talent – this was a major College-wide program development project. There was not much time to deal with that, but Hy knew that unless something positive happened it would be difficult to assemble a staff team to work with the PCs. The second issue was the makeup of the support team. If the instructors were to own the new program, they would have to be involved from the beginning. Then there was the matter of differing philosophies about trades teaching. This was going to be Hy's first big challenge since starting the job – changing a culture of comfort to a culture of achievement. It would have to be done a bit at a time. What might be some early strategic steps that Hy could take to accomplish some real change and relieve the pressure coming from the Board?

Dodging the Real Issue

Terry Castwell	Manager, Water's Edge Retirement Home (WERH)
Ben Castwell	Terry's father & former Water's Edge manager
Arden Carpenter	Facilities Supervisor, WERH
Ray Zell	WERH Advisory Council member

No one knew better than Terry Castwell that Water's Edge Retirement Home needed to be rebuilt. The old brick care facility had felt the feet of two generations – the present resident population and many of their parents. Water's Edge was a historic building in the city of Brookfield. It was the first care facility built in the region, in days when such projects represented visionary thinking. During the flood of 1935, it had provided temporary accommodation for local families as they waited for the water to subside and the mayor to authorize their return home. Terry was the second Castwell to be the Home's manager. Ben Castwell, Terry's father, had held the position for most of Terry's early years. That had led to a recent problem between the two. Ben was adamant that the Home should be preserved and Terry could already see the new building.

Nostalgia was about yesterday – this was today. The retirement home was not insulated, making it by far the most costly building in Brookfield to heat. It was an oven in May and June. It did not meet seismic standards and Brookfield was in a moderate risk earthquake zone. Chronic roof leaks had damaged the ceilings and walls; some residents had amused themselves sculpting the rotting wood around the windows. Cosmetically, Water's Edge looked pretty good, though, primarily because of the efforts of Arden Carpenter. Arden was the Water's Edge Facilities Supervisor.

Nothing was simple, Terry Castwell reflected. The Board had commissioned a facility review, and the report was clear. The building needed to be replaced, and soon. Almost everyone seemed finally to agree that there were problems, but there the agreement ended. Only the Board had managed to move beyond their memories. They had decided to build a new facility on the same property and demolish the old building. It was not an easy decision for the Board. The community was divided and feelings ran high. When it finally came to a vote, Wanda Keepit had captured it best – "We'll probably pay for this, but we really have no other choice."

Getting provincial approval was no problem. Authorization from the Ministry of Health to proceed with the project was slow, though. The community, convinced finally of the need to replace the building, was becoming impatient. The Residents' Advisory Council (RAC) meeting was evidence of that. The residents had responded enthusiastically to Ray Zell's suggestion that they send supporters to the capital to march on the legislature and lobby the members. The three-day trip was scheduled for the middle of next week.

That was when the battle lines were drawn. The division over demolition of the old building was not dead at all as it turned out. It was just covered over and the planned trip had uncovered it. Terry had predicted that there would be an open dispute over something and this proved to be the issue. The RAC had passed a motion to pay the travel and accommodation costs of twenty residents and supporters. One word described the feelings of residents and community, both those who agreed with the trip and expense payments and those who did not – *intense*. Some argued that the protest was a matter for the younger members of the community, that elderly residents should be at home playing bridge, not being used for TV news footage and as pawns in a much bigger game. Others saw it as a legitimate RAC venture and a valuable direct democracy experience for the residents. The groups facing off on the issue were remarkably similar to the two factions on the old Home/new Home issue and things had been said that would test relationships for some time to come. Much was riding on the outcome of this bitter argument. It might be labeled by an outsider as a tempest in a teapot, but insiders saw it as an awakening volcano. Terry wondered how the government would respond to the Home's demand for immediate action.

Explosion at High Valley

Pat Stanright   Principal, High Valley Secondary School
Mike Roscopic   Chemistry teacher at High Valley

It was clear to Pat that something definitive was needed to bring the High Valley staff together and change some attitudes. The Science Department would have to be the primary focus. Those teachers had an enviable group spirit but it was also exclusive. They had their own coffee room, although they hadn't cut themselves off from the main staffroom group entirely. Their achievement results were obvious. Displays, class discussions, everything reflected an emphasis on doing better than anyone else. They praised high achievers but seemed to do little extra for others. Pat wondered if they even saw the others except possibly as obstacles to ever higher average test scores. It was clear to all that Mike Roskopic was in charge, and he wasn't even the department head. Mike had been an award winner all his life and had carried that ethic into his classroom and into his relationships with the other science teachers.

It was crisis time now. For eight years, Mike and several other chemistry teachers from the secondary schools in Mountain School District had run the district-wide "Chemistry Explosion," a power test for senior students. There was an array of progressively more challenging activities with points to be won at every stage. Until now, Mike's students had *always* won, so no one had expected the ninth year's results. Not only did Mike students not win, they lost decisively. Even the local press wondered aloud what had gone wrong. "High Valley Experiments Fizzle," the headline had read.

Many were glad to see a break in what they felt had become a tiresome tradition. Nobody said much, but more than a few seemed happy to see Mike Roskopic brought back to real life. The students in Mike's classes and their parents, who had assumed that this year's group would continue an unbroken tradition of success, were openly critical. Others, who had felt that a different emphasis was necessary, thought the recent events offered a chance to make some changes in the Science Department's approach.

The effect on Mike Roskopic was not unanticipated. He was in turn angry, defensive, and quiet – mostly he was quiet. It was a problem, particularly because the department head position was coming up at year's end when the incumbent retired. Everyone, including Mike, had expected that the position would go his way. Yet Mike's attitude over the chemistry competition had raised serious questions about his suitability for the position. He refused to discuss the issue with Pat, saying angrily that nothing had changed -if he was suitable before, he was suitable now. Most of the Science Department members were used to Mike's reactions by now. They were supportive of him and correspondingly cool to the principal.

Somewhere in all of this there had to be an opportunity to 'rescue' Mike Roskopic, to alter the fiercely competitive atmosphere in the Science Department and as a result make a positive change in the whole school. But sometimes Pat doubted the possibilities. In the past, Mike had been passed over as department head by the selection committee in favor of others less volatile, and perhaps he should be again. Yet something told Pat that this could be an important decision in the life of High Valley Secondary School, if only the conflict with Mike Roscopic could be resolved. Pat wondered if there might be potential in the situation for an all-round win.

Firm Foundation

Bill D. Best	Executive Director, Future Foundation (FF)
Colin Allshots	FF manager responsible for Camp Fastwater
Stella Leader	FF library manager, advocate for adult literacy programming
Arden Carpenter	FF facilities manager
Penny Catcher	FF manager of finance

It would be a challenge, no doubt about that. The Future Foundation (FF) had struggled for several years since the departure of the organization's first executive director. Three replacements had come and gone over the following two years and some staff members had seized the opportunity provided by the lack of continuity in the executive office. Donations were down, particularly the large sustaining donations that had carried FF for many years. Some former board members had been defeated at the Society's Annual General Meeting, which had been a tumultuous call for a new look at the way FF went about its business as a broadly based service organization.

The Board's first big task had been to hire yet another new Executive Director. They had chosen Bill D. Best, an executive with a track record of success in rescuing troubled organizations and a strong interest in helping to create what he called "learning organizations." Best spent a familiarization week at FF before taking some holidays owed by the last organization, using that time as an opportunity to reflect and plan before starting work at FF. There was much to be done at the Foundation.

Bill's first familiarization trip visitor had been Colin Allshots. Colin was the manager of Camp Fastwater, the Foundation's most popular and best-supported venture. Colin had brought a scrapbook of newspaper clippings and a letter of support from the mayor, "Just as a bit of background for you to read," Colin had said. Colin was a name-dropper, Bill had noticed. He referred to the Board Chair as Tom, noting that the Chair's children were regular attendees at Camp Fastwater and that their father was "a fan" of this "flagship" program of the Foundation. Colin's main message, stated almost as an indisputable fact, was that Camp Fastwater would need a major cash infusion in the coming year's budget.

Bill had indicated to Foundation staff members that these initial conversations would be followed by a series of staff meetings to develop and recommend funding and other priorities for the next planning period. That was an unnecessary departure from a very satisfactory past practice,

Colin said. Previously, each manager had met with what Colin called "the Executive Director of the Day," then had submitted her or his own budget directly to the Board. Colin expressed concern that this expanded involvement would simply mean unnecessary meetings. He wondered why other staff should have a say in "the Camp's business."

Stella Leader was next. This was an impressive person, thought Bill. She provided a compact, clear summary of the Foundation's library service, a reading room of professional reference books accessible to staff and FF's client organizations and major donors. The list of titles was impressive and Stella seemed a thoroughly competent professional librarian.

Stella brought a copy of her proposal for a new FF service: an adult literacy program for which she had carried out a comprehensive community needs assessment. She had engaged a graduate student to design the study; it was evident that the data would be very useful. Clearly, there was both a community need and a demand, and the list of advocates was compelling – all of them people involved with the voluntary sector and community development. Stella voiced a concern, though. She thought it might be difficult to make this project look as impressive as other well-funded FF projects, and it could be overlooked in favor of, as she put it, "videos of kids on hiking trips." She seemed encouraged by Bill's plan to involve staff in the planning process and said she would bring to the first planning meeting a video of five people who had learned to read as adults.

Arden Carpenter was a man with a message – several messages, actually. The first was that he was a very capable facilities manager. Bill knew that to be the case, because Arden was well known in the area and a frequent consultant on major facilities projects elsewhere. Arden's reputation had brought a considerable amount of money to the Foundation. With his assured competence as the starting point for the discussion, Arden wanted to make it clear that his remaining on staff would be contingent on "better treatment" in both his own salary and his budget. He said he was tired of "all the money dribbling away," and asserted that FF's best advertising was to have a first-class set of facilities. Bill asked Arden to provide specifics. Arden responded only, "That's easy – a 20% increase to both. I'm grossly underpaid for my skill level, and the facilities always need more money."

It was probably good that Penny Catcher was last in the series of meetings, Bill Best had thought. What was needed now was a clear picture of the state of FF's finances and a perspective that might help in setting fiscal policy. Penny arrived with documentation – lots of it, in the form of a bulging binder of materials. Bill asked Penny for a concise summary, but Penny's response was first to ask for specific questions then identify pages where answers could be found. Clearly Penny was good on detail, but B.D. wondered whether she would be able to contribute to the larger effort – setting FF on a clear path to the future. She was most cooperative, suggesting as she left the office, "If you ever need any information, just let me know." She was also very complimentary about Camp Fastwater and Colin Allshots, indicating that she always made "a special effort" to provide "the little extras" that the camp program needed. Penny was less enthusiastic about Stella's literacy proposal, suggesting that key donors always wanted "something they could see."

To fulfill the mandate of the Board, Bill D. Best needed to understand the situation at FF. Step one was to contact a few friends for advice. It seemed there would need to be a good deal of organizational learning, including some changes in norms and expectations, if Future Foundation was to survive and prosper. The group met for an evening at a college where one of them worked. Their task? To think creatively about how their understandings of organizations could be applied productively at Future Foundation.

Français ou Anglais?

Terry Castwell	Principal, Water's Edge Elementary School
Jay McTaggart	Former Water's Edge principal
Y. & P. Duquette	Pro-French immersion parents
B. & D. English	Anti-French immersion parents

"Principal" – Terry remembered the satisfaction of finally seeing the sign on the office door. The first six months of being principal at Water's Edge had almost passed now. Until this week, the job had been a dream come true. Over the past 48 hours, though, Terry's dream had begun to fade to black.

Terry had replaced the retiring Jay McTaggart. Jay's management style, to put it mildly, had left both staff and parents ill at ease. The parents had long since given up trying to become involved with the school; few of them would even offer help.

Terry's arrival had changed all that very quickly. Word had spread like wildfire that the new principal was open, responsive, and welcoming. That initiative was aided by the tone set clearly in the School Act – it was evident that parents, and their advice, were to be welcomed in the schools as important advisers.

The fall had passed as quickly for Terry as for any new administrator. On the principal's "To Do" list, near the top, was: "Ensure Parents' Advisory Council is up and running." The problem was, there had been no time to do anything about it during the first six months.

Two recently scheduled meetings with parents, due to take place this morning, had moved the item from "Important" to "Urgent." The day before, Terry had received a letter from Yvonne and Pierre Duquette, confirming the next day's meeting with them about reactivating the Parents' Advisory Council, which had been shut down as a result of some old conflicts among the members. Just as Terry finished reading the Duquettes' letter, there was a call from Bill and Debbie English, who also wanted an appointment about the same topic. One before coffee and one after – who knew what was coming?

The Duquettes had been instrumental in convincing the Board to start the French immersion program at Water's Edge three years previously. It was ironic that Bill and Debbie English, who had been strong opponents of the idea, had called precisely when Terry was reading the letter from Yvonne and Pierre.

Terry could see it coming. It would be another round in an old battle that had been mentioned to the new principal several times – sets of parents with rival interests accusing others of trying to squeeze them out. As far as Terry knew, neither couple was aware that the other was coming to see the principal.

What on earth could be done? The seeds of conflict were certainly there; Terry knew that from previous experience. The school population was almost evenly divided between the regular English program and French immersion. Reflecting, Terry thought that maybe, subconsciously, that had been why the matter of the Parents' Advisory Council had always been pushed aside by more pressing matters. It was impossible for Terry to see how a single advisory committee could possibly work at Water's Edge. For now, though, preparing for today's appointments was a more pressing item, and it called for some hard thinking.

Fun, Funds, and Friction

Shawn Merritt	Principal, Memorial Secondary School
Colette Aday	Outgoing President, Memorial Secondary Parents' Advisory Council (PAC)
Marge Forward	Incoming President, Memorial Secondary Parents' Advisory Council (PAC)

It was going to be a lively meeting. There were at least three clear agendas and Shawn wondered whether they could be harmonized. All three had to do with Memorial's PAC: and they could be summarized facetiously as change nothing, change everything, and change thoughtfully. The problem was that all saw themselves as being in the third category.

Colette Aday had been President of the PAC for two years, following four years as a PAC executive member who was willing to take on almost any task presented. She had organized concessions at track meets, headed up raffle ticket sales and washed cars. In short, Colette had been largely responsible for the PAC's healthy financial situation. Colette's key word was *support*, and that was her view of the parents' role – to support the school in any way possible. Her gentler critics suggested that perhaps there were other dimensions, while those with harsher comments, such as Marge Forward, said blatantly that Colette was behind the times.

Marge Forward had little time for "nickel and dime stuff," as she called the PAC's traditional fund-raising activities. She saw an important fund-raising role for the parents, but in her view, bingo games were "a real cash cow." Marge felt that "penny ante" fund-raising events were far too labor-intensive to be worthwhile. Colette, on the other hand, saw them as opportunities to involve a much greater number of parents, to build school support and spirit. For a while nobody would budge. Colette, who may have felt that her efforts were being denigrated, eventually announced that she would step aside from the president's job and from her PAC involvement generally. Marge had a strong group of supporters and the PAC members saw little point in nominating anyone else.

To Shawn, it was tragic. Colette, through her enthusiasm and energy, had brought many parents a good deal closer to the school. According to staff members, there had been countless examples of cooperation and group effort over the past six years. Colette was never sulky or negative – that was one of her great leadership characteristics. Shawn could sense, though, that over the past few weeks, Colette had been drained of her enthusiasm.

Marge Forward, on the other hand, was a puzzle. She professed enthusiasm and support for the school, but she was also adamant that there was a much more important part for parents to play. She referred to them as "co-owners." In Marge's view, the school staff had an obligation to draw on parents' expertise in all key areas of decision making. The difficulty was that all of Marge's questions came across as challenges edged with suspicion. Probably not everyone shared Shawn's view though. Marge Forward was highly regarded by many people and some were beginning to echo her ideas.

In Shawn's view, there was room for both and both should be encouraged. There was a place for both big-time and small-time fund-raising projects. The school needed parents who wanted to influence policy and parents who wanted to serve refreshments. Shawn was sure that things would come to a head soon. As it turned out, there was not long to wait.

For the past five years, Memorial Secondary School had held an annual "family and friends" dinner. It had become a highly successful tradition. The dinner was always widely anticipated and fondly remembered but suddenly it looked like a disaster. The dinner had always been a pot-luck affair; Colette Aday had chaired the organizing committee and the event had been a great success every year. This year, however, things were different. Colette was to chair the committee for a final time, and things were not shaping up well. A group led by a couple of Marge's friends had argued for a catered meal on three grounds: potluck dinners raised the specter of food poisoning, parents could sit and enjoy their catered meal, and the dinner could be a great fund-raising opportunity. The contrary point of view said there had never been a problem with the food and that serving dinner was half the fun. It was a great opportunity to meet neighbors, not all of whom could afford to attend a fund-raising dinner. Besides, the family and friends dinner had a highly successful history and tradition.

This could be the great divide, Shawn thought. There was a lot at stake, far more than a dinner. Maybe it was a clash of two cultures, the helpers and the shapers. As principal, Shawn had stayed well back from trying to influence the PAC – perhaps that had been a mistake. If this was the time to get involved, where should the principal's focus be, on Colette Aday or on Marge Forward? There were risks however one looked at it .

Let's be Fair About This

Leslie Wingard	Spruce Ridge Superintendent of Schools
Pat Stanright	Principal, High Valley Secondary School
Andy Sellzit	High Valley Secondary School student
Hy and Stella Standing	Andy Sellzit's guardians, owners of Standing Timber
Needa Koolit	School trustee, Standing Timber Personnel Manager

Leslie Wingard stepped to the edge of the lake to look back at the cottage. What an incredible setting! The weekend had been a delight, spent with friends and family and talking about the future. Back to work tomorrow, though. Life as Superintendent of Schools in Spruce Ridge School District was not a lot of fun these days, with funding cutbacks and more and more government regulations – too much to keep up with, at least for anyone who wanted to do the best possible job through to the last days before retirement.

Leslie's first morning back to work got off to a good start but it didn't last long. Pat Stanright, a secondary principal, had an early appointment to see Leslie about a student suspension. Leslie opened the file to prepare for the meeting and saw a name that changed the face of Monday morning – Andy Sellzit. If there was any truth to the myth that names determine occupations, Andy's name certainly suited him. He had been suspended for drug possession before, and that was only one of his enforced breaks from school. The others probably stemmed from his drug involvement too – fights, thefts, and vandalism, mostly.

Pat arrived and explained the latest events. Andy Sellzit had been picked up again with drugs and the police had been called. The quantity and packaging of the drugs made it clear that they were for sale – as if the police had any doubt. They knew Andy Sellzit well.

Pat had tried everything to help this fifteen-year-old boy. The school had hired a child care worker who quit when Andy stole money from her purse. Pat had arranged a sponsored summer camp experience for Andy, only to find that it had led the school's least favorite entrepreneur to a whole new clientele for his drug sales. It was a petty drug operation, really, in the grand scheme of things, but Pat's concern was that Andy was being used by people with much bigger plans and activities. After this most recent episode, Pat had suspended Andy indefinitely, and this morning's meeting with the superintendent was to review the suspension report.

The school staff knew that Pat was going to see the superintendent. To a person, they were finished with Andy. He had caused endless disruption in their classes and almost everyone on the staff had found him to be unmanageable. The school had tried everything, and Pat was concerned there would be an outright revolt if Andy came back this time. Pat was adamant that he must not return. Privately, Leslie Wingard wished that the principal would soften a bit and look at the situation more broadly.

By Tuesday, Leslie Wingard knew there was trouble ahead. Andy Sellzit's guardians were Hy and Stella Standing, owners of a veneer plant that provided jobs for many of the town's work force. Their home on the top of Bear Hill was positioned over the town in what seemed to be exactly the spot Hy and Stella thought was right for people of their place in society. There was no doubt that over the years the Standings had been a pair of powerful voices in a lot of things in town that mattered and some that did not. Hy Standing was President of the Lakewood Business Council. Leslie Wingard was a Business Council member, and today was meeting day. Leslie dreaded seeing Hy because of what was coming – it was always the same.

Leslie was right. Hy Standing realized that this indefinite suspension was more serious than the others, and he and Stella were having none of it. As always, Hy was very pleasant but his goal was clear – to get Andy back in school as quickly as possible. This time, though, Hy played a trump card – if the suspension wasn't reversed, the family would file a complaint with the provincial Ombudsman, whose mandate included assessing administrative fairness in schools. Leslie didn't think the Standings' standing in Lakewood could influence an Ombudsman's investigation, but one never knew about these things. You could be sure, nevertheless, that the Standings would fight hard to have their way, and they were used to winning. Leslie also knew that a phone message from the Board's Student Services Committee Chair would be waiting back at the office.

Sure enough, there was a pink slip on the desk from Needa Koolit when Leslie returned. That conversation had a familiar ring to it too. Needa always spoke of wanting to act in the best interests of the child, although it seemed to Leslie that Needa's position as Personnel Manager at Standing Timber had to be a factor. The message was clear. Needa wanted the problem of Andy Sellzit's suspension resolved without it going to the Board and definitely without the Ombudsman becoming involved.

By Wednesday, retirement was looking more attractive than any other kind of future planning. Leslie didn't want any more bumps on the road, and this one had the potential to be a major pothole. Leslie met with Pat Stanright to indicate that it was clear the Board wouldn't support a long suspension, a transfer out, or an expulsion. It would be in everyone's interests to shorten the suspension and get Andy back in school.

Pat left the Superintendent's office feeling angry. This wasn't about Andy Sellzit, or his welfare, or the school. It was about Leslie Wingard's retirement, Needa Koolit's job, and the Standings' preservation of their image and status. It was also harmful to Andy. Pat was also a bit uncertain about next year's appointment renewal. Clearly, all of the district's administrators reported to the Superintendent, and this year was scheduled for contract renewal consideration for several of them. Beyond that, though, there was the school staff. Pat had worked hard to gain their respect over the past four years but it always seemed that there was one more test to pass.

Lobbying for Learning

Terry Castwell   Teacher, Water's Edge Elementary School
Hope Formor   Teacher, Water's Edge Elementary School
M. and S. Watching   Parents of a gifted child
Farley Shore   President of ACE (All Children's Education)

Water's Edge Elementary School, which previously had held two separate classes of special needs students transported from around the district, had been the site of the district's pilot program of inclusion/integration. The goal had been to develop a model for application throughout the district. The project had been watched closely by government and it now appeared that the Water's Edge pilot program had become a model for the whole province. The students were placed in regular classes, with support staff hired to work with individual students. Terry Castwell and Hope Formor, a key teacher on staff, were in demand as speakers and resource people for other districts and schools preparing to respond to the new provincial focus on inclusion.

There were still entrenched forces on all sides of the issue. The parents of the former "special class" students involved were both excited about the inclusion program and adamant that nothing should interfere with it. There was a new issue, however, and it reminded everyone that the Parkside School Board's pioneering inclusionary initiative still was not accepted by everyone. The budget 'crunch' had made that clear. The Board was under heavy pressure to cut costs and they were seeking community input and suggestions. Several discussion groups had sprung up around particular issues; the Board had scheduled a series of special community meetings as the deadline for finalizing the budget approached.

The determination of parents whose children were now included in regular classes had been strengthened recently by a presentation to the school board from a group led by Mary and Steven Watching. The Watchings' daughter was gifted, there was no doubt about that. Her parents were also adamant that nothing would interfere with their daughter's school life. They saw the inclusion program as an intolerable interference with their family's priorities and had fought it from the start. The Watchings were not popular in Parkside and their arguments had generally been dismissed by many as elitist and self-serving. But not by everyone.

The Watchings had gathered a group of parents around them to propose that because of the severe fiscal situation, support staffing for the inclusion program should be reduced significantly for a year. The special needs students would be grouped together for half the day as an "efficiency measure." Some wondered if the one-year parameter of the proposal was related to the fact that the Watchings' daughter would be finished elementary school by then, rather than being simply "a practical recognition" of the fact that provincial policy as yet was uncertain. They expressed concern about the cost of inclusion, extrapolating the figures to display their version of the financial implications of the province's incoming policy. In tough times, they said, society simply could not support this new and unproved venture. The Watching Group, as it had become known, was also building its connections with provincial politicians.

The Board, though, had made its commitments clear – they were going to continue the inclusion program one step ahead of the rest of the province. The trustees had a long-standing commitment to equality of opportunity; they looked forward to being a beacon for other schools and districts. Terry Castwell and the Water's Edge staff were enthusiastic and they had both the support and the determination of the Board behind their efforts.

There was an uproar in the community now, no doubt about that. Parents and others were polarized in a way Terry had not seen before. There was a new group to be considered, too – All Children's Education (ACE). Many of their children had been in the old special classes and these parents were committed to the new program. They refused even to call it a pilot. In the words of their President, Farley Shore, "We've waited a long time for this. There's no turning back now."

To complicate matters further, Terry and Hope were committed to a round of Ministry of Education-sponsored speaking engagements intended to raise awareness of and support for inclusionary educational practices. Both were away from the school more than they wanted to be and some of the staff were becoming resentful of this in view of the turmoil surrounding the school. All in all, it was a difficult situation, this collision of wills.

Midnight Madness

Leslie Wingard	Southside Superintendent of Schools
Stan Fast	School trustee
Mark Mywords	School trustee
Needa Koolit	School Board Chair

Trustee Items. Leslie knew it had no legitimate place on the agenda for the Board Meeting. It was the last item on the page, an invitation to . . . who knew what? The new Board had moved quickly to change the agenda policy and add that category despite the Superintendent's argument that it ran counter to every principle of effective board operation. They had even voted, despite a few disregarded protests from 'the old guard', to waive the Board's carefully developed 'policy on policy', which assured that all proposed changes would be thoroughly debated, with notice of motion and input from senior staff and others affected.

The new trustees, it seemed, couldn't care less about established procedure. They had added a new standing item to the end of the Board meeting agenda – Trustee Items. For this item, it wasn't even necessary that trustees advise the Board of what they planned to bring up. The staff had come to call it the "Titanic Item."

The time had come. The meeting had been unusually civilized, Leslie had thought. Even Stan Fast and Mark Mywords had been particularly polite to each other, an unusual departure for the two trustees, one 'old guard' and the other 'new broom', who usually seemed barely able to tolerate each other's presence in the Board Room. Maybe no one would have an item to discuss.

"Moving now to the last section of the agenda – Trustee Items. Does anyone have anything to raise?"

Blast Needa! She always made it sound like an invitation to a banquet. The only problem was that the entree was almost always 'Chef's Surprise' and the surprise was often for Leslie.

"Madam Chairman." (Needa always insisted on the traditional term).

"Trustee Fast."

"Before I begin, let me say that this is a matter of personnel policy, not a personnel matter, so it belongs properly in this open meeting, not in the closed session."

"Some of you may have read in the paper that Martin Weary has left his position as Superintendent in Rutherford – personal reasons, I'm told. It seems people in these positions stay only for a certain number of years, then move on. It's a tough game and I guess it takes its toll after a while. Whether that's the case or not, we've got to be prepared. We know our own Superintendent isn't planning to leave, and that's good, but who knows how things can change? I've checked our policies and we have nothing in place in the event that our Superintendent should leave. That could be a problem, especially if something should happen on short notice."

"There's a related problem, too. It's important that the Superintendent and the Board know exactly how they feel about each other. I'm sure Superintendent Wingard (how polite, Leslie thought) would welcome that."

"I'd like to propose a motion – That the Board strike a committee to develop a policy on superintendent performance evaluation and a policy on the personnel search process as it applies to the executive officers – superintendent and assistant superintendents."

The outcome was predictable. Everyone was tired. The idea seemed to make sense to the trustees, and Leslie noticed that some welcomed the motion with what seemed to be a little more than the usual 'adjournment time enthusiasm'.

"Moved by Trustee Fast. Seconder? Trustee Mywords. Discussion? . . . Ready for the question? All in favor? Carried."

Office Parties

Claire Wallace   Office Manager, Hillside Property Management
Mary Parker   Claire's predecessor at Hillside
Leslie Borden   President of Hillside Property Management

Claire Wallace's mandate was clear. Over a three-year period the head office operation at Hillside Property Management had slipped from being a competent group of 12 people clear about and committed to the company's goals. Now the sales and service staff often jokingly referred to the office as the "Hillside Social Cub." There was plenty of laughter in the office, much of it directed behind the back at clients and at staff from the Company's other offices. No one's birthday went unnoticed. *Relaxed* was the watchword.

For the previous three years, the office had functioned under the less-than-watchful eye of Mary Parker. To the dismay of those in the head office and to the relief of almost everyone else, Mary had been encouraged by the president to move on to other opportunities. The President had liked Mary's breezy style, but when clients began to complain about "slackness" in the office operation, the bottom line suddenly moved into sharp focus and things changed.

Clare Wallace, Mary's replacement, understood "work ethic." She had grown up through some tough times with parents who stressed hard work, routine and responsibility. For the most part things had gone pretty well for Claire in her jobs. Claire's style had not sat well with everyone – too brisk and rigid, some said. But no one ever questioned Claire's ability to organize, to plan, or to manage the budget.

For Claire, some things were basic. You arrived at the office in good time, ready to start work as soon as the office opened (punctually, of course). Coffee break was 15 minutes, lunch was on a regular schedule, and output was crucial – you simply must get the work done.

Claire's first year at HPM had been a challenge. Most of the office staff members were considerably younger than Claire; none of them could match her more than 20 years of experience working in business offices. Claire had a depth of experience and maturity second to none; everyone recognized her skill. A few, though, wondered whether she could ever acknowledge that her ways were not always either the best or the only ways. Sour grapes, thought Claire.

All of the office staff members were well trained and ambitious. They were phenomenal at producing finished work on time and of high quality under the right circumstances. They usually caught on quickly. Claire seldom had to repeat instructions and some staff members even challenged a few of her routines with rather good ideas of their own. If only the rest of the picture was that positive.

More than occasionally, someone would show up a few minutes late or would not be at all brisk about getting started on the day's work. Some of them were more casual about the length and time of their breaks than Claire preferred – lunch seemed to be 'a flexible feast', with 12:50 about as good as 12:30. Outside activities were not only a topic of conversation, they sometimes interfered with the wok at hand. Requests for time off were not overly frequent, but to Claire, they usually seemed unnecessary. After all, there were routines, and routines were important. A salary was not intended as a gift. Somehow they were of two worlds – the office manager who prided herself on an efficient, predictable organization and staff with impressive skills but with some impatience where regularities and routines were concerned.

Clearly, Claire's staff group was not completely happy. They were polite and cooperative enough but there was always a reserve. Claire could not square their obvious skills with their less-than-enthusiastic support for her routines. On the surface and to outsiders things seemed just fine, but Claire had a growing sense of uneasiness that under the surface all was not well.

The wall of polite resistance was growing. The work sent in by junior sales staff, some of them top producers, seemed always to be done last. If there was work to be done for the 'favored few', or if an office event was coming up, deadlines were sometimes missed, resulting occasionally in lost contracts. Phones were the company's lifeline, but Claire had begun to realize that their constant ringing was not so much an indicator of increased business as a measure of careless delays in answering.

Hillside's president Leslie Borden was becoming troubled about the state of things. The hope had been that Claire Wallace would be able to get the head office back on track. Leslie knew that the company could not afford many more 'golden handshakes' of the sort given to Mary Parker, and that staff continuity and customer perception were vital in a corporation with a client base the size of Hillside's. Leslie had a 'heart-to-heart' with Claire – things must change, and fast. The plan would have to be non-intrusive though. HPM could not afford a major upset.

In Claire's mind, the gentle approach would be a waste of time and money. Definite guidelines and consequences were needed – Claire could handle that. Clearly, though, reversing the situation would be a challenge. Usually, Claire's offices had been models of efficiency and productivity. This situation was both new and troubling.

ONE POCKET TO ANOTHER

A.J. Wrestall — Metropolitan Hospital CEO
Les Risk — Board member, Chair of Facilities Committee
Frieda Grant — Past president, Metropolitan Hospital Nurses Federation (MHNF)
Trace Watts — Supervisor of Technical Services

Values, interests, and agendas – it seemed to A.J. Wrestall that they all came out of hiding when the topic was money. The positive side of it, though, was that the debate, though vigorous and often angry, was open and continuing. At least the Metropolitan community had taken seriously the Board's request for input. The difficulty was that dollars always seemed to be the only measuring stick. Budget decisions were seen as the single best test of the Board's priorities and commitments, and the idea that there might be other ways to assess effectiveness seemed to have been lost in the latest furor.

On the face of it, the question seemed simple enough: Does cost-cutting mean automatically that all budget decisions must be reductions? A.J. thought not. After all, the decision to hire an Energy Management Coordinator during the previous round of budget cutbacks had saved far more on an annual basis than its accompanying personnel and support costs. That had been well documented in the newspaper and the program had received strong editorial support. The beauty of it was that the energy savings were easily quantified using fixed costs and past years' records as support. The latest proposal was different however.

Partnership was the wave of the future and Metropolitan Hospital was prepared to ride it, beginning with technology. The discussions with computer hardware and software companies had begun when financial times were better in the health care system. But now that tight times had come, partnering with the corporate world seemed to make even better sense. No one was under any delusions; companies had their own agendas and they knew that hospitals were a lucrative market and a good place to create product awareness among citizens. The benefits to the hospital were also clear. By becoming an experimental project site, Metropolitan could have access to cutting edge technology at a fraction of the cost, which was also the only cost this cash-strapped hospital could afford these days.

It had become increasingly clear to both trustees and senior staff that clear policy had to be in place first. The policy initiative made it clear that the possibilities of partnership were endless and as yet relatively untapped.

A couple of small bad experiences, though, had sharpened the focus on coordination – this could not be a free-wheeling department-by-department effort. Board member Trustee Les Risk had been impressed by the results of the energy management program, a project of the Facilities Committee, and had convinced the Board that hiring a technology partnership coordinator would be a similar cost-saving initiative. Creation of the new position was discussed and approved at the public Board meeting.

The MHNF and the Metropolitan Support Staff Council (MSSC), facing staff cuts in the fall, were incensed at the proposed hiring. Both groups had responded with noticeable reluctance to the Board's request for cost-saving suggestions. The MSSC had offered several suggestions that could reduce supply costs and the nurses' group had agreed to measures that would help to reduce replacement staff costs. The latest staffing announcement had brought the two groups together, and they had issued a rare joint press release decrying the decision. Frieda Grant, a past president of MHNF, had met with the press, choosing the moment to question the credibility of the Board's most recent decision.

The position of Supervisor of Technical Services had been dormant for six months, because Trace Watts, whose job had mainly involved computer network support, had been on an extended leave. Trace was due to return in a month but not without difficulties. Talk had it that Trace's absence had proved one thing – the job was not required. MSSC staff who had filled the gap saw no need for Trace's position. Trace was a longtime employee, though, and a technical expert, albeit one whose entrepreneurial talents could probably best be described as latent. Perhaps, A.J. thought, Trace Watts could simply be reassigned to the new position, freeing the Board to eliminate the Supervisor of Technical Services position. After all, the job had been one of MSSC's targets during budget discussions. This would make it clear that the Board had listened.

The two staff groups had a different view. The new position, they said, was simply a way of protecting an administrator. At the very least, they insisted, there would have to be a two-stage process – eliminate the Supervisor of Technical Services position, partly as a cost-saving measure, then hold a competition for the new job. In their view, the new position was unnecessary, though it demanded a different set of skills. "It's just another case," said Frieda Grant, "of this Board ignoring the needs of its rank and file workers."

Pressing Matters

Brian Passmore	Owner, Passmore Press
Abe Passmore	Brian's father
Bud and Stan	Pressmen at Passmore
Bonnie and Diane	Graphic artists at Passmore
Margaret Greenshade	Passmore Press accountant
Advance Printing	Competition for Passmore Press

Brian Passmore loved the printing business. Both his father and his grandfather were printers before him and Passmore Press had been a going concern for more than 50 years. One generation of the family after another had built a solid base of clients both in and out of town.

The Passmores prided themselves on three generations of efficiency and productivity. Their presses were models of maintenance. Abe Passmore, Brian's father, still dropped in to the shop almost every day to admire the equipment he had loved for so long and to reminisce with employees about the many years of unchallenged success the Press had enjoyed.

Brian sometimes wished he had trained formally for the business, but he had just 'grown into it'. "Printer's ink is in your veins," his mother had often said proudly. Times had been good and there had always been plenty of profitable work. For years, Passmore Press had been the only printing shop in town. Abe Passmore had prided himself on the stability of the company he had passed on to his son. Too much change, he had often said, wasn't good for any business. Passmore Press had always offered its clients top quality printing, and they had held costs down by limiting their product range. The lack of competition had made that a fairly simple task.

Their staff was long-term and loyal. Press operators Bud and Stan knew their equipment inside out. Bonnie and Diane were capable self-made graphic artists. All four had been with Passmore Press for more than a decade.

The family had felt confident and secure for many years. Profits were solid, business was stable, and life was comfortable. Among the employees, only Bud seemed to have been restless lately. He had been away on several training courses recently and had brought back a host of ideas for new equipment and products (all expensive, Brian mused, and mostly unnecessary – why upset things?). In fact, the tension was beginning to mount; a degree of impatience seemed to be spreading among the staff.

It was annoying to Brian to constantly see Bud talking animatedly with the others about new ways of doing things and bringing in brochures about the latest equipment. What was the problem? Salaries were good, the equipment was old but well maintained, and there had always been a generous year-end bonus for each staff member. All of that should be enough to keep anyone happy. Bud had a knowledge edge, of course, and the others recognized that. He had learned a lot about equipment-related matters. Increasingly, people were acknowledging Bud as an expert.

The other nuisance was an upstart quick-print operation that had moved in just two blocks away. That was one shop too many, Brian thought. Within three months, Advance Printing had made noticeable inroads into Passmore's business (mostly with gimmicks, from Brian's perspective). Advance advertised an array of products and options well beyond what the older company was offering, and they had some new and fast equipment. Brian knew, though, that the newcomers would not be able to fulfill all of their promises – at least not unless their business grew fast and substantially.

Bud, of course, saw the new business as an opportunity to talk up his ideas about new equipment and innovative product offerings. He asked Brian to hold a full staff meeting to discuss what he called "a changing scene that could have consequences for all of us." The meeting had been worthwhile, Brian Passmore had reflected. At least it had given Abe Passmore's son an opportunity to remind everyone of the company's basic values and commitments: integrity, stability, and satisfaction. He was sure that would put an end to the fuss.

Margaret Greenshade, the company's accountant, was also becoming a problem. Profits had shown a bit of a slip lately and Margaret seemed to think it could be a sign of things to come. She must have been talking to Bud because she too had suggested that the company purchase some new, more versatile and faster equipment. Easy for her to say, Brian thought – it wasn't her wallet.

Things suddenly took a turn for the worse. Passmore Press had always had a strong, high-profit business in invitations, stationery, and certificates. People had always preferred not to send their specialty printing out of town. Passmore had always paid great attention to detail. People had been used to waiting a reasonable length of time for a quality product from a local business. The Stanley machine had done all of that work reliably for many years. Bud, though, referred to it as a "museum piece" and "the Stanley Steamer." He knew that eventually, finding parts for the Stanley would be a problem. Now it was broken and Bud had said, "I warned you, Brian."

The new shop had moved in quickly. Their turnaround time was amazingly fast. Their options seemed limitless, not to mention their ability to offer printing at very attractive prices. Even the do-it-yourselfers and the desktop publishing entrepreneurs in town were hard pressed to keep up. Advance was undercutting Passmore's prices and people had begun to talk. Where was customer loyalty, Brian wondered. He talked to his father, which eased his mind. "Passmore Press has been here for almost 60 years," Abe had said, "and this is just a passing phase – our quality and reputation will win out." The trouble was, Advance's quality seemed to be pretty good as well.

Even Bonnie and Diane seemed restless. Bonnie, who had always been punctual and missed very little time, had been away from work several times recently and somehow she seemed less focused than usual on her work. Diane was beginning to talk about going back to school. Brian wondered why – Diane was an excellent graphic artist, producing top-notch design work even without all the latest software.

Then Bud asked to meet with Brian – that was a shocker! The new shop, Bud said, had offered him a position. The pay was slightly less, which made no sense to Brian, but Bud said he would have a chance to work with state-of-the-art equipment and even recommend purchases. Bud did not want to leave Passmore Press, he said, but he was worried about the future. Stars in his eyes, thought Brian – just the glitter of fancy new equipment that probably wouldn't last. Somehow, that didn't seem to bother Bud. He talked about "technological change" and "five-year shelf life." He asked about Brian's medium-term plans for Passmore Press (no business of his, thought Brian) and suggested another staff meeting for an open discussion.

Restoration Project

Robin Willing   Volunteer worker at the Century Village project
Colin Allshots   Executive Director, Century Village project

The words on the invitation caught Robin's eye: "Our precious volunteers – the lifeblood of our organization." The note went on to invite the group to attend an annual banquet "to celebrate our achievements in community service over the past year." That sounded good. Robin and the others enjoyed their work with the Association. This would be a great time to get together and share the highlights.

The Century Village project had captured the town's heart and imagination from the start. The once-dying town of Century was now alive with the energy of restoration and revitalization. The scenic beauty and recreational opportunities of the area were a natural draw, but that had not been enough because other towns in the Rolling Hills area enjoyed similar natural benefits. Century's competitive edge lay in the fact that several key firms had recently located there, bringing with them a vigorous and energetic employee population. This group was marked by leadership; many of them had brought their talents to bear through the Century Development Foundation, the sparkplug for the old city's Century Village restoration project.

In the early stages it had been a volunteer project led by a locally elected board with a system of committees that spearheaded specific projects. From the start, Century Village had been a going concern. As the number and complexity of projects grew it became apparent that paid staff would be needed, even though some board members and volunteers feared growing impersonality and a loss of community feeling. The board had hired the vigorous and ambitious Colin Allshots as Executive Director to lead the project through the transition to the second phase of its organizational life. The directors, rolling in the substantial income from visitors, had provided him a high-end salary. Some were suspicious that Colin might also be receiving a performance bonus based on income from visitors. Whatever the truth, the pressure was on – bring them in and get their money. The new income stream was welcome news for many in the once-sleepy town.

Not all agreed. Some volunteers had left during Colin's first year, simply saying that they were "too busy" or that they needed "more time with family." Colin seemed unperturbed. He simply hired students at minimum wage as guides and laborers, confident in the knowledge that Century Village provided one of the few such employment opportunities in town. Eventually he disbanded the Volunteer Advisory Group that previously had provided valuable feedback to the board from visitors and workers alike. "Needs had changed," Colin had said.

Robin was among the remaining group of volunteers, each with a long history of involvement in the Century Village project, each with much to offer. Just as hope was beginning to fade, Robin thought, there seemed to be some acknowledgement that the volunteers were valued. Then the details on the bottom of the invitation loomed large. The "precious volunteers" were told that tickets for the dinner would cost $25.00 each, and that following the evening's festivities, all would be "given an opportunity to make a pledge as an investment in the future of the Century Village project."

The phone began to ring. Robin was one of the first volunteers, and had recently chaired the now-defunct Volunteer Advisory Group, so the calls were not unexpected. Robin soon realized that this was more than a small matter among people torn between civic pride and a sense that something good had been lost. To make matters worse, Colin Allshots' administrative assistant was calling each of the volunteers "just to make sure you're coming to the dinner." Any who declined or hesitated were cut off abruptly. For Robin, it was the last straw when the secretary sent a message to volunteers asking for their assistance in securing donations for door prizes "to keep our costs down."

The word was out, it seemed. In Colin Allshots' absence, the board asked to meet with the members of the former Volunteer Advisory Group to address the matter. In a note, they asked the group to prepare responses to several questions: (1) Do we have a problem, and if so, what are the facts and details? (2) What are those facts and details 'saying to us?' What is the message? And (3) What should be done, immediately and over the longer term? Robin saw this as an opportunity both to respond and to educate the Board, especially with Colin Allshots away. After all, the Board had taken the initiative and Robin was their employee.

SLIPPERY SLOPES

Mary Well	Principal of Prosperville Elementary School in Prosperville
Handel Well	Spouse of Mary Well and sole owner of Handel's Sports Shop, Dollartown
Ben Waiting	Grade 7 teacher at P'Ville Elementary, friend of Handel Well
Morry Looksatit	Prosperville Elementary Parents' Council executive member
Wanda Chekkit	Manager of Robbie's Sports in Dollartown

No one would call Prosperville a wealthy community these days. Unemployment was high, mainly because Prosper Industries, the mill that everyone had assumed would be there forever, was no longer. For a few months, people had dreamed that the owners would keep their promise to re-open, but those hopes were dashed when the auction was announced. Everything was sold in a single weekend.

Prosperville hadn't faced tough times like this before, but probably because of their long history and their common occupational bond, the town had pulled together. A few people had found jobs half an hour down the road in Dollartown, and a few had started small enterprises of their own, but all in all, the outlook was pretty bleak.

Mary and Handel Well hadn't intended to stay long in Prosperville but the two or three years they had originally planned had stretched to ten. It was hard to think about leaving. The place had been good to them. Besides, Handel had opened Handel's Sports Shop, a project he had dreamed of for years, on the edge of Dollartown to serve both communities. It was off to a good start – at least it had been until the closing of Prosper Industries. Mary and Handel were surprised at how much business had dropped off until they realized that both communities had been badly affected by the mill closure in Prosperville. Dollartown was Prosperville's main shopping area. Handel's store was new and most of the Dollartown people had stayed on with Robbie's Sports, which had been around for years.

They were starting to hurt, no doubt about it. Mary was glad she had the principalship. Handel owned the sporting goods store, so in plain business terms there was no connection, but the income from the store had provided a few of life's nice extras.

When the auction took place, Mary and Handel realized it was over for Prosperville, and maybe for their store, too, unless they could come up with some new ideas. The one thing that might pull the town through was its community spirit. P'Ville Elementary, as it was called locally, had never had any problems raising money through the parents and the community. In turn, the P'Ville Parents' Council had managed their money well. They were sitting on a five-digit bank account at the moment – not bad for a school in Prosperville these days.

Handel had thought of the idea one Saturday as he drove past several children who, it seemed, had little to do – what about cross-country skiing? What a great chance for some community focus – the kids would benefit, and so would the town as a whole. Logically, given the tight times, the school should own the equipment and loan it out. And if he managed it right, there would be an added benefit – a healthy sale for Handel's Sports Shop.

Mary was the key. Timing was everything and Handel would have to make sure that the cross-country idea was sold to the parents at just the right moment. The Council had the money, they were concerned about the effects of the current economic situation on their children, and the season was approaching fast. At all costs, though, Handel would have to avoid a call for tenders because that would bring Robbie's Sports into the picture.

Handel held on to his idea until he was sure that it was too late for Robbie's to get in on the act. At that time of year, and especially in those quantities, equipment was in short supply. Handel approached Olympic Distributors. Although his line of credit was pretty well extended, Handel knew Olympic would take the chance, because his profits would mean payment of some old invoices. Olympic agreed to supply 200 sets of equipment, all they could get their hands on. They could make it available for 48-hour delivery.

Handel left it as long as he could, then proposed his idea to Mary. He was both surprised and pleased by her response. Mary knew the sporting goods business as well as Handel did, but she didn't ask the obvious question: How would the school ever get that much equipment so late in the year? Mary agreed to present the idea to the P'Ville Parents' Council that week. Handel knew it was in the bag then. Mary's enthusiasm was always infectious and the fact that she was not a voting member of the Council was not a problem. They were looking for a project that would inject some life into the community as winter set in. They passed the motion and asked their secretary to try and locate some equipment in the local area.

That part was easy enough. The parents wanted action now and Handel knew that Robbie's couldn't deliver on time. Even if Robbie's inquired with the wholesalers about delivery, they wouldn't know that Handel's Sports Shop had reserved all the available equipment. Olympic Distributors was close-mouthed with its client information, and anyway, Robbie's Sports usually dealt elsewhere. The parents were pleased to be able to buy from Handel's. Mary was well liked.

The only wrinkle was Morry Looksatit, a member of the Parents' Council Executive. Morry always wanted to ask questions, but he was also easily diverted. Handel's good friend Ben Waiting was a teacher at P`Ville Elementary and he knew Morry well. Ben's grade seven class would have a chance for a winter's skiing before moving on to the secondary school. Ben agreed to have a drink with Morry and sell him on the benefits of cross-country skiing. Ben said, "It'll cost you – if I'm going to sell skiing to Morry, I'll have to try it myself, and I don't have any equipment." Handel looked after that. The season went well. Cross-country skiing was a big hit and the P'Ville Parents' Council cheque helped to keep things afloat at the store. Morry Looksatit bought right in -- he soon became a regular.

Wanda Chekkit, Manager of Robbie's, was a problem. She had driven out from Dollartown to visit the school and take a look at the skis, and had expressed surprise that Handel's had been able to get that much equipment from Olympic. When she had called, the year's stock was all gone and there would be no more until next season. Wanda even suggested that the purchase needed a closer look. Mary and Handel discussed the matter, and agreed that for the coming year at least, it would be better not to push for a second order.

It wasn't that simple. Wanda Chekkit and Robbie's had complained to the School Board and Mary was in the hot seat. She had to meet with a Conflict of Interest Commissioner who had been appointed by the Board to conduct an inquiry. Handel decided to lend her some moral support and book his own appointment with the Commissioner. After all, business was business was business, and he was the sole owner of his company. Anyway, the Parents' Council could buy from whatever source they wished. Ben and Mary arrived for their appointments just in time to see Ben Waiting being ushered in to see the Commissioner.

Straight Goods

Weir Watson   Finance Minister, Province of New Ground
Susan Steamer   President, Centreville Hospital Employees
                      Union (CHEU)
Merritt Sachance   Negotiator for the Hospital

It had all been very clear at the bargaining meeting. After a marathon session lasting well past midnight, the Board and the Centreville Hospital Employees Union had finally reached agreement on the last few points. Both groups knew they had been moving rapidly toward a showdown, either a full-scale strike or a lockout. CHEU had ruled out any more half measures such as rotating department-by-department strikes.

That particular strategy had certainly backfired. The CHEU membership knew that their quest for more dollars on the table would be fruitless, especially since Finance Minister Weir Watson had presented the budget in the legislature. It was only a few days after that when the grumbling started among the CHEU membership. Some of them were starting to feel the pinch of several days' lost pay and the CHEU had no more money in the coffers to provide more than a token. Susan Steamer was on the spot, no doubt about that. She had masterminded the whole negotiations strategy from the beginning. She and her close colleagues were adamant about the need for strong action.

Anyway, they now had a firm offer on the table that would take care of the one contentious remaining issue – control of staff development funds. Merritt Sachance really couldn't see why a minor item such as this should hold up a contract. Merritt thought that maybe it had to do with Susan's need to save face with the CHEU members. Their vote to call off rotating strikes and work-to-rule activities, which had been moved from the floor at the recent general meeting, had been a personal blow to her.

CHEU had called a meeting to discuss and vote on the contract settlement offer. Their bargaining team had told the Board they would take the package to their membership but would take a neutral position on it – no recommendation. The Board had protested that this was not a "good faith" stance, but Susan, who had been the only spokesperson after the CHEU team's final caucus, had said that they were not of one mind about the package. "In the best interests of patient care, though," Susan had said, "we will take this back to the members and let them decide."

The meeting had taken place. The outcome, though, was unusual. Apparently several CHEU members, unhappy with the presentation made by their negotiating team, had called for a second meeting to be held a week later so that they could have time to think about the offer. The word had come back informally that Susan Steamer had controlled discussion at the meeting. It had been held on a Friday afternoon with about 80 of 800 CHEU members present – hardly an impressive turnout. What bothered Merritt most, though, was that apparently Susan had misrepresented the terms of the offer on the two remaining items and had introduced something that had never been discussed during negotiations – payout of accrued sick leave on departure.

Apparently the other members of the negotiating team had been aghast, to judge by the looks on their faces, but Susan, "in the interests of time," had moved the discussion along. It seemed, though, that she had used that non-item to allege that Merritt Sachance, as the Board's negotiator, had taken her aside and told her that the Board would withdraw the entire offer package if the CHEU introduced the item.

That was an outright lie. Merritt Sachance knew it and Susan Steamer knew it. As far as Merritt was concerned, it was an outright attempt to sabotage the outcome of negotiations. Yet Merritt had two problems. A few people who worked in the District Office were CHEU members; if word got out that Merritt knew about Susan's remarks the finger of suspicion would point directly at them. It had happened before. The other problem was that Susan's allegations were about an alleged private meeting that actually had never taken place – an effective strategy.

It was frustrating to think that this might derail things. They were so close to a settlement. Merritt knew that if the CHEU had been presented with a firm recommendation on the package from the negotiating team they would have accepted it. Yet it seemed that Susan's piece of fiction could mess things up. Clearly, she wanted the offer to be rejected. The sad part was that the rest of the team didn't seem to be able or willing to speak up.

The Board's negotiating team had called an emergency meeting. They had decided that the matter of honest reporting to the CHEU membership had to be discussed. They managed to get the CHEU team to agree to a meeting and decided that one ground rule would have to be set. Since the matter at issue was an alleged meeting between Merritt and Susan, only those two would speak to the matter. Merritt said that proposing that parameter would bring an immediate end to the meeting but the Board's team members were adamant. Thinking things through that evening, Merritt wondered if they were attaching some credibility to Susan's story. After all, Susan had said that she had been "taken aside" for "a private meeting," so who really knew the truth? Again, a good strategy. Susan would assume that Merritt was planning to apply for a senior management position. Planting the seeds of mistrust carried the potential to introduce some doubt into trustees' minds in a vital area – trust.

Takeover

Tom Stanley   Previous principal of Lakewood Secondary School
Dan Steele   Current principal of Lakewood Secondary School
Marion Corwin   President of Lakewood Parents' Advisory Council

Tom Stanley had been retired for 18 months now. Some of his most enjoyable times recently had been spent continuing his mentor relationship with Dan Steele. Tom had recruited Dan as a promising first-year teacher. They had worked together for eight years and when Tom moved to the principalship of Lakewood Secondary, Dan had moved, too, into the vice-principalship. When Tom retired it was no surprise to anyone that Dan Steele became the principal. That was the way things were in Garden City School District.

From Tom's point of view, their relationship was what it should have been – the experienced principal passing on the best of what he had learned to a younger protégé. On each of his visits back to "his" school, Tom could see that Dan had learned well. It was a source of pride to Tom to see the continuing evidence of his influence on the younger administrator.

Dan had other concerns. If his years as Tom's vice-principal had taught him anything, it was that education was a job for professionals. That had always been Tom's view. Parents were helpful, even useful, especially when the school needed computers or sports equipment. In fact the Lakewood Parents' Association had been a gold mine. Anything Tom had requested had been bought with few questions asked. Tom had always made sure that executive members themselves had support of all kinds from the school – it was only fair, he said, though not always "per policy." When it came to the school's important decisions, though, it was strictly hands off. What went on in the school was the business of those who worked there and who would be held accountable for what happened. The parents at Lakewood had been taught well by Tom.

Things ran just as they should. At least, they had until this year, Dan Steele's second year as principal. The Board's new open access policy had changed the ground rules. Their position on access was clear; parents were to be given a strong voice in areas that previously had been off limits. However, most of the parents were not particularly interested in the new influencing role the Board was offering. They were busy and quite prepared to leave professional tasks and responsibilities to the professionals.

A few, though, had seized the opportunity offered by the Board. The Corwins were the most challenging. The newspaper report on the access policy had hardly appeared in the Tribune before Jim and Marion Corwin had called Dan to tell him that they were planning to "start things rolling," as Jim had put it. They were clear about their agenda – they felt the school was not doing enough to educate students about substance abuse. Both were on a local committee set up after statistics on drug and alcohol abuse at the national and provincial levels were published in the Tribune.

Marion Corwin had been elected as the chair of the Parents' Advisory Council, which had replaced the Lakewood Parents' Association. None of the former Association executive members were part of the new advisory group. Some had considered it, but they believed that the new group was more concerned with 'running the school'. Their own role as supporters, they thought, was not of much interest to the Corwins and others who had been elected to the new executive.

Marion Corwin saw great potential in the parents. She felt that if only they could seize their new role, clearly they could be a strong force for school improvement. Something was certainly needed first though to bring the members of the old Association on side. It was too bad many had opted out when the new policy was adopted. Maybe the drug and alcohol issue would be a good place to start – a 'spark' to encourage greater parent involvement. The new mandate from the Board would certainly help. First, she would have to strengthen her working relationship with Dan Steele. She had a lot of respect for his abilities – if only he could shake off the influence of Tom Stanley – "the Ghost of Christmas Past," as she called the former principal.

Time for a Change?

Pat Stanright   Principal, High Valley Secondary School
B. D. Best   Former principal of High Valley
Barry Hookshot   Department head, Physical Education

Pat Stanright was new on the block, the district's most recent appointee to its oldest secondary school. During the late summer weeks as Pat settled in to the community and talked to staff and neighbors, it became pretty clear that the school had previously enjoyed (and for some, "enjoyed" was the appropriate word) rather lackluster leadership, to say the least. B. D. Best, the former principal, had moved to retirement in Australia after a rousing send-off from the staff. Most of them had been at the school for many years.

The only significant comment Pat could remember from a phone conversation with B. D. was, "It's my job to keep the troops happy. Downtown can worry about the rest." Pat was just beginning to realize the significance of that statement. The "troops" who dropped by the school during the summer had seemed happy all right; perhaps *content* would be a better term. The common theme of conversations seemed to be "status quo." People's major concern seemed to be that they be allowed to continue to run their own show with minimal interference from the new principal – that much was clear.

It was pretty clear also that B. D. Best had been committed to the status quo. The principal's office was comfortable in the extreme even with B. D.'s memorabilia gone from the walls. Pat knew the memorabilia had been there – bright patches on the sun-faded walls told the story. Long-term staff members who dropped in told Pat the details of items that once had hung there, probably for years. They spoke fondly of the former principal and of B. D.'s respect for the way things were done at High Valley Secondary. There were some messages here.

There were a few rumbles of discontent. A couple of staff members had commented disparagingly to Pat that other schools in the district seemed to get more attention from "downtown" at budget time. One afternoon in late August, a few teachers who had been taking a break in the middle of getting their classrooms ready for the fall were talking about the school. One, speaking with back turned when Pat came through the doorway, was saying, "It would be nice if someone cared we were here – I think if this place burned down, people driving by a week later would wonder what used to be on this corner." The teacher's colleagues had responded with vigorous pro-attention and anti-attention comments. It was clear that their remarks were directed not only at attention from outside but perhaps even more at attention from within the school. Maybe B.D. Best had not actually been all things to all people.

Pat's early assessment was that in a rather negative sense the school had a strong culture, even though a few staff members seemed unhappy to see things just drift along in 'who cares' fashion and "downtown," as Pat had found out at an early meeting in the district office, wasn't happy. They recognized that for many years the school attempted little beyond the minimum; the district office had responded by placing its discretionary funds elsewhere. There also seemed to be a strong feeling in the superintendent's office that the Physical Education and Art departments controlled the High Valley budget – the walls outside B.D.'s office and the trophy case in the hall suggested that might be the case. So to did the comments of some teachers in other departments. Pat had worked as a librarian a few years back. With that experience as a background, the High Valley library seemed lean and sparse to say the least. Pat had little previous experience in building or analyzing school budgets, though, so it was difficult to know whether rank unfairness was afoot as some had suggested. One fact was clear however; the new budget would have to be seen as equitable by not only those within the school but also by "downtown." That might mean gains for some and losses for others. It might also give Pat an opportunity to introduce a new style of leadership to High Valley.

Pat planned to present some ideas about budget planning at an early staff meeting. The item on the agenda was "Budget process – preliminary discussion and staff perspectives." The new principal hoped that out of this meeting a participative approach could be developed. There was plenty of time, after all. The current year had just started and the school's submission for next year wasn't due until February. This would be a good opportunity for everyone to offer ideas about the process.

Pat wasn't at all prepared for what happened next. Barry Hookshot, Department Head for Physical Education, arrived at the meeting with a full set of handouts for everyone – a detailed department budget for the following year. Barry's proposal was tied closely to a similar submission from the Fine Arts staff – also a significant increase from the current year, because there was to be a major logo contest and a banner design project for the gym.

Us and Them

Pat Stanright   Principal, High Valley Secondary School
Kurt Bluntly   President, Priorities in Education (PIE)

Somehow it seemed to Pat Stanright that everything came down to money. It was either that or the fact that money, particularly tight money, had a way of bringing out the worst in some people. The current issue was either simple or complex depending on how you looked at it. It seemed most people saw it as a simple one. Certainly that was true for Kurt Bluntly. "Schooling was first and foremost for citizens," said Kurt. His view, and that of the other members of PIE, was that what he called "newcomers" were welcome as long as they could be accommodated within existing programs. That certainly wasn't true for many of the recent wave of immigrants. Many of had come as refugees and none had arrived speaking any English. Obviously, there was an added cost for instruction in English as a Second Language (ESL); Kurt Bluntly expressed it as "losing our librarians and custodians." PIE was promoting a policy stating that program levels that had existed on a baseline date at the beginning of the government's program of fiscal restraint should be considered the baseline. That coincidentally had preceded any significant immigration. Any new programs, PIE insisted, should be "user-pay," and that would certainly apply to English as a Second Language. Prior to the baseline date there had been no need for ESL programs in Parkside. PIE's agenda was clear, their motives less so.

Pat and the staff of High Valley Secondary School had devoted much energy to establishing what they had termed "survival priorities." They had also developed a strong policy position that the full range of services should be offered to all students in the school's attendance area. The staff had agreed on alternatives for action should current fiscal circumstances continue and worsen. Everyone knew that some tough decisions would have to be made but, in their view and the Board's, all of Hillside's programs including ESL were safe for the foreseeable future. The Board had already decided that no new programs could be added until the fiscal situation became brighter.

That was the decision that had triggered the debate. Kurt Bluntly and others had been pushing hard during the year before to have a program for gifted students introduced at the secondary level. That could not happen now. The community generally was supportive of the Board's decision to do its best to retain what the district had but, to most, it made no sense to introduce anything new in the way of programs.

In some ways, circumstances were playing into PIE's hands. A tiny minority of recent immigrants had earned a full share of attention from police and the courts and some business owners were becoming alarmed. The Chamber of Commerce had held a symposium on public safety; Kurt Bluntly had used the question period to link the topic to PIE's agenda. The lines were being drawn but they were also becoming increasingly blurred. Pat Stanright saw the potential for trouble, especially if PIE's rhetoric heated up any more.

Trouble wasn't long in coming. One of Hillside's ESL students was arrested after a break-in and major theft of computer equipment at Memorial Secondary. People were outraged. It gave Kurt Bluntly just what he wanted – a chance to link crime in the community with the ESL program. There was absolutely no logical connection between the two but that didn't make any difference to PIE. For some people in town, the population of recent immigrants was an unwelcome intrusion and a groundswell of opposition was rising. The focus was still on the costs of the ESL program but it was clear that money was just a cover for other issues that people had chosen not to express openly.

The ESL parents' group, sensing the principal's support, met with Pat Stanright to ask for a formal public clarification of the issues. In many of their cultures, the voice of authority was an important voice that would be regarded as a definitive and respected statement. Someone needed to present the other side; the parents were looking to Pat for help. This was a difficult one. First of all someone had to make some sense of the situation and help the community sort out the real issues. That alone was risky. Not everyone wanted to operate in the light of day. Kurt Bluntly, in particular, would react strongly to any suggestion that his concerns were anything other than fiscal. He had already hinted that he might run for a seat on the Board. Pat decided to take the weekend to think through the issues before answering the parents, knowing that whatever the answer, it would have to be both plausible and defensible.

What are Schools For?

Mary Carlotti   Chair, Water's Edge Parents' Advisory Council
Paul Carlotti   Mary Carlotti's spouse
Terry Castwell   Principal of Water's Edge Elementary School

The Water's Edge Parents' Advisory Council had arranged a tremendous conference on the role of schools in a changing society. The parents who attended – and there were many – rated the speakers as both inspiring and down-to-earth, just what was needed in the face of numerous changes that were facing the schools in Parkside School District.

Mary Carlotti had come with anticipation. As chair of the Council, she had participated actively in planning the conference. Mary was delighted with the topic because her personal goals were clear. For Mary, one key purpose of the schools was straightforward – community revitalization. She had lived on the West Side for nearly 20 years. Mary and her husband Paul had settled there as immigrants, newly married and anxious to buy a house and raise a family. The neighborhood had been promising, home and children had become realities, and both Mary's and Paul's jobs were secure. Everything had looked promising until the big shift in the city's population.

It was clear that the community around Water's Edge Elementary School had changed, gradually at first then rapidly as more and more families began buying lots and building houses on the fringes of the rapidly-growing city of Parkside. Mary and Paul were worried but determined to stay. Their children were in high school, both held part-time jobs. Although many of the family's close friends had moved to newer areas of town the Carlottis were still very closely tied to the Water's Edge area.

For Mary, developing a strong sense of community that would include both long-time residents and new arrivals was vital to the future of Water's Edge Elementary School and the surrounding community. As Mary and Paul looked around for a focal point for rebuilding, it became clear in both their minds that Water's Edge Elementary was the key. The school was already running numerous programs for parents and other community members. The catalyst would be the Parents' Advisory Council.

For principal Terry Castwell, channeling Mary's energy would be a challenge to say the least. Mary could become either an untiring ally or a formidable opponent. Terry knew that both Mary and Paul had an agenda that extended well beyond what principal and staff saw as the school's mandate. The principal was also convinced that the Carlottis were correct about the future of what was on the verge of becoming a decaying community. As a school principal though, Terry felt that little could be done beyond the initiatives administrator and staff were already taking. Somehow there would have to be a meeting of the minds. After all, schools were about learning, not urban renewal.

Today was not looking good to Terry. Paul Carlotti had called to arrange an appointment with the principal. Paul was bringing the Mayor and Terry suddenly realized that matters could be getting out of hand. The Mayor was a powerful figure and the promise of an official presence suggested there was likely to be some heavy pressure.

Terry sat down over coffee with a couple of key staff members and raised the issue but was a bit taken aback by their responses. Both of these teachers saw Mary and Paul Carlotti's ideas as a breath of fresh air, perhaps just the thing Water's Edge needed to come back to life. Terry hadn't realized they felt that way, but in talking with them, it became clear that there probably was more support on staff for the Carlotti's efforts than it had seemed. At the same time, Terry knew that the Board's 'back to basics' emphasis left little room for what the trustees believed and had stated clearly were matters better left to civic officials. Terry wondered how both agendas could be met.

REFERENCES

Afonso, Natarcia. "Key Players and Groups in Schools as Learning Organizations." *Proceedings from the DELSO Project 2001.* http://www.progettodeslo.it/documents/Natercio.pdf

Baddeley, Simon. "Political Sensitivity in Public Managers." *Local Government Studies* 15, no. 2 (1989).

Bennett, Nigel, Christine Wise, Philip Woods, & Janet A. Harvey. "Distributed Leadership." *National College for School Leadership.* (Spring 2003) http://www.ncsl.org.uk/media/3C4/A2/distributed-leadership-literature-review.pdf

Bennis, Warren & Bert Nanus. *Leaders: The Strategies for Taking Charge.* New York: Harper & Row, 1985.

Blase, Joseph, ed. *The Politics of Life in Schools.* Thousand Oaks, CA: Corwin Press, 1991.

Block, Peter. *Stewardship: Choosing Service Over Self-interest.* San Francisco: Berret-Koehler, 1993.

Bok, Sissela. *Lying: Moral Choice in Public and Private Life.* New York: Vintage, 1989.

Bushe, Gervase. *Clear Leadership.* Mountain View, CA: Davies-Black, 2001.

Carter, Stephen. "The Insufficiency of Honesty." *The Atlantic Monthly*, February 1996.

Carver, John. *Boards that Make a Difference.* San Francisco: Jossey-Bass, 1990.

Crick, Bernard. *In Defence of Politics.* 5th ed. London: Continuum, 2005.

Dahl, Robert & Bruce Stinebrickner. *Modern Political Analysis.* 6th Ed. Englewood Cliffs: Prentice-Hall, 2003.

Drucker, Peter. *Managing the Nonprofit Organization: Principles and Practices.* New York: Harper Collins, 1990.

Fairhurst, Gail & Robert Sarr. *The Art of Framing.* San Francisco: Jossey-Bass, 1996.

Fisher, Roger, Elizabeth Kopelman, & Andrea Schneider. *Beyond Machiavelli: Tools for Coping with Conflict.* New York: Penguin, 1994.

Fisher, Roger & William Ury. *Getting to Yes: Negotiating Agreement without Giving In.* New York: Penguin, 1981.

Fullan, Michael. "Introduction." In *The Jossey-Bass Reader on Educational Leadership*. San Francisco: Jossey-Bass, 2000.

Galbraith, John. *The Anatomy of Power*. Boston: Houghton Mifflin, 1983.

Goodin, Robert E. *Manipulatory Politics*. New Haven CT: Yale University Press, 1980.

Greenleaf, Robert. *Servant Leadership*. New York: Paulist, 1977.

Gronn, Peter. "Distributed Leadership." In *Second International Handbook of Educational Leadership and Administration*, edited by Kenneth Leithwood et al. Dordrecht: Kluwer, 2002.

Hodgkinson, Christopher. *Educational Leadership: The Moral Art*. New York: State University of New York Press, 1991.

Hodgkinson, Christopher. *Administrative Philosophy: Values and Motivations in Administrative Life*. Tarrytown, NY: Elsevier Science, 1996.

Koestenbaum, Peter. *Leadership: The Inner Side of Greatness. A Philosophy for Leaders*. San Francisco: Jossey-Bass, 2002.

Layton, Donald & Jay Scribner. *Teaching Educational Politics and Policy*. Tempe, AZ: University Council for Educational Administration, 1989.

Mauriel, John. *Strategic Leadership for Schools*. San Francisco: Jossey-Bass, 1989.

Maxcy, Spencer. *Educational Leadership: A Critical Pragmatic Perspective*. Toronto: Ontario Institute for Studies in Education, 1991.

Milton, John. "Sonnet 19." In *The Sonnets of Milton*, edited by Mark Pattison. New York: D. Appleton & Co, 1889. www.luminarium.org/sevenlit/milton/sonnet19.htm.

Moore, Christopher. *The Mediation Process: Practical Strategies for Resolving Conflict*. San Francisco: Jossey-Bass, 1986.

Natural Resources Canada. "The State of Canada's Forests 2003-04." *Natural Resources Canada*. http://www.nrcan-rncan.gc.ca/cfs_scf/national/what-quoi/sof/sof04/views01_e.html.

Newman, William & Harvey Wallender. "Managing Not-for-profit Enterprises." *Academy of Management Review*, January, 1978.

Northouse, Peter. *Leadership: Theory and Practice*. 2nd ed. Thousand Oaks, CA: Sage, 2001.

Pirie, Madsen. "Adam Smith Institute and Micropolitics." *Adam Smith Institute*. http://www.adamsmith.org/blog-archive/000902.php.

Pross, Paul. *Group Politics and Public Policy*. Toronto: Oxford University Press, 1986.

Rilke, Rainer M. "Letter 7 (Rome, May 14, 1904)." *Letters to a Young Poet*. http://www.sfgoth.com/~immanis/rilke/letter7.html.

Sarason, Seymour. *The Culture of the School and the Problem of Change.* Boston: Allyn & Bacon, 1982.

Sarason, Seymour. *Parental Involvement and the Political Principle.* San Francisco: Jossey-Bass, 1995.

Schon, Donald. *The Reflective Practitioner.* New York: Basic Books, 1993.

Scruton, Roger. *A Dictionary of Political Thought.* London: Pan Books, 1983.

Selden, John. "Table Talk." In G. Johnson, *Memoirs of John Selden*, n.p., 1835.

Sergiovanni, Thomas. *Moral Leadership: Getting to the Heart of School Improvement.* San Franciso: Jossey-Bass, 1992.

Storey, Vernon. *Guarding the Trust.* Vancouver, BC: EduServ, 1994.

Vaill, Peter. *Learning as a Way of Being: Strategies for Survival in a World of Permanent White Water.* San Francisco: Jossey-Bass, 1996.

Wheatley, Margaret. "Good-bye, Command and Control." In *The Jossey-Bass Reader on Educational Leadership.* San Francisco: Jossey-Bass, 2000.

Wirt, Frederick & Michael Kirst. *Schools in Conflict.* Berkeley: McCutchan, 1992.